MOVIE STARS, REAL PEOPLE, AND ME

BOOKS BY
JOSHUA LOGAN

Plays

MISTER ROBERTS
with Thomas Heggen

SOUTH PACIFIC
with Oscar Hammerstein, 2nd, and
Richard Rodgers

THE WISTERIA TREES

FANNY
with S. N. Behrman and Harold Rome

Nonfiction

JOSH: My Up and Down, In and Out Life

MOVIE STARS, REAL PEOPLE, AND ME

MOVIE STARS, REAL PEOPLE, AND ME

Joshua Logan

DELACORTE PRESS / NEW YORK

Published by
Delacorte Press
1 Dag Hammarskjold Plaza
New York, N.Y. 10017

Manufactured in the United States of America

First printing

ACKNOWLEDGMENTS

Designed by Ann Spinelli

Library of Congress Cataloging in Publication Data

Logan, Joshua.
Movie stars, real people, and me.

Chronology of plays and films written, produced, and/or directed by J. Logan: p. 351
Includes index.
1. Logan, Joshua. 2. Theatrical producers and directors—United States—Biography. 3. Moving-picture producers and directors—United States—Biography.
I. Title.
PN2287.L59A36   791'.092'4 [B]   78-5657
ISBN 0-440-06258-6

FOR MY CHILDREN
Thomas Heggen Logan
and Susan Harrigan Logan

Two godsent and talented people helped bring these pages from my endless penciled scrawl into a book:

Joseph Curtis, who has been my right arm and half my brain since 1949, was, along with my wife, a constant sounding board. He also typed all the various drafts.

The other chief helper was brilliant, vibrant Jeanne Bernkopf, my editor, who carried me along on her special waves of controlled enthusiasm, kept insisting on and getting facts, and eventually managed to cut this book and me down to size.

My loving gratitude to both.

BUYER
BEWARE

BEFORE YOU BUY or even read this book, you should
know that it's not a book; that is, it's not a straight once-
upon-a-time narrative. Also, it's not a "Then I Wrote" or
a "Then I Directed" order of my movies and plays at all.

It's a revue—made up of long spurts and short jets, dark and
light, sweet and sour, in no rigid form, except always factual.
Even the fantasies are factual fantasies.

The Follies and *The Scandals* and *Chauve-Souris* were also re-
vues containing odd-sized sketches, songs, and dances (and
girls, of course). Their equivalent in the publishing field is
the same word, but spelled differently: Review. Most magazines are reviews—stories, cartoons, poems, all mixed together. So why can't a book be a revue/review? Anyway
that's what mine is.

In writing it, I followed my nose, swung with the punches,
and, when I felt like it, told a—I mustn't say it among the literati
so I'll spell it—J-O-K-E. I love to laugh, and even more than that
I love to make others laugh.

But please remember, dear browser, when the book is serious,
and especially when it seems to grow a bit wild, that it's all true,

and, amazingly enough, with all its popping about in the past, it covers my life from my first movie, *Picnic,* to the present day.

Now that you are warned, either take a chance with me or don't. But know this: I hope you do, because what are writers without readers?

CONTENTS

MOVIE* STARS, REAL PEOPLE, AND ME

DELETED
WORDS

JACK BENNY once said, "Jack Warner would rather make a bad joke than a good picture." And it's almost true. He has a strong compulsion to tell corny jokes.

Jack Warner would sit behind his enormous desk at Warner Brothers Studio, surrounded by Oscars and photographs of famous people, and answer almost every question asked him with a joke. I learned that if you laughed too loudly at these jokes you might never be allowed to get away, and so I generally had one foot out the door before he got the joke started.

I was his pal in those days because I had worked hard and "for free" in the cutting room doing him a favor.

So Nedda and I were on the A list, and one day we received an invitation to honor Her Serene Highness the Princess of Liechtenstein at Mr. Warner's sumptuous château on Angelo Drive. We dressed to the nines and hired a limousine, as no one would dare arrive at an elaborate Warner soiree in a drive-it-yourself.

Nedda was seated behind a set of silver candlesticks at one of the small round tables, flanked by two handsome celebrities. I found myself at the star table with the Princess of Liechtenstein and Jack Warner, his hair carefully coiffed, his face shining from

1

a bit of extra sunlamp, his mustache touched up. About us were Natalie Wood, Audrey Hepburn, Billy Wilder, and Richard Gully, a man often invited by Jack to keep conversation going: he was an Englishman whose moonlighting job was to feed Jack Warner jokes.

The Princess of Liechtenstein was tall, rather pale, and I think perhaps shyer than usual that evening because she was in the midst of people who spoke only English, and her English was very limited. For the first time in my life I noticed that Jack Warner was himself ill at ease.

No one could think of an opening gambit for a lively dinner conversation. Suddenly I had an inspiration. I thought of a famous man, a kind of con man, who had once worked for him, and I was sure Jack's comments on him would be amusing. I said, "Jack, didn't Wilson Mizener once work for you?"

Jack Warner happily pounced on that like a dog on a bone. "Wilson Mizener!" he shouted. "Wilson Mizener—of course! Yes, he worked at our studio, and I think it would be very interesting for the princess to hear a funny story about him."

I was terrified. Surely he wasn't going to tell the story that had made me think of Mizener. That one could not be told at the table.

"Princess! Listen, everybody! There was a fella named Wilson Mizener. He used to work for me and while he was here, you know, he tried to do a lot of fancy things. He was a con man, really—he'd do anything for money—and I mean anything."

Oh, my God! He was going to tell it. Christ! What was I going to do to stop him? I quickly reviewed the story in my mind to see if there was any way of cleaning it up.

It just couldn't be told the way I had heard it:

Wilson Mizener once caught a very rich old lady on the string, but before he married her he decided as a safeguard to get a three-million-dollar policy on her life. The only trouble was that the insurance company required that she get some kind of a medical examination. Since he hadn't told her about the policy, he faked the whole thing, forging all the details himself in a shaky handwriting meant to pass for hers.

The only item he couldn't fake was the urinalysis. He was terrified to provide the specimen himself for fear there was a detectable difference between a man's urine and a woman's. So, he sought out another sidekick of his, Oklahoma Sal, a hard-boiled lady who was running a nightclub. Wilson said, "Sal, how would you like a trip to Europe on me?"

"I'd love a trip to Europe," she said. "Who do I have to fuck to get it?"

He said, "No one. Just go into the bathroom and fill this little bottle, and you've got your trip. Simple, eh?"

Sal came back with the bottle filled with amber liquid and the stopper on tight. But when Wilson turned it in to the insurance company medics, the laboratory report came back with the statement, "Positive—evidence of V.D."

This, of course, killed the policy, and the whole thing collapsed. Mizener was so infuriated that when he next saw Oklahoma Sal and she asked, "Do I get my trip to Europe?" Mizener lashed out at her angrily, "You couldn't piss your way to Hoboken!"

And yet, there was Jack Warner already launched on that story as an opening salute to Her Serene Highness. As he got the story under way, I saw from his face that he realized he was sailing into some very rough breakers. But his manner of avoiding them, which was impromptu, was simply to grunt and clear his throat at any bad portion of the story, hoping that it would be filled in by the listener's imagination. It was much like the way the blip works on television interviews today.

" 'Who do I have to umpf to get it?' and he said, 'No umphing necessary.' He just gave the bottle to Sal and said, 'Fill this with umpf,' and she went in and umpf. Afterwards, she handed the umpf back to him and he turned it in to the medics. The laboratory definitely declared it to be umpf, which, of course, negated the policy completely. Mizener was so furious that the next time he saw Sal and she said, 'Do I get my trip to Europe?' he said, 'You couldn't umpf your way to Hoboken!' "

Now, Jack Warner was not used to telling stories in which the punch line gets no laugh, and this one got none because no one but me understood what the hell he was talking about. The princess stared blankly at him, as did Billy Wilder and the rest.

Finally, Jack, squirming in utter agony at having failed, barked out in a very loud voice, *"The trouble with that goddamned story is that you just gotta use the word piss."*

KIM NOVAK
IN A
PINCH

I WAS GOING to direct a motion picture for the first time in seventeen years.

With one telephone call, Harry Cohn had saved my professional life. And he had done it by offering me a major picture, though since 1938 all of my work had been on the stage. Granted, I'd had some big successes to my credit: *This Is the Army, Annie Get Your Gun, Mister Roberts, South Pacific, Wish You Were Here,* and the play of *Picnic.* But I'd also had two manic breakdowns and had just recovered from the second one. Harry Cohn's was the first post-illness offer I got. As they say in the fan magazines and gossip columns, this was my chance for a comeback. And what a chance: the movie of *Picnic.*

I had really loved the play. Maybe it was those teenage years I had spent in the Middle West that helped me catch fire at the story of Hal Carter, a young, muscular vagabond who rode a freight into town to see his rich college pal, Alan Benson, and stayed on to find himself involved with Alan's fiancée, Madge, the prettiest girl in town. The force of the growing physical attraction between those two led to events affecting not only them but everyone around them in the town.

4

So for Harry Cohn's sake and particularly for mine, I couldn't make the major mistake of miscasting Madge. Yet I have read often—once in Harry Cohn's biography and several times in interviews with Kim Novak—that I never wanted Kim to play the part, that Harry Cohn gave me orders that if I did not use her I would have to give up directing the picture. Nonsense.

All he asked was that I consider her carefully. "If she isn't right for the part," he said, "you'll find out, I'm sure."

And the moment I saw her I was absolutely stunned by her beauty. On talking with her, it struck me that she was very close spiritually to the part of Madge. When she told me how her family always said that she was the pretty one and her sister was the bright one, it struck me that Kim had actually been living inside Madge all her life. But if the spirits matched, the looks did not. At least not with Kim's short, slightly lavender, mannish haircut.

I went to the hair department of the studio, which made for her a superb, dark-auburn, waist-length wig. When Kim appeared on the test stage with that long dark hair, wearing a simple cotton dress, I thought I had never seen anyone as near the "girl on the cover of a candy box," which is the way I always pictured Madge.

As a test, we filmed a scene from the play. Kim was slightly nervous—but extremely good. She showed great promise along with pre-Raphaelite beauty even though she had had practically no experience. Dan Taradash, who had written the screenplay, saw the test with me and said, "She's beautiful, all right, but you can't risk this huge picture on an amateur actress."

I said, "Dan, I like Kim. She understands Madge deep down. She *looks* and *acts* like Madge to me. And surely there's nobody more photogenic and, with that new hair, more beautiful than she is."

Harry Cohn looked at the test and was delighted but he added a proviso: "Kim doesn't like the wig," he said. "She wants to play it with her own hair, and maybe she's right. She may not look like your idea of Madge, but she will look like Kim Novak. You'd be building her star image."

I told him that purple shingled hair was incongruous—it might give Bill Inge, *Picnic*'s author, a heart attack—but with a dark-auburn hairdo, I was going to do everything I possibly could to convince Dan and others that Kim play Madge.

Although I had committed myself in spirit to Kim with the

change of hairdo, I told Harry that out of sheer courtesy we should test Janice Rule who had created the role. He agreed and we set up the tests.

Unfortunately, my beloved Janice was nervous when she tested, knowing that Kim Novak was almost set, and also that she had never played a leading role in pictures. She was an incredible beauty—with her Botticelli, high-cheekbone face and pearl-colored skin. And, she had naturally the hair we wanted —waist length and auburn. But she had a feeling that no one really understood her looks, so she asked whether she could make herself up. I made a mistake when I gave her the go-ahead, for she came back to the floor with her face shaded so grotesquely that I wondered if she had used her mirror. She had painted shadows on her cheeks so thick and greasy that it looked as though she had been dragged up from the bottom of the Mississippi delta.

I sent her back and had her face made up properly. But when she tested, all that showed was her fear. She was so sure she was wrong that she practically laid the part of Madge at Kim Novak's feet.

But the issue was still not resolved. One day, Freddie Kohlmar, the producer Harry Cohn had assigned to the picture, said to me, "Who's gonna play Madge? Harry wants Kim Novak, but Dan Taradash likes that test you made of Carroll Baker."

Carroll Baker? Yes, Carroll Baker had been lovely, but I had thought her too childishly young to be a proper adversary to Bill Holden. My lovely Janice Rule's beauty had seemed to defy the camera. So there was nothing to do but convince Dan and the others that Kim Novak was right. Freddie said, "Let's take a chance and give it to Kim even if it does please Harry Cohn."

But being overcautious, I made a second test. Freddie and I were all the more convinced that Kim was Madge, the taken-for-granted beauty whom everyone envied. The sad tone of her voice, her slightly withdrawn look, proved that even to Dan Taradash.

And that, my children, is how Harry Cohn shoved Kim Novak down my throat.

Superstar Bill Holden had already been cast before I came on the picture. It was a contractual thing: he still had to work off two more pictures on an old Columbia contract. Although he was really too old for the part of Hal, he was such a vital, virile, talented man and with such a youthful body, that I felt he would be strong in the part. We had lunch and I began quizzing him.

I had one problem that nagged at me: the dance sequence between Hal and Madge was obligatory for one climax of the picture, but I had never seen Bill dance and I had not thought to ask Kim Novak if she danced. Bill was having martinis at lunch.

He said, "Aw, for Chrissake, you're worried about the dancing—look at this."

He jumped to his feet in the middle of the startled restaurant, did a kind of hurried shuffle, and sat down. His movements had nothing to do with dancing, but he seemed to feel that they did, so I agreed and said, "Of course—that was great."

He laughed cynically because he knew I didn't mean it.

Dan Taradash insisted that we couldn't find all the cast in California, so I flew to New York to make tests for the other roles, especially from the New York original cast. Among them was Arthur O'Connell, who had been such a standout as Howard, the boyfriend of Rosemary, the spinster schoolteacher, that no one could replace him.

For Madge's kid sister, Millie, I had been unable to think of anyone but the fantastic Kim Stanley. But we all knew, including Kim herself, that she was too old for the close-ups the picture version required. Then someone brought me Susan Strasberg, sixteen years old, the daughter of Lee and Paula. Her incipient beauty and spirit seemed just right to me and showed itself on the screen when we tested her.

Great as Eileen Heckart had been onstage as Rosemary, Harry wanted another big name for the picture. Harry asked me if I thought Rosalind Russell could be persuaded to play the role. Roz was an old and intimate friend of Nedda's. She had made some bad pictures and needed a spectacular role in a hit picture. She accepted the role of Rosemary almost hungrily: "Photograph me any way you want to—don't even ask Jimmy Howe to blot out my wrinkles. I want to look like a real leathery Kansas dame."

Young Paul Newman had made his debut as an actor when he played Alan, Hal's friend, in the original play. Because of that he had been put under contract by Warner Brothers. By the time our picture came along, he was too promising a star to play the secondary role of Alan.

In a few years he had become almost a leader of the new wave of actors, the freewheelers, the rebels—a far cry from the Paul Newman I had known who played the square Alan on Broadway, but who was so handsome, lithe, and athletic, I had made him understudy for the role of Hal. One day when I watched him rehearse Hal's dance, I said, "You dance well but can't you wiggle your ass a bit?"

Paul said with a twinkle in his eye, "Please, Josh, I'm a Republican."

We still had to cast Alan, good role or bad. Nedda called from New York. She had just seen a revival of *The Wisteria Trees* with Helen Hayes at City Center. The boy who played Petey, the young poet, was terribly good and would be a fine Alan. His name was Cliff Robertson. I remembered him from the Chicago company of *Mister Roberts*. He had played the innocent young sailor, Payne, who brags about his participation in a drunken brawl. He got one of the biggest laughs of the evening, and since Nedda now raved so about his Petey, we accepted him as Alan with a test.

I had asked for three or four weeks' rehearsal, but I learned very soon that getting any kind of rehearsal period in movies is a difficult and expensive thing. It means that all the actors have to start the first day, and their salaries continue: even though an actor's role may not be scheduled until the third week of shooting, he is paid full salary from the moment he starts. And, it is often difficult to get actors at the beginning of a picture, since they are frequently finishing another picture and can't break away.

But Harry felt it was important, I imagine mostly for Kim Novak's sake, for us to have a two-week rehearsal.

We had our first day of rehearsal on the sound stage. We read the script aloud and there were the usual nerves. Kim was almost impossible to hear, and Bill Holden did everything but leap on the table and stand on his hands in an effort to show that he wasn't nervous and also that he was young enough to play the part.

Roz Russell and her fellow schoolteachers, Reta Shaw and Elizabeth Wilson, were on the button—using every second of the rehearsal day to take full advantage of the time to study their roles. Betty Field as Flo, the mother, and Verna Felton as old Mrs. Potts were the same. Susan Strasberg was duly respectful of all the older actresses, and Cliff Robertson just seemed to be grateful he was in the movies at last.

It went well, I suppose, but I was far too busy thinking about how it was going to look on the screen to give it all the attention I would have had I been directing a play for the theatre.

I was happy when the two weeks were up and we could really get something on film. My God, what was happening to me? I was bored with listening to myself.

We flew to Kansas and spent two days in a town near Hutchinson called Salina. I had chosen to shoot the scene there which led to the sexual confrontation between Madge and Hal the night of the picnic. I chose the location because it gave us both the waterfall we needed and the railroad track a few feet away.

Everything was set up to start shooting. Kim was in her light pink picnic dress, carefully designed by Jean Louis to look as though her mother had made it. Her long dark wig was properly coiffed to set off her great beauty, but she was pacing up and down on Madge's four-inch heels, terrified that she wouldn't be good enough. I tried to reassure her, but she was too panicked to listen.

Bill had memorized and rehearsed the scene, and felt absolutely sure of the way he wanted to play it. It was an exciting scene, loaded with sexual promise. We had to imagine Hal had driven up in the car he had borrowed from Alan. Madge had jumped in the front seat and forced him to take her with him. Now, she had got out and run to the side of the millrace with its pouring falls. He walked over to her. We were ready to close in and shoot the dialogue scene when Kim broke from the scene and came up to me.

She whispered frantically into my ear, "Please, can I see you up there where they can't see us. Please. Please, I've got to see you."

I went back in the darkness with her near a woodpile.

"What's the matter, Kim? Don't worry so."

"I can't cry."

"You don't have to cry yet. Wait until we get into the scene."

"No, no," she said. "I'm just too taut to cry. It says in the script I've got to cry, and I don't know how. I know that I've got to have tears in my eyes in this scene, and I can't have them unless you, for God's sake, help me."

I said, "Kim, dear, I think if you concentrate on the feeling of the scene, it will be all right. It doesn't have to have tears. Whatever you do instinctively will be all right. You're perfect for Madge. Just play it the way you feel it."

She said, "You've got to help me. You don't want to help me. But you've got to do something. Please!"

"What do you want me to do?"

And then she said, "Pinch me."

"What do you mean? What the hell are you talking about?"

"Pinch my arms. Pinch my shoulders. Pinch my back. Make it hurt me so much that I'll have to cry. I can only cry when I'm hurt. I've always been like that. Please. Please! You're the director—it's your duty to help me."

I said, "I've never pinched anybody in my life and I'm not going to start now. Besides, I don't think it's worth it. You'll develop black-and-blue marks and we'll have to stop shooting."

"Please, for God's sake, pinch me. Just a little pinch. That's all I ask."

I could see they were ready around the camera so I closed my eyes, lifted up a tentative thumb and forefinger, and pinched her slightly on the arm.

She laughed. "That's silly," she said. "That doesn't even hurt. Pinch me."

I tried a little harder.

"Harder," she said. "Harder."

Finally, I grabbed her by both arms and pinched both of them with all the strength in my fingers.

She said, "Ow! That's *better.* That hurts. You're wonderful. That really *hurts.*"

She burst into tears and ran back into the scene. I went back of the woodpile, threw up quickly, and ran to the camera.

I was far more shaken by the experience, I'm sure, than she was. But she did play the scene even though the makeup man had to keep swabbing her arms to cover up those purple thumbprints.

(As I am writing this, I am remembering newspaper interviews about the shooting of *Picnic* in Kansas. Most of them were magazine pulpish stuff, completely forgettable, but there was one squib I will never forget: "Oh, he was terrible to me. He got so mad at me one night in Kansas that he pinched my arms till they were black and blue.")

We shot Madge and Hal as they climbed up a railroad embankment and ended the scene in a passionate kiss, two feet from the wheels of a moving freight train, which I hoped would symbolize, with its flashing lights and monstrous rhythm, the sexual climax of the scene since we were not allowed by the censors to be more explicit.

Two days later we moved the whole company to Hutchinson, where we were to settle down for a six-week stay at the new, multistoried Baker Hotel. We made it our home and headquarters, since many of the scenes were in a radius of half an hour from the hotel.

At the end of each day I could tell what time it was by the shout that came from Bill Holden: "Warm up the ice cubes."

Which I soon learned meant, Fix me a very strong, dry martini—and quick. He never drank before the end of the shooting day. But once we had reached that part of the day, the gin industry began to prosper. Yet somehow it never seemed to affect him. It did not alter his speech, his wit, or his warmth. He was simply a red-blooded American boy who wanted to have a good time, and believe me, he did. Quite often he would take a bunch of us to a local restaurant where he had trained the ice cubes to warm up at double speed.

Carter De Haven, my first assistant, had planned to shoot first the scene needing the largest crowd. He pointed out that on the first night of after-dark shooting in a community not used to a movie company, there were generally up to a thousand spectators who moved in just to see what was going on. So if, by some chance, they stepped into the shot, it wouldn't hurt, would it?

"You mean," I said, "you'd get them free?"

"Well, if they don't know enough to move out of the camera's range, you can't pay them for making a stupid mistake like that, can you?"

I decided maybe it *would* be nice to have a crowd in a shot.

That shot was to be of a flower-laden swan boat carrying Madge who had just been crowned Queen of Neewollah. Neewollah is Halloween spelled backwards, and it is a local Kansas ceremony—the arrival by boat of the local beauty queen—that Bill Inge remembered in his play. We were going to show it in all of its questionable glory.

Kim Novak had been extremely prompt throughout all of the shooting to date, except for the day she had forgotten her high-heeled shoes. I had warned her never to appear on the set without those shoes.

"That's what makes you Madge more than almost anything else you wear, those tacky shoes."

She had promised never to forget them again.

The night of the swan boat scene was particularly important because, as cameraman James Wong Howe had explained it to me, in order to show trees and distant hills and the details of the river, plus the lights of the bridge and the torches along the water, we had to shoot the first shot at the "magic hour" before the sky turned black. There would still be enough light to outline all of the figures, and yet it would photograph not as day but as blue night, and, more important, it would be dark enough to allow the film to register all of the man-made lighting: the blue stringed lights along the bridge, the kerosene flares along the side of the river, and the lights that are used to illuminate the actors' faces. This was to be a "production shot"—a climactic effect, very, very beautiful and exciting, but it must be done exactly on time or it would be worthless. Not one moment too light or one moment too dark.

Carter De Haven spoke to all of the crowd that had come along to see "the crazy movie people." He told them that if they wanted to stay out of the picture they must stay beyond this point, but if they wanted to step in and be part of the picture and see better, then they must move right behind the crowd on either bank.

Far in the distance, the size of a postage stamp, was Madge's swan boat, with a man sitting behind it ready to pedal it forward.

Jimmy Wong Howe watched the sky and studied his light meter and checked them both against his watch.

Things were now getting very tense. Eventually, Jimmy said, "Two minutes to go."

I spoke to the crowd on the microphone and told them to sing the song I had taught them:

> Ain't she sweet!
> See her walkin' down the street. . . .

We were going to use this silly song as the theme song of Neewollah. I even asked them to wave their arms in rhythm and said that many arms moving in unison would add greatly to the visual effect of the scene.

Finally, Jimmy said, "All right. Let's go."

I said, "Roll 'em."

At that point, the camera didn't roll, and when I asked why, Carter De Haven said to me, "Miss Novak's not here."

I said, "She's not! Good God, the daylight's going fast. I'm going to lose this shot!" I started to scream over the loudspeaker, "Miss Novak! Miss Novak, wherever you are, come here, Miss Novak! Please, Miss Novak! Get into the goddamn barge, Miss Novak."

She did not appear. Nobody could find her. I looked at Jimmy studying the light.

Jimmy said, "We have only another minute. Maybe a minute and fifteen seconds. But it's going fast."

"Miss Novak!"

"Here she is. Here she is, Mr. Logan," came from the air.

She had, it turned out, forgotten her four-inch heels and her dress shields. I pointed out that she would photograph the size of a postage stamp in the shot—we wouldn't know if she was a boy or a girl. The four-inch heels and the dress shields would add nothing.

The camera started to roll, and it looked as though we'd have a beautiful scene. The crowd sang "Ain't she sweet! / See her walkin' down the street," waving their arms back and forth. All was fine, except the barge didn't move.

I said, "Move the barge, move the goddamn barge."

The motor had stopped.

But two special effects men dove into the river and walked through the waist-high mud, pushing the barge ahead of them, and we got the shot just before the light disappeared from the sky.

The rest of the evening was taken up with cover shots of Madge in the barge as she waved to the crowd.

The only hitch was that as the evening wore on, some of our spectator crowd began to go home. Their curiosity had been satisfied and they were ready for bed. That was all right for them, but for us it was disastrous. Having established a group of three thousand people, we couldn't have them dwindle to three hundred in half a second.

Carter De Haven came to me. "You've got to *do* something to keep them here."

I looked around and there was Roz Russell. I said, "Roz, take over—keep those people here."

She got up like the great trouper she was and started speaking, and because she understood what most people want to hear, she began telling them tales of Hollywood—little intimate details of who had been to dinner, and where, two weeks ago. She went on for another half hour. And they stayed.

We still had to shoot the setting for the famous dance between Hal and Madge, which I had restaged so it could be played on a low platform, a sort of boat landing very close to the water, and we could take advantage of the reflection in the water of the

Japanese lanterns which surrounded the landing. With the opposite bank crowded with people, the general feeling would be of an intimate sexual scene taking place in the middle of a crowd.

One afternoon, when we came early to prepare for our night shooting, I saw the beginning of a sunset that was dramatic to me. It changed by seconds and looked like fires burning in hell reflecting some sudden Armageddon. I planned to put Rosalind Russell's voice over it, saying, "Look at that sunset, Howard."

But none of us knew at the time what was inside that sunset. As the night wore on and we moved to shoot the dancers around the little concrete dance floor, we heard the harsh, grating bark of the public fire warning. It was so loud that it nearly shook us off our feet. It sounded four times. Anyone from Kansas knew what that meant, but I was not from Kansas.

While I was still trying to photograph, one by one the cast was beginning to disappear. Within two minutes or so I was alone, shouting, "Where is everybody? Where the hell are you going? I'm shooting a picture—this is costing Columbia money—come back here!"

Then I began following a few people, calling after them to come back. As I passed a certain spot in the path, I heard a voice saying, "Josh, get down here." I stopped and looked down in a ditch; lying flat was Rosalind Russell.

I said, "What the hell are you doing down there, Roz?"

She said, "You get down here, too. That's a tornado. It's right at us."

By that time I did notice that there was a funny change in the air—it felt thick and humid. I heard a large whooshing sound, and about fifty yards away I saw a can being lifted in the air and whirled around, and I dove into the ditch on top of Roz. We waited there, still, for two or three minutes before it happened, and then there was a roaring of winds and cracking of trees and branches as I had never heard in my life. It felt for a while as though we were inside the cave of the winds.

But just as fast as it had come, it went on, and the two of us leaned up out of the ditch and looked around. Others were emerging from their hiding places. There were even a few hurricane cellars that had been built into the park; Kansans were used to anything anytime. "If you don't like our weather," they said, "stick around for five minutes."

That tornado, by some freak of nature, did not actually land in the center of our picnic ground. It landed in a town a few miles away and destroyed it. We took our trucks and our biggest lights down there and all of us helped uncover bodies, clean streets, and load injured people into ambulances until early the next morning. It was outrageous, but in the middle of all that agony I kept thinking to myself, At least we got the sunset.

Spit. It has always seemed to me the most insignificant of substances, and yet I am accused by enemies and friends alike of building my career on it. "Your whole reputation in films started with one spit bubble, and a baby's spit at that." But they don't know how hard it was to get that spit and how nearly it was lost to the world forever—and how expensive it turned out to be.

For the daylight shooting of the actual Labor Day picnic at the picnic ground, we had our three hundred paid extras who worked with us daily and who in real life were housewives, merchants who had found someone to take their place at the store, schoolchildren who had been let out early by the teachers because they thought it was an educational experience—ordinary, nice, warm, hearty, corn-fed Kansas people. They did everything: sang harmony, played games—the potato-sack race, the three-legged race—volunteered for the amateur contest, whatever we wanted.

When lining up the Kansas extras on benches for community singing, I noticed on one young woman's lap a baby calmly blowing one spit bubble after the other. I had never seen a baby who was that bored before and I longed to photograph her to cut into the picnic sequence. Looking through the script, my eye lighted on the words, "Labor Day speech by Mayor." Oh, now I had to have the bubble shot. After some especially pithy remark by the mayor, we could cut to the baby blowing a spit bubble. It would be a kind of visual raspberry and would prove the baby had good taste.

Jimmy Wong Howe lined up a shot so close to the baby that only the young mother's arms showed. The operator reloaded the camera so as to have plenty of film. The young mother assured us that the baby would blow bubbles all day long. The crew set the lights and the focus while I kept watching the little baby girl. Bubble followed bubble as though there were a machine inside her.

So as not to disturb things, we didn't call out or use a clapper to start the shot: it was all done in pantomime. The camera rolled but the baby, hearing the motor, stopped blowing bubbles and stared at the camera, fascinated. Her young mother was humiliated. She tried to recapture the baby's mood by slithering her finger across the baby's lips.

Jimmy Wong Howe signaled for us to keep on running. The film cranked on, and the baby kept on listening to it. Everyone tried to distract the baby from the camera sound. She was not to be distracted. Three hundred extras, an entire cast and crew waited while we rolled film on a baby girl's eyes looking right into the camera.

A camera has only a thousand feet in one roll of film. I wanted to give up, but Carter and Jimmy wanted to go on. The mother slithered her little girl's lips again, then jumped her up and down—and just before we ran out of film, the baby got bored with the sound of the motor and blew another bubble. And we had it on film. We cut it into the picture during the mayor's speech and got about the biggest laugh I ever got from anything I ever did. It was the high spot of the picnic sequence and was mentioned by many critics as a Logan touch. I am still very pleased when other directors say to me, "How on earth did you ever get that baby to blow that bubble?"

If the bubble of spit was a high spot of the onscreen *Picnic*, two nights later we reached an offscreen high spot.

We had got to the games section of the Labor Day picnic, and the night before shooting we had all got together in Bill Holden's suite on the fourteenth floor of the Baker Hotel. Roz Russell's suite next door furnished extra rooms, and so the party grew.

Bill, who had been warming up the ice cubes since before he left the set, was so amusing, lively, and funny that he gave me an idea.

I said, "I need to film you in action in some way. Hal is always telling people he's the champion of this and that. Do you suppose you could do any kind of gymnastic trick?"

Bill smiled charmingly and said, "My father was a gym teacher."

"Good," said I. "Then you can stand on your hands?"

Bill said, "I stood on my hands on top of that big Aurora Bridge in Pasadena, and it made my brother so mad he got arrested."

"Bill, you've had too many martinis."

"No. My brother wanted to prove to my father that he was

better than I, so he did a handstand on the Brooklyn Bridge and got arrested, so they would notify my father."

I turned gray. "You mean way up high?" I could feel my spine growing limp at the thought of height.

"What's the matter?" said Bill. "Don't you like heights? I mean, for instance—" He got up, carried his martini to the windowsill, opened the window, climbed out, and holding himself from the fourteen-floor drop by resting his bent left elbow over the sill, he raised the glass with his right hand and said, "Is this the kind of thing you mean, Josh?" Still holding his glass high, I could see that his legs were swinging over all that emptiness.

I melted onto the floor, not able to look.

"Get him back, somebody," I mumbled. "Get him back in, get him back in."

I was crawling toward the hallway with such vertigo I was unable to rise. I could hear Roz Russell's high, hysterical imprecations. "Bill, dear, you've had your fun—now crawl back into our midst." And then higher. "Bill, dear, we're getting pretty bored with that athlete stuff. Get the hell back in, dear. Bill, get back in here before I drop dead."

"I'll come back," said Bill, "if you make Josh watch."

And I did. And he did.

I decided to go down to the ground floor for a while. While I was sitting there, Kim Novak came in from midnight Mass, picked up her key at the desk, and came over to me.

"You won't believe what I think I just saw. When I got out of my car, I happened to look up, and halfway up I thought I saw a man hanging out of the window. But of course I probably didn't."

"Oh, really," I said. "I wonder who that could have been—that is, if you saw anyone."

"Well, you know, it's funny—as a matter of fact it's ridiculous that I should even think such a thing—but the way he moved and the way he kind of hung there so calmly, I thought just for a minute, that's Bill Holden."

"Bill Holden?" I said. "That *is* ridiculous."

"Of course. Well, good night—see you in the morning."

To me, the greatest scene in the picture was Rosemary's begging Howard to marry her. We shot it in daylight but with a porch canvased in to imitate night. Roz Russell and Arthur

O'Connell had worked hard on it with me. It was what the English call "close to the knuckle." In other words, it would be delicate, sensitive if done right; one step further, it would be ridiculous. There was always the fear that when Roz dropped to her knees, the audience would laugh.

As they were nailing the canvas down, I heard a strong wind coming up. The sound man said, "I think I can hold that wind down to seem natural." I asked Roz if she was ready to go ahead. Her makeup was streaky. Jimmy Wong Howe had lit her according to her own instructions, showing shadows in her neck and under her eyes, with wrinkles on her forehead and temples. She was a woman at the end of her rope, a desperate human being clinging to one shred of hope—the hope that Howard would marry her.

It was such an emotional and fevered scene that we decided to shoot it all in one shot. The camera would start far enough back to establish the porch and steps, and then it would move forward imperceptibly until Roz dropped on her knees, and then move in intimately.

We were ready. I said, "Roll 'em," and the camera turned. Roz started. Suddenly, there was a flap, flap, flap. I looked around. Some part of the canvas was loose in the wind, but no one could figure out exactly where. Roz was playing with a bitter resignation and controlled fury. I let her go on. The wind continued, but the flapping died down a little. Eventually, she fell shamelessly to her knees and the scene was over. I said, "Cut." And that small group of cynical technicians burst into applause. It's the only time I've ever seen them do that.

I asked the sound man if we could use it, and he answered, "We've got to use it. It's a once-in-a-lifetime thing. We may have to dub a few lines."

We tried to do another take, but the wind roared in and blew off part of the canvas. The wind seemed to be directing the picture.

The shot that now meant the most to me was at the very end when Madge boarded the bus to follow Hal to Tulsa. I wanted the camera to follow the bus for a while and then move over to show Hal's train headed in the same direction, to show that the two young people would be in each other's arms before nightfall. All we needed was a helicopter shot to connect the two vehicles.

Carter De Haven had planned everything perfectly. The helicopter was behind Mrs. Potts's house. The bus and the train were ready to take off. The young camera operator who was going to shoot the scene for us was from Chicago. He was Haskell Wexler, on his first important mission. He climbed in the helicopter and wrapped his right leg around the pole, the only thing holding him in.

I said, "I'm sorry—I can't stand it."

"It's quite simple. Don't worry about it."

"But can't they strap you in?"

Haskell said, "No, it's impossible. It's right this way. If I stay in a safer position, I won't be able to lean out enough to see both the train and the bus, and I want you to have your shot."

Carter De Haven said, "It was your idea, Josh."

I said, "Yes, I know. All right, let's try it."

The helicopter took off. Haskell gave a signal and the bus started. The helicopter rose, photographing the bus, and then swept across the fields, roads, and woods until it centered on the moving train.

The helicopter came down. Haskell stepped out and said, "That is the shot you'll use."

That young man was soon to become one of the greatest cameramen and finest directors we've ever had.

At the studio, I immediately sensed *Picnic* was going to be a hit. There is no praise written by a newspaper critic that compares with the greeting you receive from the doorman of the studio when you come back from location. Everybody connected with the studio has heard how well it's going or how badly. From our doorman's reaction, ours was obviously better than the best. I walked about with a smug face and arrogance in my heart.

By this time all of them, including Kim Novak, felt at ease in their roles. More than that, Kim, who had started out on the defensive, had become an enormous contributor to the whole mood of the picture. In the first place, she kept in character always. She had innate good taste about where she should stand and how she should react. As she blossomed, life was better for all of us.

Now we were to go into night shooting at the duplicated picnic grounds at a studio ranch near Burbank. They had dug and filled a river, along which they had built the exact landing platform from Kansas. Japanese lanterns had been hung, and there was a string of blue lights across a token bit of bridge.

Here was where I got my first taste of the magic of matching shots. It became not only a game but a ruling passion of mine. I was constantly thinking of ways to tie this location with Kansas without the audience ever guessing. We were to photograph some major footage: the famous dance sequence between Hal and Madge, and the fight that takes place following it, when Roz Russell as Rosemary pulls them apart and pulls Hal toward her, tearing his shirt, and then turns furiously and storms away, followed by Howard.

In Kansas I had shot the scene from far away to establish it geographically: we had the group arriving at the platform and then leaving it. The important work, the detail, was now to take place.

The dance between Hal and Madge has become a kind of minor national monument, and so I guess it's difficult for anyone to understand why I was so nervous about shooting it. But one reason was that the dance had been such a high point in the Broadway production that I couldn't bear the thought of its not reaching the same level in the film. The fact that Bill Holden was not really a dancer and that Kim Novak was not much better was a big worry to me.

Miriam Nelson, who was to help me with the dance, had rehearsed two doubles for Kim and Bill for the long shots and had worked very hard on Kim and Bill themselves, hoping we could catch a few moments of them really dancing so that the audience could feel their closeness, their sexual attraction. It all went very well the first night in the establishing shots.

I asked Jimmy Wong Howe, "How can we photograph them and not see their legs, which are not quite in rhythm?"

He said, "Well, I can photograph them from their waists up if they can move in the proper sphere."

I said, "Is there anything extra you can do to make up for what they lack?" By now our nerves were frayed, and he suddenly screeched at me, *"Just tell me, what kind of a shot do you want?"*

And I screeched right back at him, *"You're the cinematographer —you figure it out!"*

He turned on his heels abruptly and left. But by the next day he had figured it out. He said, "I know what you mean by something extra. It will be so romantic, so beautiful and distracting that we won't worry about seeing their feet. All we'll want is just to gaze at their faces and read their eyes."

He planned to move the camera slowly across the platform, following the two walking in rhythm. Up above the Japanese lanterns, he had rigged tiny spotlights with different colored gelatins, so as Kim and Bill danced, or rather, walked, across the platform looking into each other's eyes, their faces would move in and out of constantly changing colors.

This is the shot we made that night, and surely to the naked eye it was breathtaking. Still, I kept worrying, Will the audience wonder whether they are actually dancing or not?

This shot was to be played to the accompaniment to "Moonglow." It had to last a certain amount of time or the effect of Hal's and Madge's attraction for each other would not register as important enough in the audience's mind.

Much later on, after the picture was cut and looked at carefully, we found that the main shot did not sustain the mood as long as it should.

I showed it to Morris Stoloff, our musical director, and said, "Morris, this dancing shot doesn't last long enough for the sexual excitement it needs. Do you think we should make some change musically?"

Morris said, "George Duning has written a very effective *Picnic* theme to use under the love scenes. Since this 'Moonglow' arrangement has no melody to it, I could bring in the *Picnic* theme over this rhythm on a hundred violins and a full orchestra, and I think it would be very effective."

It was. The dance music became a single record that was played all over the world. It got me my best notice, which I can prove from a letter I got from Jess Gregg, a friend of mine. Jess wrote me that he was at a roadside diner sitting next to a booth in which there were a couple of old gals. Someone put a coin in the jukebox and out came the rhythmic *Picnic* dance record. One of the gals said, "Isn't that the theme from *Picnic?*"

And the other one said, "I don't know, but every time I hear it I want to get laid."

BOGEY
AND THE
PETALS

HUMPHREY BOGART, long before he was "The"
Humphrey Bogart, was a very casual fellow—at least he
seemed so to me. I never saw him hotfoot the pave-
ments daily from agents' offices to producers' offices, "making
the rounds" as we did.

He was even casual about the roles he played. He seemed to
accept the fact that he was doomed to play poor parts in bad
plays. For a while he even was a "replacement" for a juvenile.
Six months after a play became a hit, Bogey might step into the
role while the original actor went on to bigger things—a new
play or a role in a movie.

It was Bogey who, in the unavoidable white flannels and
white-and-brown shoes, would lope through the room, calling
"Tennis, anyone?" He used to entertain his friends by reading
them from his scrapbook of bad notices (the only ones he kept):
"Humphrey Bogart adequate. Bogart played the young man
with no dash at all." Perhaps that's why Bogey seemed so devil-
may-care to me; he was branded as the perfect actor for poorly
written juvenile parts. He was shackled to mediocrity.

I first laid eyes on him at the Lambs Club in 1934 or 1935 at one

22

of their time-killing, Sunday-afternoon billiard contests. Out-of-work actors had to do something to stop thinking about being out of work. But Bogey wasn't playing billiards—there was no cue in his hand. He was the umpire, the most affable umpire I ever saw. If one of his decisions met with an argument, he reversed it at once. Nothing was worth a raised voice or a raised fist—not to Bogey. He'd given up fighting long ago.

And then came *The Petrified Forest* and world fame. Gone was the antiquated juvenile. Now there was cold steel in every word, mounting threat and terror. Bogey was a world symbol of the killer, especially for the ladies. He was the best bad man around —the best looking, the most virile. In short, a star of the highest power.

Where was all this talent last year? Simple. It was buried in bad writing, flat, silly dialogue, tired, overfamiliar plots. Actors try as hard as they can, but eventually are drowned in wetness of thought. Most of these unfortunates are too poor to refuse a bad part or a weak play. They can feel themselves being stereotyped, as I'm sure Bogey did, but rather that than not working.

Bogey shone when surrounded by girls. Men liked him, but women had him for breakfast.

I found that out while I was in Hollywood in 1936 working with Walter Wanger in *History Is Made at Night.* Bogey was shooting *Dead End* for Samuel Goldwyn on the same lot, and often came over between takes. Wanger, an aging Dartmouth smoothie, was all excited because he was about to start shooting *Vogues of 1938,* with the eight most beautiful models in the world.

I could tell he was in an amorous haze when I saw him staring at a slip of paper as though he were reading a pornographic novel. He handed me the slip. It read, "Tomorrow morning at ten o'clock we are testing Miss Aldredge, Miss Cawley, Miss C, Miss D, Miss E."

I said, "I sure would like to meet those girls."

Wanger jumped up suddenly with a startling thought. "You've got the setup"—I was sharing a house with Jimmy Stewart, Hank Fonda, and John Swope— "you'll give them a party. All of you at the house. I don't want any of these Hollywood press agents to make the girls feel commercial. This affair has to have class. I'll send over the food and drink, but you've got to distill the guest list. No other girls. Fuck them. At least two men for every girl, and they must be (1) single, (2) tall, dark, and handsome; and (3) gentlemen in evening dress—and, if possible, famous. Above all, eligible. Now, call me if Jimmy, Hank, and Johnny Swope agree."

I called him and accepted his conditions, because my roommates fell over themselves approving. When I tried out the idea on several friends I again found roaring acceptance. One friend even offered to pretend to break up with his girlfriend until the party was over, but we wouldn't allow that.

I spent so many hours on the telephone extolling the exquisite perfection of these girls that I began to fantasize them as creatures descending on a light-blue-and-rosy cloud from the land of Venus halfway up the rainbow.

We signed up dashing Alan Marshall and bulky but affable Dick Foran and a few others, but I was aiming for the big time —Bogart. At first, he wasn't sure, but then I began my poem on the juicy wonders of these New York vestal virgins—the tactile loveliness, the curvilinear fleshiness of them—and before I knew it, Bogart had caught the fever. Although there was a very low-key, underlying hint of sex to the whole thing, the filthy word was never so much as mentioned. Deep down, though, I was a little bit afraid that I oversold Bogart because I had a feeling that he was expecting to walk right into a Botticelli gang bang.

The anticipated day arrived and still none of us had laid an eye on any of the girls, although we had heard raves from the people in the studio who had met them or worked on their photographic tests.

Eight of us were assigned to pick up one girl apiece at eight o'clock Saturday night. We dressed in our white tie and tails and took off for the various addresses. John Swope picked up Katherine Aldredge and I picked up Olive Cawley. Olive was dark, perfectly featured, with a glowing ivory skin and black, twinkling eyes. Katherine Aldredge was taller, blonder, full of vivacity, and almost perfectly formed. The other six were either their equal or slightly more perfect.

We arrived at the house and I began serving drinks, but none of the girls took a drink. All they wanted was lemonade. This, of course, made the anxious men take slightly larger whiskeys.

When the girls in their pastel dresses were scattered about the living room, they were like beautiful petals fallen from a perfect magnolia blossom—unstained, unscarred, with pulpy fragrance. And the language in the room became a little more circumspect. "Damns" and "hells" were increasingly difficult to find and certainly never "goddamns" or "Jesus Christs." I was beginning to be afraid that there was going to be a sudden avalanche, that the men were just going to storm out of the place, yelling bloody murder that they had been hoodwinked.

But not at all. Instead, they soon stopped drinking, too, and after dinner, for want of music to dance by, we began playing games—charades and musical chairs. Jimmy did a few card tricks. It was perhaps the most innocent evening any of us had spent since we were adolescents.

When the party was over and we had driven the magnolia petals home, we came back into the room and found that everyone had gone but Bogey, who was sitting there in an inkily thoughtful mood.

Thought I to myself, Oh, my God, he'll never speak to me again. He was expecting a good wrestle in the hay with one of these girls and he got nothing. He'll be so frustrated I'll hear about it at the studio for months to come.

Jimmy and Hank and I went over to him to offer him a drink to lift his spirits. "What's the matter, Bogey? Did you have a bad time?"

He looked up at us with the most profound emotion and said, "Anybody that would stick a cock in one of those girls would throw a rock through a Rembrandt."

Picnic. William Holden and Kim Novak in the famous dance sequence. Susan Strasberg watching. (Columbia Pictures Corp.)

Picnic. Roz Russell: "I danced so hard one night I swooned." Arthur O'Connell watches. (Columbia Pictures Corp.)

The actual picnic scene. Left to right: Susan Strasberg, Arthur
O'Connell, Rosalind Russell, William Holden, Kim Novak, Verna
Felton, Cliff Robertson (back), Betty Field. (Columbia Pictures Corp.)

Bus Stop. Marilyn Monroe performing "That Old Black Magic." Note kick light switch in lower-right-hand corner. (Zinn Arthur)

Marilyn on Don Murray's shoulder watching the parade before the rodeo. Note four-year-old Susan Logan at Marilyn's right elbow. (Zinn Arthur)

Don Murray ready to rope a calf. (20th Century-Fox)

"Daddy, why is the snow yellow?" Tom Logan, age five, on *Bus Stop* set. (Zinn Arthur)

Edward G. Robinson in *Middle of the Night*. (Jos. Abeles Studio)

GOLDEN GOLDWYN DAYS

BEFORE I FIRST went to Hollywood, I had studied, even memorized, all the Hollywood legends. It was very much like the way I had learned New York by heart from the Rand McNally guidebook when I was nine and still in Louisiana.

A large part of the Hollywood legends, of course, was Sam Goldwyn. I knew that he was a brilliantly successful producer whose name had been Goldfish and that he was considered wildly egocentric because he insisted on his name being on the main titles sometimes as many as five times: Sam Goldwyn presents A Sam Goldwyn Production produced by Sam Goldwyn. Et cetera, et cetera.

I also knew about the Goldwynisms that were starting to become famous at that time, lines that may have been made up by his press agents. "Include me out" was one of them. But one of my favorite Goldwyn stories was about Sam and Maurice Maeterlinck. When Sam discovered that there was a new and great writer in Europe who had never been to America, Sam decided to bring him over, give him the royal treatment, and maybe squeeze a hit picture out of him. He located Maeterlinck, got him to Hollywood, gave him a house, a chauffeur-driven car, and secretaries—anything he wanted.

Maeterlinck told him it would be impossible for anyone to see him until he had written something he really liked and believed himself.

Soon, in a mysterious way, all the Goldwyn publicity about Maeterlinck disappeared from the papers. The author of *The Blue Bird* seemed to have flown off where the bluebirds fly. Finally, a reporter friend of Goldwyn's went to him and told him that it was rumored that Maeterlinck had gone back to Europe. "What happened?" the reporter asked Goldwyn. "Did you have a terrible fight?"

Goldwyn looked up at him a moment. "Do you know what that son of a bitch did to me?" he screamed with a red face. *"His hero was a bee!"*

I appeared on the United Artists lot every morning at eight-thirty and sat in my office wondering when they were going to put me to work on *History Is Made at Night.*

Since I really didn't have enough to do and was anxious to work and learn as much as possible about motion pictures, I was delighted to hear that the fabled Sam Goldwyn had requested me to direct an acting test for him.

The next morning I was outside Mr. Goldwyn's office, knocking at his door. His high-pitched but slightly husky voice called, "Come in, come in."

I entered, and we faced each other for the first time. He was trim, slightly wrinkled, with an apple-shaped head and a foam-rubber face, but he was vigorous, and showed real enthusiasm for our meeting. He picked up a couple of photographs of a large, very handsome young man. It was Frank Shields, the tennis champion, who was still very young at the time and who evidently was trying to break into the movie star business.

Goldwyn said to me, "Frank Shields sleeps with all the beautiful women in Hollywood and nobody has ever caught his sex appeal on the screen. I want you to make a test of him with it all over the screen."

I said, "I'd be delighted to, Mr. Goldwyn—at least to try."

"No," he said, "I don't want you to try, I want you to do it —full force. And there's a girl I want you to test at the same time. Her name is Sigrid Gurie. She's from some place up in Scandinavia and she's very pretty, and I want to see her work with Frank Shields."

I said, "I'll have to find some kind of a test scene that shows them both off."

He said, "Do it for Shields. She's just an also-ran."

I walked away from his office, trying to think of any scenes in any plays that showed all-out sexuality in a male. The sexiest scene I'd ever read in literature was in Hemingway's *A Farewell to Arms* when the hero is in bed stripped and getting a sponge bath from a beautiful nurse. Every few seconds during the bath he says, "I've got to have you," and urges her to get in bed with him.

I got the book from the library and fashioned a scene.

Frank Shields and Sigrid Gurie both read it and were delighted. I've always found that you can get an actor to play any part if it includes a scene in which he falls on the floor or takes his clothes off. Frank, who had probably one of the best physiques in the world at that age, was delighted at the prospect of revealing it to the girls via a motion-picture camera.

I asked them to read the scene aloud. To my surprise and horror Frank's face became rubber and moved all over the place. This often happens with amateurs who are trying to put over a scene. They don't realize that the simplest movement is the most effective. Finally, I said to Frank, "Read it now and don't move your lips at all. Just read it *through* your lips, as though they were frozen together." This he did, and suddenly there was a glimpse of life.

The next morning, on the set, Frank was propped up in bed with part of his bedclothes just covering his crotch, and Sigrid was leaning over him, letting the light play on her face to see whether it would cast improper shadows on Frank or on his body.

Rudy Matte, the great cameraman and director, was photographing the test himself. He was trying to please Mr. Goldwyn by having Frank look as naked as possible.

I said, "Be sure that his shorts do not show at the side where the bedclothes go off at an angle."

Rudy kept looking through the camera and asking us to pull the shorts down a little farther and a little farther, and finally he said, "I'm terribly sorry, but if we really don't want to see the shorts he's got to take them off."

Frank grinned and looked at Sigrid and said, "I hope you've got brothers," and reached down and pulled off his shorts, exposing for a moment all that Uncle Adam had given him. This did make a difference when they lined up the shot. It was now quite obvious that he was without a stitch, as they say.

We shot the scene several times, sometimes with Frank never moving his lips, sometimes with them moving a tiny little bit, and, at my urging, with Frank never making any attempt to be an actor, which deep in my heart (and in his too I'm sure) I knew he was not.

The next day, I spent quite a bit of time with the cutter eliminating mouth movements and getting the best performance from the film we shot. The whole thing was to be shown to Goldwyn the following morning, first thing.

I didn't have to wait long for a reaction.

The hall to Goldwyn's office passed several open-door offices, most of which were empty except for secretaries. At the last doorway I heard someone hail me. I looked in and found four youngish men. George Haight, whom I had worked with in New York, introduced me to Jock Lawrence, Goldwyn's head publicity man, and his assistant producers, Merritt Hurlbut and Frederick Kohlmar.

Jock Lawrence said, "You're a hero. He likes it. First thing he's liked in God knows how long."

Freddie Kohlmar said to me, "Bess Meredith, the dean of screenwriters, saw it with him, and when it was over she applauded, which impressed him beyond compare. You're this morning's genius. Go on in—he's waiting for you."

I looked back at them and they were all smiling. Evidently, most mornings were not as smiley.

I knocked on Goldwyn's door and I heard the same high-pitched, flawed voice call, "Come in."

I entered. Goldwyn was dictating to a secretary. He turned his billiard-ball head up at me and he said, "Frank Shields sleeps with all the beautiful women in Hollywood and we are the only ones who got that on the screen. He's a sexy stud and he can be a star—but I don't want to take any chances. I want you to make another test with him. With Sigrid Gurie, if you want. Just to see if he can do anything else but that scene."

I said, "Of course."

"I want you to do a lot of tests for me. You know how I think. In the meantime, do you mind if I show that test to some other people? I want to see if I can get Shields a job."

I said, "No, no, of course."

I didn't realize that his friends were going to run the Shields test very much as they would stag films. I had heard of a Hollywood character, Bobby, a young page boy who was very well endowed sexually, and who was hired by various semi-impotent producers to walk through their rooms naked in front of a prospective lady bed partner, and when Bobby's natural gifts excited the lady sufficiently, Bobby would disappear and the producer would take over. Evidently, that's somewhat the way Frank Shields's test was used, and pretty soon I got the reputation of being the dirtiest director who had come to Hollywood in years. Yet I'm sure that same test was congealed innocence by today's standards.

But I did keep looking for a second test scene for Frank, and having seen Gary Cooper in *Morocco* fairly recently, I decided to try and improvise a bit of that, complete with Arab music and street sounds. I made the test with Frank wearing part of an American marine uniform in the tropics and Sigrid Gurie dressed like a combination of Dietrich and Sadie Thompson. Rudy Matte filmed it, and the new test so excited Sam Goldwyn that he signed Frank Shields to a seven-year contract. I was sure he was throwing his money away, and so was Frank. Frank took me out and bought me a bottle of champagne and wondered how long Goldwyn would be fooled.

There was one thing the test did achieve, however: I became the regular test director for Sam Goldwyn. In the next year I made between ten and twenty elaborate casting tests for Goldwyn's pictures.

But one day, Goldwyn called me into his office and said, "I'm very anxious to get the part of the rich girl in *Dead End* for my contract girl, Andrea Leeds. She's a fine young actress but she's rather quiet and shy. She doesn't know how to project. But she's beautiful and I think she can make it with you putting some fire under her. But Willie Wyler's the director and he doesn't think she can act. Let's show him."

I said, "I'll do my best," and I got Andrea Leeds and began rehearsing with her. Soon I grew very fond of her, because she worked and was so terribly attractive and, I found, very talented. However, it was difficult for her to really let go, to do a big emotional, angry scene such as she was asked to do in the text. We went over it and over it and over it until she knew it perfectly. We were to film it one morning with Gregg Toland at the camera—the great Gregg Toland. He got excited about her too and decided that, instead of cutting it from close-up to long shot, he should move the camera in and out on her so we could make the whole scene in one shot and the emotion would never cool off. We rehearsed with the camera as well as with Andrea, and then we did two takes. I was ready to quit when I suddenly thought, no, maybe we'd better make one that's even a little more emotional, in order to get the quality Goldwyn wanted.

We did and I printed that last test. Of course, I should have printed one of the quieter ones, too, but since he had emphasized the bravura side so much, I sent him only that.

I came to my office early the next morning and waited for his reaction.

When he had not called me by eight-thirty or nine o'clock, I got a little worried and rang Freddie Kohlmar. "Have you heard from him this morning?"

He said, "No, I haven't, but I know that he and Bess Meredith saw the test the moment they came in. I don't know what they thought."

I called George Haight and Merritt Hurlbut and Jock Lawrence, and they were also in the dark. But there was a kind of strange tone to their voices that made me very nervous. Eventually, I decided to beard the lion in his den, and I went across the lot and knocked on Goldwyn's door.

"Come in!" he shouted, and as I went in the room Goldwyn stuck his finger in my face and said, "You stink! You made her overact. You made her scream. You ruined her chances of getting the part. I can't show that test to Willie Wyler. He would hate her more than I did. You stink! Don't ever come in this office again."

I called Andrea and told her the sad news, and she said, "Maybe you should have printed the second take."

I said, "I'm terribly sorry, Andrea."

She said, "Don't blame yourself. It was me. We both tried it and we both failed, and that's all right. We'll just do something else, that's all."

I will always love her for that.

But a bit chastened I went back to work for Wanger on the next lot and really never saw Goldwyn except by accident one morning several days later when I was going to the commissary for a cup of coffee. I passed him in the areaway between the big sound stages. When he saw me, he stopped, turned his back directly to me, and held his nose in the air until I passed. I don't think I've ever been as famous on any lot as I was on the Goldwyn lot after that.

I sneaked out a copy of the Andrea Leeds test and showed it

to some of my friends, all of whom said, "I don't know what he's objecting to—I think she's wonderful."

However, someone else got the part and Wyler started shooting *Dead End.* When it was about a third of the way through, I again found myself on the lot walking toward the commissary and passing Goldwyn. Expecting the same cold shoulder, I was not only surprised but almost overwhelmed by his reaction at seeing me.

He broke into a beneficent smile, came over, pumped my hand hard, and said, "You're a genius! You really know how to direct. You're an absolute genius!" And he walked past me quickly.

I walked back to my office in a daze. I just couldn't figure him out. And it wasn't until I met Willie Wyler coming back from the same commissary several days later that I learned what had happened. Wyler walked over to me, introduced himself, and said, "Are you Joshua Logan?"

"Yes," I said.

He said, "I want to tell you that I was terribly impressed with that test you directed of Andrea Leeds. I didn't know she had that kind of ability. If I had seen that test, she would have had the part. Will you tell her that?"

I said, "Of course I will, Mr. Wyler, and thank you very much."

He said, "It's just tragic that that foolish old character didn't have enough sense to show me that test. Just tragic." And he walked away.

I took Andrea to dinner. We toasted ourselves with a bit of champagne—and that was the only high moment we were able to glean from that ill-fated test.

I got busy with *History Is Made at Night* after that, and of course was not available when Goldwyn asked me to do several other tests later on. I left Hollywood when my term expired and didn't come back for many years because I did one play or musical after another, and whatever movie offers I got were for seven- or five-year contracts, which I had determined never to sign.

But I finally did get back to Hollywood for *Picnic* and *Bus Stop* and *Sayonara.* It was during this more affluent time of my life that I found myself at a dinner party at which Sam Goldwyn was one of the guests. After dinner, he got me off in a corner and he said, "I like your pictures, Logan. I think it would be a very good idea for you to do a picture for me."

I said, "Are you sure, Mr. Goldwyn? I have a feeling that it wouldn't work out, much as I would like it to."

He said, "What do you mean, it wouldn't work out? I'm the best producer there is. All directors want to work with me."

I said, "Well, all except, say, Joe Mankiewicz, whom I just saw last week, and he told me that you'd locked him out of the cutting of *Guys and Dolls.*"

"Aw, that's nothing, that's nothing," he said. "He'll forgive me later—I'll win him over. You ask Willie Wyler what he thinks of me."

I said, "What good would it do? I'm not Willie Wyler. I wouldn't know how to deal with you. I haven't got that kind of reputation, that power."

"You don't have to do anything about it," he said. "Just say yes and I'll find a picture for you."

I said, "It wouldn't work, Mr. Goldwyn; don't you remember me?"

"What do you mean?"

"Don't you remember how I used to make tests for you years and years ago when you borrowed me from Walter Wanger? I made a test of Andrea Leeds and you absolutely hated it. You snubbed me on the lot. You thought it was badly done. Quite honestly, I don't think I could go through that again, especially on a big picture."

He said, "You never worked for me one hour of your life. What are you saying?"

"Mr. Goldwyn," I said, "there's no point in our arguing about it. Just go back and look at your records. I made quite a few tests in 1936. You'll find that it's true. So I really don't think we ought to talk any more about my directing for you until you've looked it all up and decided what you really feel."

I left him as nicely as I could, and as firmly as I dared. I did not see him again for three or four weeks, and again we were at a party. As I came into the room with Nedda, I turned when someone introduced me to Mr. Sam Goldwyn.

Mr. Sam Goldwyn looked up at me and started to scream, causing quite a group of people either to crowd around or to get far away.

He said, "You stink! You're a liar! You never worked for me as long as you lived. You didn't work for me for five minutes. I talked to all my people, all my associates! They never heard of you in those days. You never did anything with me. How dare you say you worked for me and cause me all this worry! How dare you! Get away from me! And stay away. Liar! Liar!"

And he went on screaming as his wife pulled him away to the other side of the room.

It was hard to believe that this man with the tantrum of a three-year-old had made some of the greatest pictures of all time —but he had.

WILL ACTING SPOIL MARILYN MONROE?

NEARLY MISSED one of the high spots of my directing life because I had fallen for the popular Hollywood prejudice about Marilyn Monroe.

It certainly wasn't her fault that I became involved with her in the first place. I had no intention of working with her. I was out to make a movie of James Michener's novel, *Sayonara.*

But a joint lawsuit had been launched against me in 1953 by William Goetz, Metro-Goldwyn-Mayer, and Twentieth Century-Fox over the sale of those movie rights.

The case was dragging on, and we were going into a tedious pretrial examination when Lew Wasserman, the Great God Brown of MCA and my agent at the time, said to me, "With appeals for delay, you'll never win this case before the Korean War's over and the story's become dated. You've got to marry your enemies."

"How's that?"

"Let William Goetz be the producer of *Sayonara* and share half and half if he will drop his part of the suit; direct an extra picture of their choice for M-G-M; and appease Twentieth Century-Fox by directing another picture for them. Josh, I've gone to all of them and they agree in principle. You do *Designing*

Woman for Metro with James Stewart and Grace Kelly, and *Bus Stop* for Twentieth with Marilyn Monroe."

"Oh, no!" said I. "Marilyn Monroe can't bring off *Bus Stop!*"

"Why not?"

I answered, as though someone pushed a button. "Because she can't act."

I could gargle with salt and vinegar even now as I say that, because I found Marilyn to be one of the great talents of all time.

But I met with Bill Goetz, who was an established producer, about the idea of collaborating with him on the production of *Sayonara*, and in the course of the meeting asked him what he thought about Marilyn Monroe taking on the part Kim Stanley had done so brilliantly on Broadway, and he said, "Well, of course Marilyn's a very popular actress, but is she good enough to play that *Bus Stop* role?"

My heart sank.

Back in Connecticut, I sat in our front room talking to Lee and Paula Strasberg. Paula and I had become good friends when I directed the teenage Susan Strasberg in the movie of *Picnic*. I had read a great deal about how Marilyn Monroe had left Hollywood and moved to New York "to study acting with Lee Strasberg." The columnists couldn't stop making jokes about it. "Will acting hurt Marilyn Monroe?" But Marilyn had always been a butt of jokes. It seemed an accepted conclusion that she was a beautifully formed but stupid blonde. That was her fixed and nailed-down professional label.

Lee Strasberg, I must admit, had always struck me as a bit smug and pedantic, but I also knew he was worshiped by his students. Besides, Paula was so warm and earthy that I somehow believed every word she said, and her being Lee Strasberg's wife gave him a certain reality for me.

One day, when I asked Lee what he thought of Marilyn, he assumed one of his poses, looked out into the air for inspiration, and said, "I have worked with hundreds and hundreds of actors and actresses, both in class and in the Studio, and there are only two that stand out way above the rest. Number one is Marlon Brando and the second is Marilyn Monroe."

I was astounded. It was the first time I had heard Marilyn praised by anyone in the theatre. But I made the decision to go ahead on Lee's say-so. If he turned out to be wrong, I could kill him later.

I called Lew Wasserman and said, "I'll go through with the deal. I'll be delighted to direct Jimmy Stewart and Grace Kelly in *Designing Woman*—and I would be delighted and excited to direct Marilyn Monroe in *Bus Stop.*"

Lew laughed and said, "That's extremely lucky, because you happen to be one of the six directors she has *agreed* to work with. I won't tell you which number you were on her list."

Although Nedda and I had seen Marilyn at a couple of big parties, neither of us had ever met her, so a dinner meeting was arranged for us by Milton Greene and his wife, Amy. They had a house in Connecticut where Marilyn was staying.

Marilyn had always had such bad advice about her financial affairs that Milton Greene, one of the front-ranking magazine photographers, had given up his profession at least temporarily to take over Marilyn, run her affairs, help choose her pictures, and give her whatever advice she needed. He had persuaded her to head a corporation of which he was the vice-president. He was a very bright-eyed young man with a pleasant smile and a brain that ticked away night and day.

We drove up the Merritt Parkway from our place in Stamford to the Greene house. I was so excited about meeting my new star that I was the one who grew most impatient when she didn't appear for dinner. I asked Milton where she was.

He said, "Oh, she's dressing for dinner."

"But dinner's over."

"I know," he said, "but she's still dressing. She'll be down in a while. Don't worry."

Later, I learned that Milton had known she was going to be late for dinner. He said she was determined to make herself look exactly like Cherie before I saw her. And it was then that I began to realize what a passionate thing it was for her to give the right impression.

Eventually, after quite a delay, she did appear—beautiful, perfectly groomed, but with a slight bit of disarray that made her even more appealing. She greeted us, ate a bit of food, then sat on the floor and talked about *Bus Stop*—the story of a little, beat-up, hillbilly singer at a local nightclub and of Bo Decker, a wild cowboy who falls for her.

She obviously had loved Kim Stanley's performance and was planning to see it many times so as to get Kim's Southern accent —to me the greatest Southern Texas accent I had ever heard, a true distillation of the ignorant South. But it turned out that Marilyn had also been in the South a great deal of her life and that the accent was not going to be a problem. She drawled a few words and I was reassured.

I began to warm up. Of course she was the perfect girl to play the part. Kim Stanley had had to readjust her looks, her height, her weight, and everything else to appear as this girl, but Marilyn *was* Cherie, presto in the flesh.

Marilyn got a telephone call. I don't know who it was on the other end of the line, but evidently whoever it was hadn't talked to her for a while, because with childlike enthusiasm she said, "Hello, Billy, this is Marilyn; I'm incorporated."

It had been said that Marilyn was always late for any form of public appearance, and particularly for the camera. Directors had ground their teeth on the subject.

I made a quiet decision that night that her being late was never going to bother me. If she were as attractive as she was that night, I didn't care how much time she needed to get that way.

All pretty girls, especially stars, it seems to me, have a problem in life that most of us plain folks don't have. They have been forced to rely so much on the perfection of their face, the freshness of their skin, the brightness of their eyes, and most particularly on the youth that must radiate from them at all times, that they are mistrustful of their looks every minute of the day—and especially before they face any judgment.

They feel they must study themselves carefully to cover a wrinkle with a bit of hair, color a blemish with a tiny bit of makeup, reassure themselves that they are not one minute older than they were a minute ago. They are terrified of the glare of scrutiny awaiting them. And I'm sure that this study of themselves takes sometimes only a few minutes, and sometimes a few hours. If you're as beautiful as Marilyn, it might be longer.

So although others might have been disturbed by her behavior that evening, I was exhilarated. She struck me as being a much brighter person than I had ever imagined, and I think that was the first time I learned that intelligence and, yes, brilliance have nothing to do with education.

Certainly, Marilyn was not a finishing-school product, although she had recently decided to improve herself by reading as many "good books" as she could.

But her wit, her quicksilver laugh, her accurate reactions to each well-made point were so reassuring to me that I began to glow with the thought of what was going to happen to all of us during this production.

That night she was an ambitious, young, bright-faced girl who longed to be a great actress. She spoke in dreams. Perhaps someday someone would let her play Grushenka, the sensual girl in *The Brothers Karamazov*. And then as though she sensed doubt in the room, she said, "She's very erotic, you know."

The only thing she felt herself an authority on was eroticism; therefore, anything that suggested sensuality or sexuality gave her instant, joyful confidence. It was as though Dr. Einstein were mired in a conversation about wheat when someone accidentally and happily brought up the subject of mathematics. Delicate as were her skin and coloring, Marilyn was at heart a physical girl. Whenever the subject of sex came up, there was a twinkle in her eye. Sex was obviously fun and infinitely desirable. Up until her new educational phase, sex had been her finest hour.

In the next few weeks I saw a great deal of George Axelrod, who was writing the screenplay. George was a fun-loving American boy who was married to a warm, blond, and extremely smart girl named Joan. George and Joan became our great friends quickly. George had turned his play *The Seven Year Itch* into a movie for Marilyn and had as big an enthusiasm for her as I now had. He wrote the part of Cherie expressly for her and let the entire story be guided by his feelings for her.

Of course, Bill Inge's original play of *Bus Stop* was used, but while the play had taken place in one room—a bus stop in the mountains—George decided to go all over the map in the movie —on moving buses, to the rodeo at Phoenix, and to the café where Cherie sang "That Old Black Magic."

The two of us conceived a girl who was half Inge and half Monroe. Our Cherie was a little girl, coming from the Ozarks, who had always felt in her heart that fate had given her a "direction." This "direction" she had marked out on a beat-up road map with her lipstick—a straight line from the Ozarks to Phoenix and then, as she pointed out with a great leap of joy and her arms waving in the air, to Hollywood and Vine, that "wonderful place where you get *discovered* and *tested* and *everything!*"

Several weeks later we were all in Hollywood, George had completed the script, and we were making a few tests of costumes, makeup, and hair.

One night, I took Marilyn to see my picture *Picnic* which was playing in Beverly Hills. I was very proud of it, and wanted to use it to reassure Marilyn that she had not made a mistake in agreeing to me as a director.

She was entranced with the picture, thought it was beautiful, and kept nudging me and talking to me all through it. When it got into the sexual scene where Bill Holden talks about having sex with two girls in a motel, Marilyn nudged me again, and I looked over and she rolled her eyes heavenward. I said, "What is it?"

She said, "How did you get *away* with that? This is the dirtiest thing I ever saw in my life on the screen. They never would let me do a thing like that. Oh, it's wonderful—absolutely wonderful." Much as she loved art and culture, that sex scene was for her the biggest achievement of the evening.

The costume designer brought in the designs for her clothes. We looked at them and felt a bit sick. They were too grand, too movie star—not pitiful, comic, and humorous enough for Cherie. There was supposed to be a very skimpy, homemade showgirl's costume for Cherie's "That Old Black Magic" number. The designer had come up with something too well made, too rich, too slick.

But Marilyn jumped up and started wiggling with excitement. "Go ahead! Put it in production! It's perfect, I love it." She pushed the designer out of the room.

After she closed the door, I said, "Do you really like it? I thought—"

"I hate it! I hate it the way it is." But then came that rippling laugh. "But it isn't gonna be the way it is. You and I are gonna shred it up, pull out part of the fringe, poke holes in the fishnet stockings, then have 'em darned with big, sprawling darns. Oh, it's gonna be so sorry and pitiful and it'll make you cry."

I was beginning to feel that she had always been brilliant. No one seemed to have listened to her before.

Marilyn said, "Let's you and I go over to the costume department and rummage through the racks."

That's exactly what we did. Cherie needed a skimpy little coat to wear—a coat that was her idea of a grand coat but would photograph as the opposite. We found an almost disintegrated, wrinkled, green-gold lamé coat on which we asked the costume department to add a skimpy border of moth-eaten rabbit fur dyed brown. It turned out to be an inspiration. All the rest of the clothes were found in the next half hour. We chose the oldest, the most worn, the saddest, but each with a kind of reach that exceeded its grasp.

Meantime, Milton Greene was supervising the makeup for Cherie. He wanted to eliminate the usual "Petty Girl," honey-colored Marilyn the screen was used to. He decided on a light opalescent color, very thin and white. Milton worked with great care, but with daring. Marilyn was enthusiastic, and so were George Axelrod and I. We felt that a whitish pallor was exactly right for a little nightclub singer who always went to bed at five or six in the morning after drinks, and woke up way past noon to a breakfast of black coffee and aspirin—a girl who never really saw the sun.

But that makeup almost got me fired from the picture.

One day, during the shooting, Buddy Adler, the producer assigned to the picture, said to me, "All I hear at the rushes are two complaints. One is that Marilyn's face is too light and the other is that Don Murray is shouting too much."

I explained to him that the clownish makeup was part of Marilyn's characterization. It made it possible for her to wither like a sad hothouse flower.

"I know," said Buddy, "but they all think it's lousy, and I'm the producer. There's a rule in the makeup room—Marilyn must always be tan, honey-colored. And she's not as beautiful as she should be."

I said, "Well, maybe she's not quite as tan as they're used to, but at least she's in character. And as for Don, he's playing the part of an untamed young man. The only plot there is to *Bus Stop* is that a young, wild animal is tamed by a weak young girl. The reason Don yells onscreen is because that's the one way he can show the public he's wild. If he stops yelling and talks normally, then he doesn't need this girl to calm him down. If we follow all that advice, we have no plot. So, tell everyone to stop sending me messages about Don's yelling and Marilyn's makeup."

He paused a moment, and then he said, "Josh, you're right. You'll never hear those complaints again."

I never heard any more about it, and I'm very happy it worked out, too, because both of those elements are outstanding contributions to the success of *Bus Stop*.

Don Murray, who played the cowboy who falls in love with Cherie, was twenty-four and this was his first part in a movie. He was a tall, lean, and handsome young New York actor who immediately married a meltingly beautiful young girl named Hope Lange, who also had a part in the picture, the small role of Elma who worked behind the counter at Grace's diner. Don was an experienced actor who had been brought up in the legendary theatrical trunk. Both his father and mother had been stage managers, and I suppose by this time Don really knew almost all there was to know about acting. He was entirely convincing as the exuberant, roaring, physical young animal who would win all the events of the rodeo.

But there were two things wrong with Don as Bo Decker. One was that he was terribly thin. This we cured by putting a sweatshirt under his extra-sized shirt. We found out about the other problem just before we put him in action.

We had to start filming the picture in Phoenix, Arizona, on March 15 in order to be able to take advantage of the huge parade which always preceded the Junior Chamber of Commerce Rodeo. That parade was the most spectacular event of the year in Phoenix, and consisted of an endless line of cowboys, Indians, girl bands, groups of old scouts, the ladies' auxiliary, and on and on throughout the day. Tens of thousands of people sit watching each year on bleachers on either side of the street in downtown Phoenix.

We had arranged that our first scene was to be photographed during the parade so that we could use the crowd for the background.

I learned ten minutes before it happened that there was to be a parade of cowboys called the Grand Entry, consisting of a long line of horses, two by two, ridden by the contestants in the rodeo. I realized it would make a great shot to have Bo and his friend Virge (Arthur O'Connell) riding side by side.

I said, "Don, would you mind riding with Virge in the line of cowboys?"

He said, "Oh, not at all. There's only one problem—I've never been on a horse."

I said, "You mean you've never been on a horse ever in your whole life?"

"Never. I've never even put my legs around the back of a horse."

At that point, I decided to give up, but Marilyn Monroe of Marilyn Monroe, Incorporated, said, "Well, why don't you do it anyway?"

Don, never to be daunted, and certainly not by Marilyn, said, "Sure," and went toward the horses.

I can only say that eight minutes later Don rode past the camera with Arthur O'Connell, smiling and waving at the crowd, and he even took enough time, had enough control of himself and his horse, to smile and wave at Marilyn. And we made plans to give him riding lessons.

The remarkable thing about that day's shooting was that, just before the parade started, I made an announcement over the loudspeaker to the spectators in the immediate foreground—perhaps five thousand people who were in the camera's range. I urged them to watch the parade and please to look neither at Marilyn nor the camera, and just before I finished my little speech, I thought of the clincher. I said, "Because if you look at her or the camera, we will have to cut that part out of the film. So, if you want to be in the film, please watch the parade." It worked perfectly.

As George Axelrod put it to me, "You're lucky, because there are three fundamental basic urges in the human being. One is the will to live, two is the will to propagate, and three is the will to look into the lens."

Before coming to Phoenix I had got a call from Milton Greene saying that he would certainly understand it if I said no, but that he had to tell me Marilyn had requested that Paula Strasberg, who was to be her dialogue coach, sit on the set during the filming of the picture.

The thought of Paula's sitting there and approving or disapproving of a reading or of a take that had just been shot was very disturbing to me. I took a chance and said it as gently as possible. "I love Paula. She can come and work with Marilyn as much as possible, as long as she *never* appears on the set."

So Paula remained in Marilyn's dressing room or someplace available to her in case she wanted to run over her lines, but never sat in view while we were actually shooting or rehearsing.

I decided to write Laurence Olivier about this, because Olivier had agreed to direct as well as to star in *The Sleeping Prince* (later released as *The Prince and the Showgirl*) with Marilyn as soon as I finished *Bus Stop*. As an old friend of Olivier's I wanted to tell him as much about working with Marilyn as possible.

"First of all," I said, "be sure that you do *not* have Paula on the set. I'm sure she's going to be with Marilyn on your picture, and I think it would be most disturbing for you to have anyone there in authority except you."

I described to him the great beauty and talent of Marilyn, but added, "Please do not expect her ⁺⁻ behave like the average actress you have worked with.   ⸴ ⸴nstance, don't tell her exactly how to read a line. Let her work it out some way herself no matter how long it takes."

I got very nice answers to my letters. I remember one that said, "You have absolutely reassured me about this venture, and I will not get upset if I don't get everything my way. I will iron myself out every morning like a shirt, hoping to get through the day without a wrinkle."

Unfortunately, as I learned later, he was unable to carry out his resolve.

Marilyn was a totally satisfying professional during all the shooting in Phoenix. She was always on time. She sat for hours under a sunshade while we lined up on the various horses and crowds around her. Her hillbilly accent was impeccable. It was as though she had been working on this character all of her life.

Yet everybody who talked to me about her told me what a problem she was going to be: the old cameraman, the carpenters, the members of the crew.

I was walking with Ad Schaumer, who was our second assistant director. He said, "The only thing that can spoil this picture is if this dame gets your goat. If you see to it that she never gets your goat no matter what she does, you'll be all right."

He said it just in time, because the next day Marilyn almost got my goat.

There are very few things that cause me to let my nerves get the better of my self-control on a motion-picture set. I am prepared for the fact that almost anything can happen, and actually sometimes I welcome the unexpected—as, for instance, when a gust of wind brings dust into a shot and gives it a sense of reality. Variables add to the reality of filmmaking; they make people realize, even unconsciously, that we were actually on location, that the scene wasn't reproduced in a studio with paint, gelatin, and filters.

But there is one thing about filming outside that is invariable. I'm speaking of the sun. It always rises and it always sets; it can't be told to go back and start again. And now the light was fading quickly.

I felt my blood pressure rise because we were in danger of losing the shot we were set up for. We were to film a sequence of Marilyn running through the streets to the Phoenix bus station in an attempt to escape from Don Murray. I was particularly excited about the shot because it would establish the fact that it was actually made in Phoenix.

I had gone over and over the scene with the extras and with the cameraman and with the double who was doing the action that Marilyn was to do later, while Marilyn was getting ready for the shot.

But by now we all began to sense that something was wrong. The sun was dropping fast—and there was no Marilyn. I kept getting reports from the assistant director that she was on her way, but she didn't show. Finally, I turned to the cameraman and said, "How many more minutes before we have to shoot or lose the shot?"

He looked at his watch and at the sky and at his light meter, and said, "Three minutes."

I took off like a superannuated hummingbird and plummeted toward Marilyn's trailer, which was about five hundred yards away. I dove into her dressing room. The poor dàrling was still looking at herself in the mirror. I didn't ask any questions. I grabbed her wrist and pulled. I didn't even listen while she ran behind me explaining that she had actually been on her way when I arrived. I ran all the way past the camera, pulling Marilyn behind me, plopped her into her starting spot, and shouted, "Roll 'em!"

She didn't run in the exact light we had set up, but we got the shot, and without that shot we would have had to have spent an extra day in Phoenix, which would have cost the picture another $20,000 to $50,000. That sun can be expensive.

The rodeo was held every afternoon in Phoenix for a week, and we had permission to shoot during it as long as we did not interfere with the various events. I became obsessed with the idea that we had to have one shot that would show the public that Marilyn was actually there, a shot that would prevent people from thinking the rodeo was done with doubles or rear projection or the various other tricks that are used to create illusions in motion pictures.

And the only way I could think of was to put the camera back far enough to take in both sides of the huge rodeo ground and its stands while showing the activity in the center of the arena.

I dreamed up a scene in which Cherie would make a mistake while trying to escape from Bo who had planned to marry her during the rodeo. According to the script, she simply ran from the rodeo grounds and was later seen hurrying down the streets of Phoenix. But that didn't seem to show the location well enough, so we decided that Cherie, in panic, would run the wrong way, push her way through a gate, and run across the arena while Bo Decker was bulldogging a steer. She would run past him, getting away because he was using all his strength to hold his steer's horns to the ground.

The only way to shoot this excitingly, of course, was when the stands were filled, and the only time the stands would be filled and still allow us enough time for the scene was during the ten-minute break between the two halves of the rodeo. But we rehearsed the scene early in the morning, before the rodeo started. Bo knelt and held the horns of the steer down. Cherie ran, followed by her waitress friend, Vera (Eileen Heckart), while Bo shouted for her to stop and come back. In rehearsal I found it such an exciting shot that I wanted something that would make it last a few seconds longer. After all, we had ten thousand people on the left side of the screen, six thousand on the right side; all of the cowboys and horses down at the end of the field; Don Murray in the near foreground holding the steer; Marilyn and Eileen running wildly past. It shouldn't go by too quickly.

"Couldn't I lose my shoe?" Marilyn asked.

And that's what happened. At intermission I made an announcement over the loudspeaker, saying that we would like to shoot a scene from a forthcoming movie called *Bus Stop* and asked everybody to remain in the stands to participate in the scene. I explained what was going to happen and asked them all to react as they would if such a scene happened in an actual rodeo.

We pinned the steer down with stakes. Bo knelt next to it, pretending to hold the steer's horns into the ground. We had several cameras set up. I gave the command, "Roll 'em," then "Action," and, as the cliché goes, all hell broke loose.

Cherie ran across as fast as she possibly could in her tight little satin skirt, followed by gawky Vera calling to her to come back, saying, "Be careful of those animals, you're going to get killed." Cherie passed Bo, who screamed, "Wait a minute, Cherie— somebody hold this thing, please—come on back, Cherie, come on back."

Cherie saw him and realized she was too close and might get caught, tried to run faster, lost her shoe without realizing it, ran almost to the exit gate of the arena, discovered she had lost the shoe, ran back past Bo, and grabbed the shoe, picked it up, and, with Vera following her, disappeared through the gate into the crowd.

When I finally said, "Cut," the entire audience applauded wildly.

The main sequence to be shot in Phoenix was the series of cowboy events which Bo Decker had entered and which he performed during the afternoon while Cherie sat in the stands with Vera. At the end of each event Bo won, he had to run to the center of the field, wave his hat in the air, and jump up and down with joy and triumph. He then was to make an elaborate bow to the audience in the background, and then whirl toward the camera and shout, "HEY, CHERIE, WHAT DID YOU THINK OF THAT? CHERIE, HOW ABOUT THAT?" And he was to shout it so loudly, causing all the thousands to crane to look at her, that Cherie was tremendously embarrassed.

These shots of Don taking bows had, of course, to be done during short breaks in the rodeo with the crowd's cooperation. The actual scenes of Don competing in the contests were, of course, doubled by one of the real contestants dressed in Don's shirt and trousers and green neckerchief. All the rodeo events —the bulldogging, calf roping, steer wrestling, and riding the Brahman bulls—were covered by a second-unit camera. Our stunt men were professional cowboys, and we found many of them who were young and slender enough to look, at a distance, like Bo Decker.

Only a few of Marilyn's shots were made during the actual rodeo, because most of her bleacher shots could be done in the studio against a sky background with the help of hired extras. But it was while we were at the rodeo that we filmed a moment that many people feel was the funniest Marilyn scene in the picture. Sixteen thousand people are shouting and jumping up in the air as they watch the exciting events. The camera pans down to Cherie in the midst of the sunny bleachers. She is asleep. Although it is the start of afternoon, she has never been up that early in her life.

By the time we left Phoenix, I was beginning to know Marilyn a little, but we were both so busy with our particular jobs that we didn't have much chance to sit and talk until we went to our second location: Sun Valley, Idaho.

What we were after now were sequences of the bus arriving at the little bus stop in deep snow and getting stuck fifty yards away from the small frame building; shots of Marilyn and the rest of the cast running through the falling snow to the warmth of the bus stop. All of it went very well. Again, I had no problem with Marilyn's acting or performance. But we did have difficulty getting the proper falling snow. A machine for it was a new invention of one of the propmen at Fox who had figured out a way to throw wet detergent into the air and blow it in front of the camera with huge fans. It fell like snow, it looked to our eyes like snow, and as it landed on people's shoulders and hats, it melted very much like snow. And, fortunately, it didn't come down in gobs as real snow would. We had shot hundreds of feet of film in detergent snowstorms, when one day my son Tom, then aged five, came out to see the shooting. I thought he would be impressed by the way Hollywood recreated "real storms." He was standing next to me when we put on the machines and the blowers, and after a few seconds when the storm reached climactic proportions, Tom turned to me very quietly and spoke into my ear over the din.

"Daddy," he said, "why is the snow yellow?"

We immediately shut down the machines and everybody began to examine the snow. Indeed it was yellow. We spent the rest of the day working on it to whiten it up, but didn't get very far. The only consolation was that when we finally showed the film in theatres, only little Tom seemed to have noticed the color of the snow.

In the evenings at the Sun Valley Lodge, we began to meet as a group for the first time. There was a band, good food, and dancing. Marilyn was in a high state of exuberance.

Bus Stop was her first production as Marilyn Monroe, Incorporated, and she had a vision of a future in which she could choose her directors, her stories, develop herself as an actress. Her hopes were high. The very eagerness with which she grasped anything that smacked of culture, education, wit, mental stimulation made my heart break thinking of how much had been denied her before. I wonder how anyone seeing her then could have imagined the tragic things that were going to happen to her in the fairly near future.

She was always the most beautiful person in the room, and certainly the most fun to talk to, to listen to—warm, witty, and with the enthusiasm of a child. Innocent, yes, but she was never ignorant, stupid, or gross. She was in my opinion extremely bright, totally involved in her work. I think she was at some kind of peak in her emotional as well as intellectual life.

Certainly, the work she had done with Paula and Lee Strasberg had stimulated her basically. She talked constantly of Stanislavsky, for instance, and she wanted to know all about my studying with him in Moscow. She wanted to know all about the way the actors lived and acted there. How Stanislavsky talked to them and they talked to him—intimate details.

I think that Lee had opened a locked part of her head, given her confidence in herself, in her brainpower, in her ability to think out and create a character. But sometimes she acted as though she had discovered something that no one else knew. Words like "Freudian slip" and "the unconscious" and "effective memory" would appear in her conversation at the oddest time. If they didn't fit in, she made them fit.

But she was never so serious about herself that she didn't give her remarks a kind of wistful, comedic twist. It seemed to me that she was a combination of Greta Garbo and Charlie Chaplin. She was so beautiful that she could have played almost any romantic part that was physically suited to her, and yet I do believe she could have put on those baggy pants and that little mustache and made a fortune with slapstick and a sad, tearful twist.

All of this showed wonderfully in a scene we did the last day outside the bus stop in the snowy Idaho hills. The bus was waiting, ready to go off to Bo Decker's ranch in the north. Cherie came out of the bus stop, joining the rest, and was ready to step into the bus. Bo dashed ahead of her in his big, fleece-lined jacket. He had promised to try to be as much of a gentleman as possible, and here he was doing the ungentlemanly thing of preceding her. Cherie scolded him, and he, as though to show how much he had changed, how much he had become the knight in shining armor she dreamed of, said, "Cherie, what are you doing in that skimpy little coat? You're gonna freeze." And she stood there with her teeth chattering but with a look in her eye that said, "Yes, yes, go on." He whipped off his big, rough, fleecy leather coat and held it out for her to put on. In an ecstatic fairy-tale trance she slid her arms into the sleeves of the rough jacket as though it were made of chinchilla. There was in her eyes and face a look of fulfillment, reward, and a peaceful hope that was most moving, yet at the same time truly comic.

The first time Marilyn had tried the scene she put the coat on rather quickly, but I explained, "No, no, you must relish it more. It must be . . ." And then I tried to describe the various moods I thought she should have going through her mind while the action was going on. At one point I said, "Slowly, as though you were sliding into a bubble bath." I didn't really mean that; I was just trying to find a way of getting to her, when all of a sudden I heard a voice behind my ear saying, "Yes, Marilyn, he's right—that's a good image; you're enjoying a bubble bath." That was the only time Paula Strasberg entered a *Bus Stop* scene.

The rest of the picture was done on the back lot and stages of Twentieth Century-Fox, which is now mostly occupied by the vast complex of buildings called Century City. When I see them now, I don't really mind those enormous monoliths. I like to think that the higher they go, the more of them there will be to remind me of Marilyn.

It was here we did the major acting scenes of the picture, and the first one was in the nightclub that George Axelrod had created for Cherie's singing of "That Old Black Magic." George's idea was that it was the type of place where cowboys met to talk while drinking soft drinks or beer the night before the rodeo. They had come to swap ideas and boasts and challenges, but because it was a predominantly male clientele, the manager had allowed this little woebegone singer a chance to entertain. He didn't give her much time and certainly was not giving her much money, and although there was a small band to play music for the crowd, it didn't do much for Cherie's song.

In working out the "That Old Black Magic" sequence, I decided that Cherie might be ambitious enough to try for the theatrical effect of a change of lighting during the song. Maybe she could stand on a little platform of glass bricks which had under it some red spotlights. She wouldn't be able to persuade anybody to help her with the lighting, and she couldn't afford to hire anyone, and so she would have to do everything herself, changing colored spots in the middle of the song with her foot by kicking a homemade switch on the platform below.

We practiced the song and she did it with almost an instinctive comic genius. But I knew she could not ever concentrate enough to sing the song to a playback, and then sing it for the camera by lip-synching. She could never memorize exactly the way she had sung it, breathed it, performed it, and still make it sound spontaneous.

I went to the head office—Buddy Adler—and said I would like Marilyn to do her song *live*. The way he looked at me, I might have been asking him to cut off one of his arms. But still, he agreed to a conference with Al Newman, head of music at the studio, and Ken Darby, who did the song coaching.

At first they all said it absolutely could not be done. It hadn't been done in Hollywood for thirty years. It would waste money and time. We would lose the good smooth sound that could be achieved in a studio after many rehearsals. But I was insistent. I knew Marilyn would fail if she had to resort to that mechanical way of reproducing the song. Finally, it was agreed that we would shoot the song in two parts—since there was a pause in the middle where Bo Decker did some yelling to the crowd— and that we would record it as we shot it, with two cameras of different-sized lenses.

Two cameras were set up on Marilyn, one a full-length shot which showed the way she kicked the switch and waved her handkerchief (a corny old trick which she had learned from a makeup lady) and the other camera had a lens cutting her at the waist but showing much more detail of her face, lips, and eyes and, of course, performance, as well as the wiggle and wave of her body.

And that's the way it was shot—with two cameras, live, and with a hidden orchestra that was baffled by cardboard and canvas screens. With the two cameras Marilyn was free to perform the song as she wanted to; she never had to worry about lip-synching or anything other than her own feelings. It worked perfectly. We took one long close-up with a bit of lip-synching but mostly for her eyes, and an extreme long shot showing her position in the room.

Eventually we had a memorable musical sequence, primarily because we gave a great artist, a superb comedienne, the freedom to perform the way she felt.

There has been a great deal of comment on Marilyn's inability to remember lines. I will admit that in some of the scenes with lengthy exchanges of dialogue, we had some difficulty, but never because of memory, only because of anger and frustration.

Marilyn played with feverish concentration. But if I cut the scene and wanted to do a second take, Marilyn would have lost this concentration—be thinking about her hair, or chatting with a makeup man or an extra. It might take minutes, sometimes half an hour, before I could get her back into the state of mind she had been in before the interruption. But the moment the camera turned, it was just as though someone had pressed a button: she was immediately acting. And no distraction could keep her from playing the part until the word "cut." She was owned by the camera.

There are certain great actresses, even great beauties, who seem to be rejected by film, lessened by it, who are welcomed by footlights and beautified by the distance at which they are seen in the musical or legitimate theatre. But not Marilyn. Whether in close-up or a long, long shot, she was always recognizably graceful, lovely, and fascinating, but there was actually a certain suspense to watching her. What will she do next? And she must have subconsciously known that because the moment the camera started turning, Marilyn "turned on" with it.

And so, I invented a new technique for filming Marilyn. It used to drive the experts at the rushes crazy, but I really didn't care. I would let Marilyn play a scene, and then without cutting, I would put the first prop back into her hand or reach out and turn her head to the position it was in when she started the scene, and I'd say, quietly, "Action—go ahead."

All this time the film would be rolling. And by the third or fourth take I could cut together a magic scene. But I had to keep taking these scenes until the film ran out, and then print the whole thing in order to get a concentrated, word-perfect performance from her. It is true that as the scene progressed, or, rather, as one scene overlapped the other, I would sometimes get a better performance, sometimes not as good a one, but each one was interesting—never dull or routine—and would give me a chance to piece bits and pieces of brilliance together until the final scene shone.

Marilyn worked so hard to give a good performance that sometimes she would stop and wrinkle her face as though in pain before she could continue. I began to suspect that what was the matter with her was that she was in some private chamber in the side of her brain, looking at and listening to herself and disapproving of both. Her little fire of creative acting was extinguished as though with cold water whenever she thought she had been a whit less good than she dreamed of being.

So I instructed my dialogue director, Joe Curtis, to prompt her whenever she seemed to dry up. Since as long as the camera turned she never stopped acting the part, she just picked up the prompt calmly and continued to the end of the scene.

In the final version of *Bus Stop*, Marilyn plays a tender scene with Don Murray in which there seems to be a long pause in the midst of dialogue. The reason for this is that Joe Curtis gave her a line, and we later removed his voice from the sound track. But the scene was so beautifully played, so touching, that I was never able to find a take anywhere near as good—and, besides, the pause didn't hurt. Marilyn had a way of filling pauses visually and keeping an audience in her spell.

Everything was going well. It looked as though we were going to come in on schedule, or certainly very close to it.

We got to the spot in the story where Bo and the bus driver have a showdown in Grace's diner as to how Cherie is to be treated. Bo wants to force her to a preacher and the bus driver prevents him. They challenge each other to a fight outside in the snow.

Of course, when a fight is called for in Hollywood, there are always, whether you want them or not, a few stunt men who appear. We started to film the fight out in the phony snow that was packed around the exterior of the bus stop.

It was during the first day of the fight that someone came to me and said, "Marilyn Monroe has been taken to the hospital." I couldn't believe it. She didn't seem ill, but she was always a bit trembly and tentative, and certainly the white makeup might easily have been covering a white face.

There was no doubt about it. The doctors had examined her: she had a bad case of pneumonia. I asked the front office what to do about the shooting and they said, "Go on shooting around her." That was difficult. There was a scene between Bo and Virge which took up one day, and there were a couple of other small bits here and there that we could photograph, but Marilyn was in every foot of the rest of the picture. The only scene that could have been filmed without actually seeing her was the fight, since we could later cut in her face watching it.

So, I set about filming the fight. We shot it in reverse, we shot it from the right, from the left, in close-up, in long shot. I don't think any pitiful little fight between two men ever got that much attention. We filmed it for fifteen days: in the final cut it lasted half a minute.

Milton Greene and Paula were around all the time, worrying about Marilyn, assuring each other that she was going to get better. But the bug held onto her and she didn't get better.

About the tenth day, Nedda decided to go down to the hospital and call on her. We had all been warned not to go because the doctor felt she needed all the rest she could get. Nedda told me that when she was being led to Marilyn's room by the nun in charge, the nun said, "Oh, Mrs. Logan, she's so terribly sweet —but really she's too sweet. This morning she complained of the cold and said she had been freezing all night long. I asked her why she didn't ring the bell to ask for a blanket, and she said, 'I didn't want to disturb you.' "

When Nedda returned from the hospital she reported that

Marilyn was terribly nice, and I said, "Is she worried about holding the picture up?"

Nedda said, "She didn't mention it."

The only thing Nedda learned was that there was a telephone right next to her bed and that she talked on it constantly, and she had a feeling from the way Marilyn spoke that she had been talking regularly to Arthur Miller. Arthur Miller was in constant touch with Marilyn, and it was hinted that they were going to get married.

Meantime, the windup fight went on, until the day Marilyn walked in, dressed, ready for the next scene. The adrenalin that shot through that crew and cast was almost enough to win a war.

The last big love scene was to be played near the wood stove at the bus stop. I knew we had no other technique to give to this picture except the performance and the beauty of Marilyn—and the fine work of Don Murray as Bo—but I remembered Garbo's big close-ups and went to Milton Krasner, the cameraman, and said, "How near can we get to Marilyn's face in CinemaScope?" This was a lens that elongated the side of the scene and was a little bit, as they used to say, like looking through a post office slot. I said, "I feel we have here one of the great faces of all time—let's really see it."

Milton said, "That won't work in CinemaScope. The face becomes distorted once you bring it closer than five feet away from the lens."

I said, "But it would make such a difference to the end of our picture if we could really see these two people looking at each other intimately." I made such an issue of it that the camera crew got together and decided if they could get a diminishing lens, or several of them, we could get maybe as close as four and a half feet; the diminishing lenses would redistribute and eliminate possible distortion.

The day we were to do the scene, Marilyn was dancing around like a child in anticipation of having a big head closeup as Garbo had had. Garbo and Dietrich were her goddesses. When we had arrived in Phoenix, the Chamber of Commerce had come out to meet the plane in an old-fashioned stagecoach, and Marilyn was to ride on top of the front seat next to the driver and be photographed for the local press. They had handed her a big cowboy hat to wear. She had plopped it on her head enthusiastically, but then suddenly pulled it off her head and handed it back to the man.

I said, "Marilyn, what's the matter?"

She said, "It just came to me. Dietrich wouldn't have done it."

But Dietrich and Garbo would certainly approve of a huge close-up. I think it was the thrill of imagining her face so enlarged that nothing showed below her mouth or above her eyebrows, the lens so carefully focused that every vein, every tiny bit of facial fuzz, the watery depths of her eyes, the detail of her skin, her nostrils would leave an indelible impression on the world. But more than that, it was new—that is, so old it was new. It was a daring move. And Marilyn, since it was her first picture as a coproducer with Twentieth Century-Fox, wanted to be fresh and daring.

We started by lining up on Don Murray so as, in a sense, to use him as a testing case. The diminishing lenses were in the camera, the focus was made—he was only four feet from the lens. Everybody was waiting for the decision of the operator, who was looking through the lens very carefully, watching everything he possibly could so he would not make a mistake. The close-up idea had been forced on the whole camera crew, and they were nervous. Finally, the operator spoke.

"I can't see the top of his head."

For a moment there was a shock of disappointment, and then Marilyn said, "But everybody knows he's got one. It's been established."

This caused such a laugh that all doubts about the lens were dispelled, and we shot the scene. The single heads went so well that I decided to do an intimate two-shot with the same lens, to include two faces. Now I had to figure out a way to get the two heads on the counter sideways. We had Cherie sit at a bar, and after a few moments, put her head down on the counter in despair: Bo was going back to his ranch and she was going in an opposite direction.

But Bo decided to try again. So he came back to the bar, went over to Cherie, whose head was still on her folded arms, bent down and put his head right above hers, and told her that Virge had said since she had had so many lovers and he had had none, it evened things out: "I like ya like ya are, Cherie, so I don't care how ya got that way."

Cherie answered, "Oh, that's the sweetest thing anyone ever said to me," and lifted her head away from her hand and agreed to go to the ranch with him.

When the film was developed and blown up to the size it would be on the screen, we noticed that as Marilyn raised her mouth from her hand there was a thin line of saliva that pulled away from her mouth and for a second hung in the air, joining her mouth and her hand. It was very delicate and showed great emotion, but it had not been noticeable to the naked eye or through the lens.

The next time I saw the film I noticed that the segment before she raised her head had been cut. The front office had decided the public does not want to look at spit. I started to yell and before I stopped I had screamed at everybody in the entire organization. It was only after I had a sworn statement from Buddy Adler that the spit would remain in the film that I was willing to go on shooting.

As far as I am concerned, this is the most beautiful scene in the picture, spit and all.

There was a wonderful scene that too few people ever saw. Cherie and the others were all riding the bus at night through the snowstorm. Cherie sneaked away from Bo when he fell asleep and relaxed for the very first time since the trip began. She told Elma (Hope Lange) about her dreams and confided her childhood ambitions and her discouragement because she had never achieved what she aimed for.

As she talked and played this scene, Marilyn was so sincere that you could see her skin flush and tears begin to form in her eyes. By the end of the scene, the tears were slipping down her cheeks.

I used my newfound technique and handed her the first prop, turned her head with my hand to the proper direction, and said, "Begin again, Marilyn," which she did. Of course, she began with the tears still in her eyes, but she got more and more emotional as the scene went on.

When the scene was printed, all of us who sat there in the projection room felt that this was a genuine performance. No one had blown menthol in Marilyn's eyes to cause false tears; they came from her true feelings, perhaps from feelings she had had since childhood.

But in the final squeeze of editing and pleasing all those in authority, the question came up of cutting the scene. Certainly, from the point of view of understanding the plot of *Bus Stop*, it was unnecessary, and yet it revealed an extra dimension of this little girl and gave a new view of Marilyn's acting. I urged that it be kept.

Unfortunately, Buddy Adler asked the opinion of some of the

heads of the studio, and they agreed that it should be eliminated, and much to my despair I was overruled.

There was nothing I could do about it; it was eliminated. But I did write a piece for *The New York Times* about Marilyn, praising her ability, and I spoke of her with highest enthusiasm in countless interviews.

There are still those of us who remember that extraordinary performance, who know how badly she was judged by most of the world, including her so-called peers, how stupidly she was written about. Like Cherie, she was never able to feel what she yearned for—respect.

I think my favorite moment during the shooting of *Bus Stop* was in the funny old boardinghouse in Phoenix where Cherie lay in her bed trying to sleep off the night before. George Axelrod had indicated in his script that Cherie is asleep under a sheet, with obviously no other covering, when Bo bursts into the room and pulls up the window shades to rouse her for the rodeo.

Before the rehearsal I said to Marilyn, "Just put on something and rehearse it."

She said, "Oh, no, it's supposed to be a sexual scene. It's a nude scene. I've got to be nude in order to play the scene."

I wasn't quite sure why she found it so important, but since she wanted to do it I was willing, and I looked around at the crew who watched me with blank faces, hoping I would let her. I said, "Go ahead, Marilyn," and she arrived a few minutes later in a terry-cloth robe.

She climbed into the bed and then, from under the sheet, which was bouncing and bumping around like a circus tent being put up, she handed out the terry-cloth robe, and we packed the sheet around her so that we could give some idea of what a beautiful figure there was underneath that thick sheet.

We started to film the scene. Bo strode in. "Wake up, Cherie," he said. "It's nine o'clock—the sun's out. No wonder you're so pale and white."

At that point, Cherie, whimpered, "Please go away. I didn't go to sleep till five." She was tousled and white, and sleepily angry.

The whole scene was set up so that Bo could try to prove to her that he had more than just physical ability, that he also had a brain. And when she didn't want to hear about his brain, he paraded his gray matter by climbing in her bed and reciting into her ear Lincoln's Gettysburg Address. We shot the scene another time and finally I said, "Just one more time. Try it again."

So, Bo appeared again, lifted the blinds, and said, "Wake up, Cherie, . . . no wonder you're so pale and scaly."

I said, "Wait a minute—cut! Don, I'm terribly sorry, but you said 'scaly' instead of 'white.' "

He said, "Oh, lord, I'm very sorry."

The operator said, "Sorry, we have to reload." That meant about a three-minute wait, so Don sat down on one side of Marilyn's bed and I sat down on the other, and we rested while the camera reloaded.

A voice, whispering and excited, came from the head of the bed. "Don," Marilyn said, "do you realize what you did? You just made a *Freudian slip.*"

Suddenly, Marilyn raised herself from the bed, holding the sheet to cover her nakedness, but with a look in her eyes that showed she was in the midst of an intellectual experience.

"You see," she said, "you must be in the proper emotional mood for this scene because it's a sexual scene, Don, and you made a Freudian slip about a phallic symbol. You see, you were thinking unconsciously of a snake. That's why you said 'scaly.' And a snake is a phallic symbol. Do you know what a phallic symbol is, Don?"

"Know what it is?" he said. "I've got one!"

It was the perfect nonmeeting of the minds.

On the last night of shooting, Marilyn invited me and Nedda to Trader Vic's in Hollywood for a personal thank-you-and-farewell occasion. When we got there, Marilyn was waiting for us with a package. She said, "I think you should open it now." We did. It was a large picture of Marilyn in a silver frame, and it was inscribed in white ink, "With love and thanks to Nedda and Josh from Marilyn."

It was her favorite picture of herself. Milton Greene had photographed her in one of the old costumes of the Twentieth Century-Fox collection, and in it she looked like a girl from the turn of the century. It was very beautiful and we were touched. Beside it were a dozen yellow roses.

"It's lovely, Marilyn. Thank you so much. I can't imagine anything I would want more. And the roses, too."

She said, "I thought you'd like it—and you know, I think it would look awfully well always with yellow roses beside it."

I didn't see Marilyn again until Europe, but in the meantime I learned that she was going to marry Arthur Miller, and Nedda wanted to give her a wonderful wedding present.

In a recent issue of *Harper's Bazaar,* Cecil Beaton had published a picture he'd taken of Marilyn. On the opposite page he had written a most beautiful tribute to her—to her looks and to her spirit and to her personality. It was so flattering and so well written that Nedda thought it would be a good idea if she could have Cecil write it out in longhand on two pieces of paper and put them on either side of his photograph in a silver, triptych-like folding frame.

Cecil was most obliging and worked out everything according to the measurements Nedda had sent him, and when it was finished, it really was a spectacular yet personal thing. We sent it to her the day she was married, had it delivered to her house, but we never heard a word from her about it.

But we did meet her several times in England while she was shooting the Olivier film, *The Prince and the Showgirl.* And the first time, she showed her fangs. I had gone to see her in her dressing room but she didn't let me past the door: "Thanks for what you said about me in *The New York Times*—but why the hell did you cut out that scene in the bus? I'll never forgive you as long as I live. I was going to show it to Arthur and I couldn't. I was never so angry in my entire life, and I'm just as angry now as I was then!"

And she banged the door of her dressing room in my face.

I knew exactly how she felt. She obviously had waited for her new husband to see this scene she was proud of, and when it was cut out it was just too painful to bear. But I was never able to explain it to her because she didn't want to talk about it after that, and really I didn't either.

Laurence Olivier gave me a bad time too. He got me alone and said, "Thank you so much for writing me all those letters. It was terribly thoughtful of you—but, my God, why didn't you tell me it was going to be like this?"

I said, "How is it?"

He said, "That beast Paula Strasberg is on the set all the time, and every time I do a take, Marilyn looks at her to see whether or not we should print it."

I said, "But, Larry, I told you not to let Paula on the set."

He said, "But you were so nice about it, I thought it wouldn't matter."

I said, "But you mustn't let anybody on the set who has any authority. You know that—or you should."

He said, "But that's not the worst of it. What did you do when you were explaining how the line should be read and acting it out yourself for her so she could see and hear the way it's to be read—and she walked away from you before you were finished and started talking to somebody on the other side of the set? What did you do?"

I said, "Well, I really don't know, because I've never tried to read a line for her. But I did tell you that she was terribly talented and to let her have her way. She's on intimate terms with the camera. You know every facet of acting, directing, drama, the whole theatre art is yours. All she has is brilliant instincts and the mystery of a frightened unicorn."

But for years Larry had been used to a prescribed way of working with well-trained, obedient co-workers. You can't teach an old director new tricks, and directors' suggestions rolled off Marilyn's back like so much water.

I was amazed that so many people had troubles with her when mine were minimal. John Huston didn't like the way she sneered at Arthur Miller during *The Misfits*. Billy Wilder called her a "mean" girl to a reporter during *Some Like It Hot*. Later, Arthur Miller wrote a bloodcurdling portrait of her in his play, *After the Fall*, though he denied it was a picture of his then-dead wife. But I never saw a "mean" side. All I know is that together with her I hit my peak, and as far as I'm concerned she hit hers.

Toward the end of her life we received bits of news about Marilyn from various friends, but we never saw her again. When we read the news of her death it was a personal shock for us because both Nedda and I had grown very fond of her and we both felt that *Bus Stop* linked her to us with a strong emotional tie.

We knew none of her family; the nearest person to her whom we knew was Paula Strasberg, so we called her to say how much we were feeling Marilyn's loss and to show we sympathized with Paula and Lee and their family at their loss.

Paula said, "She loved it, you know."

"What?" I said.

"The silver frame with the Cecil Beaton picture with his personal writing. She always showed it to everyone. It was the gift she loved the most."

MIDDLE OF
CHAYEFSKY

PADDY CHAYEFSKY is a square. I don't mean that he is mentally square. Mentally, he is a squared puzzle, a cube: cut up into a million pieces and then fitted back together again. When I say square, I'm talking about his physical appearance and effect.

Paddy is built something like an office safe, one that fits under the counter and is impossible to move. He is the only man I know who was that way when he was in his late teens and is still that way in full-fledged manhood.

I knew him off and on all along. First I discovered him through hearing and loving his lyrics in a soldier show that I attended in London during World War II. When those diamond-bright lyrics came out from the cast—much funnier, much clearer, much more professional than anything I had heard in a long time—"The Air Corps, the Air Corps, That cozy, easy chair corps"—I was so impressed that I made a trip backstage to meet the lyricist.

The bulky office safe in suntans came trundling up with a chip on his shoulder and a square haircut and said, "I wrote 'em— Paddy Chayefsky. P-A-D-D-Y."

I told him how much I liked them, expecting him to warm up

a bit and become a very friendly person. Not at all. He knew they were great—he'd written them.

The next thing I knew of Paddy Chayefsky was when I was in Hollywood, finishing the preparation for *Picnic*. Freddie Kohlmar urged me to come see a new picture he heard was excellent, and the two of us attended an early showing of *Marty*. When I saw Paddy Chayefsky's name on the title, I knew it was going to be good, and it was superb—so good, in fact, that that year it won the Academy Award over my picture *Picnic*, which was pretty good, too.

I was so excited by Paddy's writing that I decided I would find him come hell or high water, and it turned out that he was living in the same hotel I was, the Beverly Hills Hotel. I sent him a note saying how much I loved *Marty* and how much I wished I could do something with him. Did he have any new ideas, any new plays, any movies? And before I knew it he was on the phone and we were meeting downstairs.

He had two acts written for a play to be called *Middle of the Night*. I took the script to Columbia that day and Freddie Kohlmar and I read it together, each breathing down the other's neck.

I can't explain what the play did to me. It was so truthful and touching and romantic and brave—the story of a dignified Jewish industrialist and a lovely young girl. The only trouble was that Paddy had no third act.

I said, "Look, I'll take a chance, Paddy. I'll do it and guarantee to get it backed without the third act," and after a bit of hee-hawing, hemming and hawing, he agreed. But I also knew who *had* to play the older Jewish man, and that was Edward G. Robinson.

Paddy was terribly excited at the idea of Edward G. Robinson, as well he might have been, since Robinson was one of the greatest names and talents in our profession. He left all the persuading to me and I had many visits with Eddie. I reminded him that this kind of part did not happen very often for a man in his full years. His fiancée agreed with me, and before long we had a project going.

Paddy had a bit of trouble writing the last act because he couldn't decide whether to make it a happy ending or a rueful one. I urged him to leave us with some hope, and before long he had a sparkling, warm, and uplifting finish that I knew was going to appeal to an audience.

The biggest problem I had was in directing the show with Paddy in the same room. I had been in the habit of being sacrosanct while I was directing. No one would bother me or dare approach me until a scene was having a break, but Paddy had no such feelings. He sat or stood beside me and whispered instruction into my ear the entire time—whether I was talking or thinking or doing neither. At first my instinct was to yell and scream and object, but my better sense told me that Paddy might have something interesting to say, and therefore I wanted to hear it.

While we were preparing the play back in New York, and before Paddy had actually signed the contract, it became Christmastime and New York was covered with snow. I was particularly anxious by this time to please Paddy and to compliment him and give him confidence, because he still had not finished the third act and really hadn't committed himself to my doing the play—on paper, that is.

One afternoon we had a date to meet at our apartment at five-thirty in the evening, but he was late. It was during the Christmas rush and I figured that was the trouble. But not at all. He came in later through our kitchen carrying an enormous package, thin but wide and long! An electric blanket he had bought for his mother. Because he looked like Paddy Chayefsky and was carrying a huge parcel, the doorman had refused to let him up the front elevator. So, much to my humiliation, he was directed past the garbage cans and into the kitchen. I was infuriated, but Paddy found the doorman thoroughly justified.

"I look like a delivery boy. I always have. Why should they let me up the front? I wouldn't have any respect for this place if they did."

When *Middle of the Night*, with a topnotch cast headed by Eddie Robinson and beautiful young Gena Rowlands, Martin Balsam, Anne Jackson, and Lee Philips opened in Wilmington, Delaware, Paddy was in a morose state.

"But it went well, Paddy," I said. "Honestly it did. Really. I know. I can tell what an audience is feeling, and they love the show."

"They love it too much," said Paddy. "I don't like all those laughs."

"Don't you realize you've written some of the funniest lines ever put on the stage?"

"Not one of you has said this is an august play," Paddy said.
"An august play?"

"Yes," he said. "It has nobility, it's a serious play. It shouldn't get all those laughs. It's that Robinson—he's cueing them when to laugh."

"Oh, no, he's not. You're cueing them when to laugh with your funny lines. Now, come on, please, watch it for a while before you make up your mind."

He said, "I'm not going to change my mind."

I said, "Don't be square, Paddy."

"I *am* square, and squares don't like those lightweight laughs. This is an august play." But he didn't make too many changes before our Philadelphia opening.

When the play opened at the Locust Street Theatre in Philadelphia, it had only a six-thousand-dollar advance, which was enormously small for any play, much less for one with a star of the magnitude of Edward G. Robinson.

The papers were ecstatic, but Paddy still worried. "It's getting too many laughs. It's not supposed to be that funny."

"But it's a comedy, Paddy—it's not a tragedy. The man marries the girl, not kills her, they are happy together, he wins out over the young man. It's an amusing idea even though it's got some serious sides to it."

"It's an august play," he said. "You're not going to talk me out of it."

Even the fact that by Wednesday matinee we had sold out for the entire two weeks we were in Philadelphia did not change Paddy's mind. He kept complaining that there were too many laughs, and eventually, since I felt Paddy was such a brilliant guy, I decided to find out exactly which ones he didn't like, and why.

Eventually, he took out five or six of the biggest laughs in the show, and how I was able to persuade Eddie Robinson to give them up I don't know. By the time we opened in New York the laughs were out, and it wasn't as effective a play, but Paddy felt better about it.

It was only years later that he realized how foolish he was, and apologized to me for having forced me to make a judgment against my own.

The play opened in New York to the strangest set of notices I think I ever read. Although the critics were impressed with the play, they kept harping on one note. They called it tape-recorded dialogue. Paddy had a perfect ear and used it to translate his perfect memory into perfect dialogue, and yet he was being blamed for it. I will never get over that. They have long since given up that complaint about Paddy, but he has never given up his ability to put true speech onto the screen and stage. Paddy Chayefsky is and always will be a sparklingly brilliant man, and I was terribly proud that I was not only the director but the producer of *Middle of the Night*. It ran well over a year and was a tremendous financial success, but Paddy kept saying to me on the side, "Robinson's terrible; he's wrong for this part."

I would say, "But, Paddy, he was made by God for this role. You'll never find anyone who's anywhere near him."

Paddy said, "Well, he sure ain't going to be in the movie."

I said, "Well, you'll sure be sorry."

He had made a contract whereby he controlled the movie rights as well as the making of the movie. I had nothing to do with it. Soon after the play finished, he went to Hollywood and made the movie. Why he turned it into what we would call a goy play, I do not know. Fredric March played Edward G. Robinson's part, and great an actor as Fredric March was, he didn't touch Robinson. He wasn't within half a mile of winning the race.

Gena Rowlands was substituted for by the less effective Kim Novak. It was a very poor movie. Paddy controlled everything, including the direction, and if ever a great piece of work failed, that one did.

A year later, Paddy called me and said he would like to have lunch with me at Sardi's. My heart leaped. I thought he might have a new play. We sat down and he began talking about this new play he had written, and I could tell from the tone of his voice and his excitement that he was madly in love with it. It was going to be called *The Tenth Man*, and it was about a minyan —a group of ten Jews—who got together to rid a young girl of a dybbuk.

He talked on and on about a cold-blooded young rabbi, and laughed as he talked. I was growing more and more interested and more and more nervous that he had never brought up any word of a director. Finally he said, "The director's got to be really smart, really sharp, really chic. I really think this can be one of the best things I've ever done."

After a short pause, I said tentatively, "Paddy, is it by any chance something that might be right for me?"

"Oh, good God, no!" he said. "This one needs class."

"Class?"

"Yes," he said, "somebody very classy—somebody like Moss Hart. Oh, no, you'd be terrible for it."

I saw it later done by Tyrone Guthrie and I kept looking for the class.

Paddy and I didn't get together again until he did a treatment for the movie of *Paint Your Wagon* years later. It was an ailing play on Broadway and was still an ailing script as it was being prepared by Paramount, with Alan Lerner in charge, and Alan had the brains to give it to Paddy Chayefsky, who was a specialist at writing original stories. His was the idea of digging tunnels under the city until the entire city collapsed building by building. That ending was and still is the most spectacular thing about the film, and so here we are back at that square but brilliant Paddy Chayefsky.

In recent years, he has swept the motion-picture industry with a violently critical picture called *Hospital,* and even more with a diatribe against the television industry called *Network.* Perhaps he'll never stop, and that will be all right with me. You can't build for the future with nice, polite people. They're too round. What you need are concrete blocks like Paddy.

A PARTY FOR PRINCESS MARGARET

PARTY FOR royalty is something we never planned on or trained for or even wanted, until we found ourselves giving one for Princess Margaret and her Tony Armstrong-Jones on their first trip to America in November 1966. We had given plenty of parties for our friends, and we never cared whether they were theatrical friends, civilian friends, rich friends, or poor friends. There was only one requirement: they had to be interesting. In addition, it was Nedda's theory that a successful party came when you filled a room with exciting people, gave them enough to eat and drink, and provided a bit of music somewhere. So far her theory had seemed to work.

We gave parties for twelve or twenty-eight as well as for seventy-five, but somehow it was always more fun when crowds of friends were spilling about. So our parties got bigger and bigger, and people began to expect it.

I guess the idea of the Princess Margaret–Tony party started years before in London when we first became friends with Oliver Messel, the delightful and brilliant English stage and costume designer famous for his decor for Sadler's Wells (now Royal) Ballet, numerous operas, motion pictures, and plays. He and we soon became very close, and whenever we were in London he gave us a party, and when he was in America ours was his home. At one point we saw him daily as he painted Nedda's portrait.

When Oliver came to New York, he often brought his young nephew Tony to us for cocktails. Tony was a talented photographer who was trying to get a foothold here among the fashion magazines. He was enormously friendly and as quick to laugh as his uncle.

But Tony turned out to be more than Tony. He was Tony Armstrong-Jones, and he didn't marry Jacqueline Chan, his favorite model. Instead, he married Princess Margaret and became world famous.

We hadn't seen him for the several years they had been married when Oliver wrote that Tony and Princess Margaret were going to take a belated trip through the United States, and asked whether we would have a lunch for them. Of course we said yes, but soon Oliver felt it should be a little bigger, and we suggested dinner.

Oliver sent us a list of the guests they would like, we added the friends we thought they should meet, and it soon became a downhill sleigh ride headed for a proper bash.

Everything had to be protocol. There had to be the perfect menu, proper seating, the loveliest dress for Nedda. And we had to be careful about the guest list. Our apartment had limits. It could accommodate a crush but not a riot.

As is usual in New York, we knew few people who lived in our own apartment building, but we began to hear rumors that our neighbors at River House were planning to be walking through the lobby casually when the distinguished couple arrived, while other owners would be slowly parking their cars in the courtyard. Within a short time we became very famous—in our block. We got spectacular service at the drugstore, the grocery store, the meat market, and from the boys who delivered the papers. Each of them had come up with an idea: "Do you suppose I could deliver the papers while the party's going on?" "Could you order something at the last minute from the drugstore that I would have to carry while the princess is there?" Our elevator boys were drawing straws as to who was to bring the princess upstairs.

That was just the start of it. As the day approached, Secret Service men appeared to make a tour of our apartment to see whether there was any possibility of intruders climbing up over our balcony and what was the easiest way of intruders getting up the service elevator or entering the building through the back entrance. All personnel were screened.

We had decided to invite people we thought would interest our British visitors the most, but even that list spread into dozens, and therefore we had to eliminate some of the ones we loved to make room for those chosen by Oliver and Tony. Our apartment could, at a stretch, hold slightly over a hundred when filled, as it would be for the major part of the evening.

We decided we would have thirty-two people for dinner at four round tables in the dining room, and ask the largest crowd to come in afterward.

Impulsively, Nedda said, "This mustn't be a stuffy party. We're theatre people—artists. Surely we should have entertainment."

"Oh, no!" I said. "You can't invite people to a party and then ask them to entertain. They'd never know whether they were asked because they could entertain or because we felt that Princess Margaret and Tony would like them."

She said, "But we always sing around the piano or 'do turns,' as Oliver says. Certainly we can ask *somebody.*"

And after much deliberation we decided we might just dare ask Ethel Merman if she would be willing to sing, and when we called her, it was almost as if she was already planning to.

"Of course I'll sing," she said.

Well, now that we had one, Nedda's ambitions began to grow. She started to think about our neighbor in Connecticut, Benny Goodman. Could we possibly ask him to bring his clarinet? Nedda called him and talked around in circles, and got almost a completely circular answer.

He said, "Oh, I never entertain at a party. I'm sorry—I could never bring myself to do such a thing. It would embarrass me."

She said, "Well, couldn't you accidentally bring your little tootie toot anyway, just in case you change your mind?"

He said, "I cannot enter the room carrying a musical instrument. Everyone would think I was a hired musician and had come through the kitchen door. No, I can't do it, Nedda. I'm awfully sorry. But I love you and I'll be there."

Then, to Nedda's surprise, Benny said, "Oh, I think you ought to ask Hank Jones. He's the greatest jazz pianist in the world, and in case you want anybody to . . . oh . . . accompany . . . uh . . . someone else—you know, for jazz—well, he'd be the best."

We did ask Hank and he said yes.

And we decided to invite all the stars who happened to be playing in New York. We knew Tony and the princess would welcome the chance to see and talk with Broadway celebrities. And soon we had acceptances from Sammy Davis, Jr., who was playing in *Golden Boy* on Broadway at the time, Barbra Streisand of *Funny Girl,* Tommy Steele, then on Broadway from London in *Half a Sixpence,* plus celebrities such as Rosalind Russell, Alan Jay Lerner, Betty Comden and Adolph Green, Leonard Bernstein. We invited the famous couple's nontheatrical hosts, Mr. and Mrs. Jock Whitney, and Betsy Whitney's sisters, Mrs. William (Babe) Paley, complete with husband, and Minnie Fosburgh with her husband, Jim.

But Mr. and Mrs. Whitney decided they couldn't come, as Tony and the princess were staying with them in Manhasset and the Whitneys wanted to be there when they arrived.

Pleasance Mundy, our designer from the flower shop we once owned, spent the day creating her famous Monet–Fantin-Latour bouquets, and the great Horst, a friend of Oliver, was sent by *House Beautiful* to photograph them. He even took a picture of my favorite hundred-year-old bonsai tree, a miniature pomegranate with a single piece of fruit hanging from it like a lonely Christmas ball.

I worried all day about how to bring up the subject of entertainment.

Nedda was calmer. Stavropoulos had fashioned her a graceful dress of crimson chiffon with panels of orange chiffon, the loveliest she had ever had.

It was protocol, we had been told, for the host and hostess to go down to the front entrance to welcome the princess and Tony as they got out of their limousine. The doorman had assured me that he would clear the courtyard of all other cars.

But an elevator man came upstairs, trembling. "Mr. Logan, you've got to go down. Mr. Privet won't move his Rolls-Royce. It's sitting in the middle of the courtyard and *he's sitting there in it!* You know he's got that terrible loud horn that plays the 'Colonel Bogey March.' He's gonna play it full blast when the princess arrives! My God, that'll be a disgrace for The River House! You've got to go down and talk to him."

"What can I do? He owns an apartment here—he has a right to sit in his car."

"Go down, Mr. Logan," said the elevator man.

"Go down, Josh," said Nedda.

So, I went down. There was the Rolls in the middle of the courtyard, a grinning driver sitting behind the wheel with his hand on the horn. I was nervous that he might start playing it the minute I approached him, but we came together instead like a couple of wild animals sizing each other up in the forest. I stood outside his car, still and silent, holding myself as steady as possible. He looked me over while I looked him over.

"Hello, Mr. Logan. What do you want?" said Mr. Privet.

"I was just curious to know whether you had a horn that played the 'Colonel Bogey March.' "

"Yes, sir, I have. A beautiful thing it is, too. I'm going to serenade you all with it later."

"Will it make you very happy, Mr. Privet? Because from all reports it will certainly make everybody else unhappy."

"Why should it? It's a beautiful tune. They played it in *The Bridge on the River Kwai.*"

"Yes, I remember. It was suitable there. They were all prisoners of the Japanese. They whistled it for courage. Are you trying to threaten our guest of honor, Princess Margaret, or is it just that you feel very American tonight and you hate the English?"

"Oh, it's not that at all. If you don't want me to play it, I won't play it."

"I certainly would be relieved if you gave up the idea. And maybe you could also move the car out of the courtyard so the Secret Service wouldn't be so fidgety."

"Why, of course, Mr. Logan. I'd be delighted. You see, I'm really a nice guy."

And with a toss of his head he put the car into gear and pulled away. I went back upstairs feeling like Muhammad Ali, and yet I hadn't even delivered a punch. If I live to be a thousand I will never understand what Privet planned to do. I think he was just curious to see what was going on and figured that was the best way of finding out.

All the dinner guests had been told to arrive before the guests of honor. For the first time in our lives, everyone was on time.

And then the sirens came. Fifty-second Street had been cleared, and the police on motorcycles, two abreast, came screeching down the middle of the street, followed by a black limousine. Nedda and I were already down and were standing at the front door of The River House when the car pulled up.

Tony got out first, shook our hands, and then the two of us helped Princess Margaret out of the car as Nedda curtsied. They preceded us into the hallway and I turned to Nedda. She was crying.

"What's the matter?" I asked.

"My Irish grandmother came over in the eighteen hundreds, steerage, and now look at what's happened to a Harrigan."

Upstairs, Tony and Princess Margaret were presented to the other guests who had arrived: Leonard Bernstein, who was to sit next to Princess Margaret; Lennie's lovely wife, Felicia; two of the three Cushing sisters and their distinguished husbands; Prince Amyn Aga Khan; Rosalind Russell and her producer husband, Freddie Brisson; and all the rest of the first wave troops. We stood about drinking champagne and cocktails. At the appointed time, the doors of the dining room opened and we went in to find our places for dinner. I seated Princess Margaret on my right and we all settled ourselves for a gala meal.

The curtains of our dining room windows were open to allow the full view of New York's skyscrapers with their lighted panes. The sight fascinated Princess Margaret.

"Oh, isn't it beautiful!" she said, and then she turned and looked over her shoulder. A phalanx of waiters was entering. She turned to me. "This must be the smartest party ever given."

"What makes you say that?"

"You've even got Sol Hurok as a waiter."

I looked, and the waiter was indeed a replica of Sol Hurok. And we all laughed to think of Sol waiting on tables, and everyone began having a good time, particularly me.

After dessert and coffee there was a roaring sound outside the dining room. It reminded me of the crowd crashing the rodeo in *Bus Stop*. Everyone who had been asked for after dinner seemed to arrive at the same time. The elevator was pouring them into our front hall. The living room was soon jam-packed, and the crowd got turbulent.

My sister, Mary Lee, a born social director, said, "You must get the entertainment started right away, Josh."

I said, "We haven't got any entertainment, darling, except Ethel Merman."

"Well, Ethel must go on immediately."

I said, "I wouldn't dare ask her this early."

"I will," she said, and she went right up to Ethel and said, "Will you sing now and stop an inundation?"

And Ethel said, "Sure," so I stepped quickly into the crowded living room, wondering what on earth was going to happen if one more person came in. I shouted, "Ladies and gentlemen, please be seated. Miss Ethel Merman is going to sing."

Immediately, the living room became an auditorium. Everyone sat down on chairs or on the floor, exactly where they were. It was really quite miraculous. The trio we had engaged—accordion, violin, and piano—was going full blast, and Ethel trumpeted out "I Got Rhythm." During the singing I watched Tony and Princess Margaret; they were obviously ecstatic. When Ethel finished a chorus and a half with a high note, the place went into cheers and shouts, and Ethel started again. This time it was "There's No Business Like Show Business," which inspired more cheering, except that halfway through it I got nervous again. What was going to happen next?

I ran to Nedda. "What now? They're sitting there expecting a night of entertainment, and this is all we have."

She said, "Well, maybe we can ask Benny's friend, Hank Jones, to play the piano."

He said he'd be happy to play, so I announced that one of our greatest American pianists would now render a jazz selection for us. Hank, smiling, sat down, and the sound of his fingers playing a syncopated, wailing tune delighted the room.

We will now shift scenes to downstairs in the lobby of our building.

Joe Curtis, my assistant, had been standing at the downstairs elevator door as a kind of St. Peter at heaven's gate; he was to let the right people in and keep the wrong people out. Now he had come upstairs, but he had left behind at the lobby elevator a secretary who was to call Mrs. Jock Whitney in Manhasset the moment Princess Margaret and Tony left, so Mrs. Whitney could get into a pretty negligee and meet them, as per protocol, at the door of her beautiful home.

When the secretary saw the signal summoning the elevator to our fourteenth-floor apartment, she decided it had to be Tony and Princess Margaret leaving the party early, because they were the only ones who could leave first. So, she ran quickly and telephoned Mrs. Whitney to expect them in half an hour.

But it wasn't Princess Margaret and Tony who came down in the elevator; it was Benny Goodman. When he stepped out of the elevator, everyone in the lobby was astounded that he would leave the party before the guests of honor, but he walked calmly past them, got his clarinet from his car, and came back up.

Hank Jones was still playing when Benny returned. The crowd sitting on the floor saw a strange man walking across the room, playing a clarinet. No one dared guess who it was, but he sure could play. Benny sat on part of the piano bench and continued playing. I shouted over the music, "Mr. Benny Goodman!" and the floor almost caved in with the excitement. They just sat there and applauded.

Princess Margaret, who was seated on a small slipper chair, seemed to have no thought of leaving. And everybody else must have decided that we had planned it that way and that the entertainment was going to go on for hours. I had no idea whom I dared call on, but I decided the best thing to do was to get up and be honest with the room.

"Ladies and gentlemen, this room is filled with great entertainers, but I'm sure none of them came prepared to entertain you. If there's someone who can, I just wish he'd take over and save me, because I'm standing here very embarrassed with no one to introduce."

Sammy Davis, God bless him, stood up and said, "Will I do? The only thing is, I want to work with Tommy Steele, and there's Tommy Steele over there. Now, I know the lyrics because I made a record of a song he's singing in *Half a Sixpence*. Tommy, I'm Sammy Davis, Junior. Do you suppose you and I could do that song together even though we never have?"

Tommy Steele was up in a minute, and our wonderful trio was faking the music that Sammy hummed for them—and soon one of the most original duets I've ever heard in my life was sung by two men who had never sung together before. Of course, it was ideal for the occasion: an Englishman and a black American. Patriotism was flowing all over the floor.

Roz Russell got up and did a song from *Wonderful Town* in gospel shouting voice, and everyone cheered as though they had just heard Marilyn Horne.

While she was singing, my agent, Irving Paul Lazar, who I'm sure had a further scheme in his mind, came over and whispered in my ear, "Alan Lerner sings very well. Get him to do 'I've Grown Accustomed to Her Face.'"

So when Roz finished I stood up and said, "Ladies and gentlemen. The next person to sing does not even know that I'm going to ask him, and he doesn't know what I'm going to ask him to sing. But let's just see if it works. I give you Mr. Alan Jay Lerner in 'I've Grown Accustomed to Her Face.'"

Everyone applauded and Alan got up and started to sing in the kind of voice that most composers would like to have but don't. But when the climactic moment of the song came, Alan went absolutely, totally blank and couldn't remember a word. The idea that Alan Jay Lerner couldn't sing his own lyrics struck everyone as hilarious—except me, because I've always found that composers and lyricists forget their own lines quicker than anybody who sings them.

There was someone who had come later sitting in the back of the dining room, spooning food into her mouth as fast as she could. It was Barbra Streisand. Several of us went over and asked her if she'd sing, but she kept on eating and just shook her head. She didn't come there to sing, she said, she came there to eat.

Neither Tony nor Princess Margaret ever realized she refused to sing for them. But a minor revolution broke out on one side of the room when the guests who had entertained learned about Barbra.

The guests of honor stayed until early in the morning. As they went downstairs I realized it had been quite a while since Betsy Whitney in Manhasset had supposedly started standing at her door in her negligee. I've always wondered whether she was still there when they finally got to Manhasset.

The next day, Nedda and I received a huge bouquet of flowers and two charming notes from Tony and Princess Margaret, and whenever we have seen them after that, they have always remembered to say that that party was a highlight of their trip to the United States. I can believe it. It was my highlight, too, and Nedda's. After that, no party ever came anywhere near it, no matter how hard we tried.

Nedda and Josh welcoming Princess Margaret and Lord Snowdon to
River House. (*Women's Wear Daily* photo)

Miiko Taka and Marlon on Japanese bed. (Warner Brothers Pictures
Distributing Corporation)

Marlon clowning for girls at a geisha party.

Sayonara. Marlon saluting as Miiko crosses the bridge. (Warner Brothers Pictures Distributing Corporation)

Directing Mitzi Gaynor in a scene from *South Pacific*. Oscar Hammerstein, right center, bare-chested with cap. (20th Century-Fox)

South Pacific. On island of Bali Ha'i. Nedda, Josh, Buddy Adler (the producer), and Tom, age seven, dressed as a native. (20th Century-Fox)

AT HOME
WITH
GARBO

CROSS THE STREET from The River House is a very imposing building called The Campanile, with fantastic views of the East River. For a while, Mary Martin lived there, and Drue and Jack Heinz, owner of the 57 Varieties. We went over there also because of our friend George Schlee and his wife, Valentina, the great designer, who had a luxurious river apartment with a most elegant living room—a Savonnerie rug, rich paneling—the perfect background for any kind of regal affair.

We often went to the Schlees for cocktails, and sometimes five or six of us would sit around the coffee table, eating caviar and drinking vodka. At these gatherings there was always a most exciting but agonizingly shy lady: Greta Garbo. She seemed to love being in the Schlee home, and people began to wonder why she was so close to Valentina and George when she seemed so distant with the rest of the world.

Of course, back when George had managed Valentina's business, Valentina had designed Garbo's clothes. Now, however, the Schlees had got out of the dressmaking profession, but Garbo and George had grown very close. How close we will never know.

Garbo trusted George. He helped her in all her business affairs; he invested for her, and well. I think perhaps George Schlee made Garbo independent for life by these investments on her behalf, and in turn gave her the chance to live the kind of life she wanted most of all—a life of solitude.

As long as George was alive, the two ladies pretended to be friends. But it was accepted that George came without Valentina when he was escorting Garbo.

In all the times we had been with Garbo, it was never in her own apartment, which we knew was a few floors down from the Schlees and directly on the river. She never invited anyone to it—that is, no one I knew—and for some reason that stimulated my curiosity. But then, Garbo fascinated me totally.

I decided I *had* to see her apartment. How could I go through life pretending that I knew Garbo without ever having been in her apartment?

So, the day that Nedda and I found ourselves going down in the elevator with Garbo at the end of a Schlee party, I seized my opportunity.

I said, "Don't you live somewhere around here?"

Garbo said, "Oh, yes, I live . . ." and she gave me the number of the floor and said, "You must come and see it sometime."

She got in the "sometime" a little too late, for the elevator had stopped and I was out of the door and walking to her apartment.

She said, "Oh, I didn't mean—"

"That's all right," I said. "I don't mind."

"But it isn't ready now for anybody to see."

"That doesn't matter to me. I'd just love to see the view and where you're located in the building, and so forth."

And before she knew it, I was inside the apartment, with a fascinated but embarrassed Nedda pattering close behind.

We first stepped into a small, empty hall, shiningly clean as though someone had waxed it a few minutes before. There were two doors open off this hallway and as we passed them I glanced in and saw empty rooms—again spotlessly clean—but truly empty, without a single picture, rug, or piece of furniture.

On the other side of the hallway the door was closed. That must have been Garbo's own bedroom and bath.

We went on farther as she opened a door, and we stepped into a small nook, the corner end of an L-shaped room. A bulky television set faced the door we had just come through, and in front of it was a low table on which was a half-eaten TV dinner, and a forbiddingly straight chair used evidently for eating dinner and watching TV. From this chair she could not see the rest of the room or the window. When we rounded the television apparatus, we could see the rest of the L, the main room of the apartment, and that turned out to be strikingly beautiful and in exquisite taste. It was hung with small but great pictures—a dazzling Soutine, a small, perfect Renoir of two girls' heads, a few other charming Impressionist works and fine cut glass and ormolu sidelights. On the ceiling was a small chandelier, and at the end of the room through rich draperies was a widespread window looking out at water as far as you could see.

Garbo didn't offer us a drink—I'm sure because we might accept—so after a while we excused ourselves and thanked her for the tour. By this time Nedda had forgiven me for my crash entrance.

Nedda and I had some wonderful intimate evenings with Garbo and George Schlee, and there was an endless line of presents between us. I'd always heard that she was very careful about money, but certainly not with us. She was profligate. After she saw *South Pacific*, she was so overcome by it that she sent me two round, red Venetian ashtrays which she said were the nearest things she could get to shrunken heads, and after seeing a preview of *Sayonara*, she sent me two rich and handsome Japanese dolls, a warrior emperor and empress seated on battle thrones. They stand above two bookcases in our dining room now, making it Garbo's room.

But the most fun I ever had with her was making her laugh. At a restaurant one night George Schlee asked me to tell her my story of Marlene Dietrich and *The Garden of Allah*. It's a ridiculous Hollywood story of my first day as a dialogue director, trying to teach Marlene and Charles Boyer to pronounce some dreadful Hollywood English dialogue. It has always been one of my surefire stories; I've told it six thousand times, and I was used to the places in the story where I got big laughs, but I never got the kind of laughter Garbo gave it. I guess the fact that she had been through the same kind of agony in learning English that Dietrich had, and the fact that Marlene was a rival of hers at one point, did it. She laughed until she folded in half on the banquette at the restaurant, and at one point she laughed so violently she flipped and would have fallen on the floor had George and I not grabbed her.

I had never seen her laugh like that except in *Ninotchka*, and I had thought then that that was the loveliest performance I'd ever seen. But now I saw her close up and real—filled with the true, wonderful, bawdy laughter that was obviously buried somewhere in this sphinxlike character. The next day she sent me two beautiful ties and said, "Thanks for the laughter, thanks for the funny story. Love. G.G."

It is ephemeral and changeable, her quality. She still has great Nefertiti beauty, despite no lipstick, no rouge, nothing to help it along. And she seems to be truly naive. Her humor is the humor of a fourteen-year-old boy, just past childhood, just entering manhood. He laughs, and blushes when he laughs. She becomes almost awkward. She loves to wear shorts and will do so on any occasion, but she is feminine, too.

When we bought our new house on Old Long Ridge Road in little Long Ridge near Stamford, the first people we asked for lunch were Garbo and George Schlee. We got so excited when they accepted that I went out and bought a visitors' book, but I was too embarrassed to put my own and Nedda's name on the outside, so we pretended that it belonged to Tom Logan, our then baby boy.

She and Schlee arrived and we wandered around the garden. When she saw the swimming pool she opened her bag and pulled out a little suit which she changed into in our Japanese studio by the pool. She was into the pool in a moment.

It was a great day, a great lunch, and we had a lot of laughs. We took her down the street and showed her a Victorian house we'd always admired. And then because we realized what fun she would have in a crazy store in Bedford Village, we drove her to the little shop called Trela's. It had everything in it that the mind could encompass, piled up on counters on three floors, and she wandered about the cheap trinkets with the same childlike fascination and excitement.

It was only after Garbo and George took off for New York that Nedda said, "Oh, my God, we forgot to ask her to sign the book." And we couldn't get her back to sign it for another three years.

When I was making *Fanny* in Marseilles, George called us and asked us to come to Cap d'Ail, where he had bought a lovely house with classic columns. We made the trip one Sunday and saw what was known in the neighborhood as the Garbo house. George had bought it at a great bargain, and he and Greta Garbo enjoyed that house as much as any children ever enjoyed a tree house. They could swim in the ocean or in the pool; they could pick flowers or plant them; they could cook or be cooked for. It was a warm home, and I'm glad that he had some fine years there, because he was a good friend and a nice man.

Now that he is dead, Valentina still lives in their old apartment and Garbo still lives in hers. They never meet in the elevators because the elevator man has instructions that when both bells ring he answers only one, and must bring that person to the main floor before going up for the other.

Once in a while, my daughter or my wife sees Garbo on her little trek across Fifty-second Street toward First Avenue, where she browses in antique stores, and they speak briefly, but we never hear from her and she has never been back to our house. She came once and admired the children and some of the porcelain we have. But when we asked her a second time and she learned from our elevator man that there were two more people upstairs than she expected, she wouldn't come up—and never accepted again.

MARLON
BRANDO-SAN

B Y 1957 *Sayonara* had become a cause for me as well as an excitement.

I had been looking for years for a story that would try to explain something of the East to the West, and vice versa. James Michener's novel had struck me as one that contained a lot of fascinating information on both cultures. Now Bill Goetz and I were going to coproduce it.

We both wanted Marlon Brando to play the lead, and Bill was going to take care of approaching him. I had missed before when I tried to get Marlon for the move of *Mister Roberts*. But Brando refused *Sayonara* at first because he didn't feel it was a serious enough story for him. We then offered it to Rock Hudson. But Rock Hudson had too many obligations at Universal, and Bill just turned around and said, "Let's just get Brando."

I said, "All right with me. I'll help. But you have to make the first move."

For a while, Bill and Edie Goetz came back to Connecticut and stayed in our guest room while we had further conferences. Then we decided we could never do this film unless we found out ourselves what it required, and the four of us took off for Japan.

We went first to Takarasuka, a little town at the end of a railroad with a theatre and an all-girl opera company designed as a come-on for people to use the railroad.

Michener had written his story about Takarasuka and its all-girl opera troupe which lived as a sisterhood by strict rules and were treated like nuns as far as men were concerned.

We saw the actual opera several times. Certainly, as a show it was good. The performances and the performers were beautiful, and the production spectacular, as is all Japanese musical theatre. The Japanese have an extraordinary ability to use color and light and to fill the stage with surprising movement.

But as we walked about the theatre grounds, the general atmosphere didn't look very photogenic, certainly not as lushly romantic as James Michener had made it seem in the novel.

Then we went looking for the famous bridge the girls used to go from the theatre to their sleeping quarters. In the book it had sounded like the bridge to heaven; in actuality, it was the most disappointing thing of all. It looked like a walkway for crossing railroad tracks without stepping on the third rail. It was simply a metal arch with side rails of wire netting. It offered no hint of young love or sexual suspense. So we decided to take a trip through Japan to find a really beautiful bridge.

Before we left, we saw several outsized, wild Kabuki plays, with men stars playing the women's parts. Kabuki had thrilled Nedda and me when we had come through Japan in 1950. Much to my delight, they thrilled Bill Goetz and Edie as well. We agreed we must include a Kabuki actor in the screenplay to give us a legitimate excuse to show the Kabuki theatre. Then we took off on the bridge hunt.

There were plenty of little piddling bridges, but no majestic ones. And we wanted something of great beauty and size. We went to every municipal garden and every royal garden, and after a while we took a boat to other islands, the islands of Shikoku and Kyushu.

It was on Shikoku we saw our bridge. We walked into the biggest and the most beautiful Japanese park yet. Most of them up till now had been miniatures, the kind that fit on trays, and we had got used to smallness—dwarf bridges, trees to shade miniature dolls, and benches for them to sit on. This park was on a magnified scale, and although the bridge here was a high arch, a graceful, humpback bridge, it was lyrical, photogenic, and obviously something that would be beautiful for the girls to walk across if they could move up and down it with slippery clogs.

We then boarded a charming, comfortable, but small steamer that went around the Inland Sea. In Osaka we saw the Bunraku puppets in the classic puppet theatre. The night we were in the audience they had stepped away from the classic Japanese stories and were playing *Hamlet*.

What techniques were involved. For the Hamlet-Laertes duel, three men managed each puppet: one for the sword arm, one for the head, and one for the feet. This meant that three men had to skip or leap backward across the stage while three other men plunged forward in fast duel. Then both groups exchanged violent cross swipes and lunges until one side won over, and the vanquished danced backward across the seemingly endless stage to defeat.

But Michener's book had asked not for *Hamlet* but for one of the classic double-suicide stories with Kelly and Katsumi watching from the audience and deciding to do the same themselves.

We saw one ancient Noh play with its strange, moody tales and production—very underplayed action, singing, and movement, with a man as the heroine in a smoothly carved wooden mask lacquered white—his face so languorous that it seemed as though it were asleep. I wanted to get a bit of the Noh theatre into the picture, too, as it was almost a symbol of old Japan. And Bill said, "Okay, if we can."

We went to Tokyo to see the head of Shochiku Company, because the Takarasuka Theatre company had objected to our sexually explicit picture and had refused to cooperate with us. They would not allow us to photograph any member of the sisterhood of the Takarasuka company, the exterior of the theatre, the bridge, nothing.

But Shochiku told us not to worry about the entertainment side. They had two all-girl opera companies, one in Osaka, which we could use freely. We could also use their Kabuki companies and their puppets, and they had the only double-suicide play extant in their present repertoire. We were especially lucky about that because Shochiku was the only company in Japan which owned the Osaka puppets.

Bill negotiated with the head of Shochiku and got the use of all these companies for a decent and feasible amount. He got letters of agreement signed and we flew back home, convinced we were in good hands.

We still did not have Marlon Brando, but Marlon had said that he would be willing to talk to us on the subject. We met—Marlon, his representative, Bill, and myself—in Bill and Edie's front room. First off, Marlon told us he didn't like the attitude of the book's Americans toward the Japanese. He felt that in its general attitude of white supremacy it belittled the Japanese.

I said, "We will change that. Paul Osborn will rewrite every scene you wish him to. I will not only guarantee it, you will see it."

Marlon talked interminably. When he gets rhetorical it's like a tapeworm. He wanted to make sure that he was going to be safe, that we would back him up. In most stories, he told us, the Asians are treated as second-class citizens; he wouldn't be party to any such stereotype. Again, I said we would make the changes and he could read them for himself. He left, saying he would like to think about it and maybe have another meeting. He was perfectly right, except that I wondered if he would ever listen to anyone else talk but himself.

I went back to New York. Marlon came to New York for an entirely different reason and wanted to have another meeting with me and Paul Osborn in our River House apartment.

While he was there, he and I walked out on our terrace to discuss the picture. Paul stood and listened. By accident, I noticed as I talked that one of the plants on the terrace had a few dead leaves, and, still talking, I knelt down and began pulling them off. I noticed Marlon looking at me strangely.

"What's the matter?" I asked.

"Is that a lemon scent you're using?"

"What do you mean?"

"I have a very sensitive nose. It's lemon, isn't it?"

I had shaved just before he came and used Guerlain's Imperiale cologne, and I realized for the first time that perhaps it was lemon. It was Guerlain anyway, and I said, "Why?"

He said, "Nothing. I think I'll go now."

And he left, as enigmatic as ever. Paul rolled his eyes to the sky. When Bill Goetz heard about the lemon scent, he felt it was all getting crazy.

I was beginning to get pretty tense. Bill had wanted to start the picture in January, but if we didn't have a leading man we couldn't cast the other people.

Bill said, "Listen, why don't we get a girl star for it instead of a goddamn male star? Let's just take any good leading man, whether he's a star or not, if the girl's a star."

I said, "But who can we get who's a real star who looks like one of these Takarasuka girls?"

He said, "Listen, don't you remember in Japan, every time we passed a poster or looked at a magazine, one of us would say, 'Look at that—it's Audrey Hepburn.'"

It was true. The Japanese girls had taken to imitating Audrey Hepburn's hairdo and many of them had managed to look exactly like her.

Bill said, "Let's get Audrey Hepburn to play the girl, and screw Mr. Lemon Scent."

I didn't bother to think about it very much. All I knew was that I was desperate to move fast.

Bill said, "Listen, you fly to Paris and see what she thinks about it. I'll have her prepared for you."

Nedda and I flew to France the next day. Sure enough, Bill had arranged for us to have dinner with Audrey and Mel Ferrer, who was her husband at the time.

Audrey was totally charming. No one could be more so. She had the prettiest, sweetest, dearest valentine face, and she said in her dearest little sweetheart voice, "I couldn't possibly play an Oriental. No one would believe me. They'd laugh. It's a lovely script. I'm longing to see it and I would love to be able to play it, but I can't."

I said, "I don't suppose I could persuade you to?" with not too much enthusiasm in my voice.

"I don't think anyone could persuade me to," she said. "I know what I can or can't do. And if you did persuade me, you would regret it, because I would be terrible."

We had a lovely meal and two more glasses of wine, and flew back to New York.

Bill called me from California. "Get out here tomorrow morning and we'll have another meeting with Lemon Scent."

I got there, but I was exhausted. My eyes wouldn't stay open.

Marlon talked and talked and talked and talked, and I agreed and disagreed and agreed again. We talked all the weary day. He seemed to grow closer and closer to it. I could tell that he had really thought it over, but something was holding him up. We plugged on to the end of the day, all of us panting, walleyed with exhaustion from the pressure, words, thinking, fatigue, whatever, and finally I said, "Marlon, are you going to do it or not?"

Marlon said, "No. I can't do a picture where the American leaves the Japanese girl like the arrogant ending of *Madame Butterfly*."

I said, "Would you do it if he married the Japanese girl?"

"Would your writer agree to such a change?"

I called Paul Osborn, and after the initial pause for shock, Paul said, "Of course. I'd like that better—it's less cliché. We only thought we had to use that ending because Michener wrote it that way."

After thanking Paul, I turned and said, "There! Now what do you say? Will you do it or not?"

Marlon started to squirm. He said, "Let's have one more day's conference."

A deep yell came up from my innards and filled the room. It was uncontrollable. I shouted, "No!" as loud as any man who ever played Oedipus. *"Not one more goddamned minute!* You either do it or you don't do it—and tell us now. I'm not going to say or hear one more sentence, one more syllable, nothing! I can't take it. I'm mentally paralyzed. I can't take it. You either tell us now, Marlon, or—"

Marlon said, "Quiet, please, Josh. I'm going to do it. I decided to do it when you were crumbling those dead leaves on your terrace. I didn't know you were sensitive enough to care for flowers and I didn't know you wore lemon scent."

We got quickly into the business of tests. Flame-haired Martin Baum, who had helped me as an agent and casting director for the stage play *Fanny*, made what I thought was a wonderful suggestion for Kelly, the lower-class kid who marries a Japanese girl. It was Red Buttons.

I knew there was no one in Japan to play the Kabuki actor because I had looked everywhere there among the theatre people to find a virile man who would look romantic to an American girl and could speak enough English and who could dance as a woman in a kimono. And I also had done some looking on the way back when we stopped in Hawaii. So I persuaded Ricardo Montalban to play the part.

Solly Biano, one of the most talented of Warner Brothers talent scouts, had insisted that I meet Miyoshi Umeki. And the moment I saw her, there was no doubt. She opened her mouth and I melted. She could win any man or any three men, and charm all the birds off nearby trees at the same time. I have never known such enchantment from a human being at first glance in my life. Of course she would play Kelly's wife.

Now we were approaching the greatest casting trouble of all. It was the Takarasuka girl, who had to be tall enough to play men's roles in the company, beautiful enough to be the woman that Marlon Brando fell for, fluent enough in Japanese to play the Japanese scenes, and fluent enough in English to keep from sounding too comic when putting across a thought or an idea. She also had to be able to dance enough to be in the Takarasuka revue and to sing well enough to be the leading lady of an opera company.

We had sent representatives, coached by Solly Biano, to Hawaii and Japan looking for this paragon. We were going to search the world. I flew to France and made a test of a Japanese actress who was then living in Paris. She couldn't speak Japanese. I also tested, outside of London, two beautiful girls who looked Oriental. One was a famous director's wife who was talented but unconvincing as an Oriental.

But that was all in the past. Now we were at the jumping-off place. We had three weeks to go before we would actually start shooting in Kyoto, Japan. We had not found our leading lady, and it looked as though we were going to have to sign a girl who was far too old for the part but was at least a famous and talented Japanese actress who could speak English.

But Solly Biano would not give up hope. "One of these girls is going to walk through the door, just you watch." And she did.

Two tall Japanese girls walked through the door that evening —Japanese-American girls, that is. They worked in a travel bureau. Each had goaded the other into coming down to see these movie people. Both were lovely, but one seemed righter than the other. Her name in Japanese was so difficult to pronounce that we didn't bother about that. I simply started talking to her.

"Have you ever acted?"

"No."

"Have you ever done amateur theatricals in the living room for your mother and father?"

"No."

I could see Marlon off at a distance giving her the old Marlon Brando size-up, and he was obviously pleased.

I said, "Would you mind trying to read a scene for me? Only don't read it with that very strong nisei-American accent of yours. Read it with a little bit of a Japanese accent. Do you think you could do that?"

"Yes," she said, as though she understood, and she went off with the scene to study it.

Marlon said, "Could I rehearse with her?"

I said, "Of course."

He took her off in the corner and the two of them knelt down looking at each other. Marlon talked very gently to her, and after they had whispered for half an hour, I strolled over and said, "How is it going?"

"It's going to be all right," said Marlon.

The girl then read the important scene in which she tells him that in spite of her strict background she is willing to love him. It was a rather odd accent, but charming and understandable and, yes, authentic. I really couldn't believe my eyes or ears. She looked like the girl and sounded like the girl, but she had never done anything like that before in her life.

I asked her, "Would you mind if we got a dentist to replace that blackish tooth?"

"Not at all. I hate that tooth, but I couldn't afford another."

"Do you sing, by any chance?"

"I sing a little bit."

"And do you dance?"

"Well, I don't do traditional dance, but I could learn."

"What's your name again?"

"Why don't you call me Miiko Taka."

I had met one of the great ladies of my life.

But for the moment I was still fearful. The production was going to cost slightly less than five million dollars. Everybody was booked on the airplane and in the hotels of Kyoto. Marlon Brando, whose uniforms had been already fitted, was actually signed to play the lead. Somehow, I felt this girl was too big a chance to take, but I did like her and she looked far better for the part than the girl we had considered.

I turned to Bill Goetz, who had been standing in a neutral corner. "What do you think, Bill?"

"She's it," he said. "Let's go—and what's more, she's got full, fleshy lips. Flat lips are sexless."

Two days before we took off for Japan I got a body blow. Bill Goetz told me *The New Yorker* magazine had called him, saying that Truman Capote wanted to go to Japan and watch our shooting so he could do a piece about *Sayonara* for the magazine. They had published his piece, "The Muses Are Heard," on the American tour of Russia of *Porgy and Bess*, and it was such a success they were sure he'd do a good piece on our picture.

When I heard this I almost stripped gears. "The Muses Are Heard" was vicious and personally humiliating to everyone, especially Ira Gershwin and Leonard Lyons. It treated human beings like bugs to be squashed underfoot. And Truman would have even juicier fodder to chew on with us. Boorish Hollywood invades Japan, and with golden ladies' man, Marlon Brando. I knew from his conversation at many parties that he had it in for Brando and wanted to shatter his powerful image.

Both Bill and I called *The New Yorker* and complained vehemently. We also wrote letters through our lawyers. We said we would not cooperate and that Truman would be unwelcome on the set. But with all our protests, I had a sickening feeling that what little Truman wanted, little Truman would get.

We took off on the vast project with ninety-nine percent professionals and one unknown quantity, not knowing that it was that one unknown quantity that would save our bacon.

We landed in Japan two or three days before New Year's Day and tried to get organized for shooting as quickly as possible. We thought we would be able to roll the cameras perhaps two days after we arrived, or at the most three days. We didn't dare waste time or money.

But we were not taking into consideration the Japanese. For twenty-four to forty-eight hours we tried to reach our associates on the telephone, and it was impossible. We then tried to buy a few things we needed for the first day's shooting, and the stores were closed. If we peered in, there seemed to be people in the back of the store, but none of them would come to open the front door. Two days went by. The same damned thing. By this time it was New Year's Day.

When we got to an American reporter, he explained, "Don't try to do anything around New Year's. This is when all Japan decides not to work. They might be full of saki, they might be up looking at the snow scenes on the mountain. You never can tell. The only thing to do is relax and swing with them. If I were you, tomorrow morning I'd go and call on the emperor and leave your calling card."

When we learned he was serious and that everybody did call on the emperor and leave calling cards, we got out our own calling cards, those of us who had them, and those of us who hadn't wrote them up. Then we walked to the palace in the midst of thousands of Japanese, past the table where the calling cards are left, and dropped ours in the pile. We figured it might bring us good luck, and, besides, what else was there to do?

The Warner Brothers people in Japan had organized a press conference two days after we got to Tokyo, and most of us appeared. It wasn't very successful because so many Japanese newspapermen did not appear. The Warner Brothers man introduced the director, the stars, and the producer, and we all left, rather let down.

I went back to the hotel suite with Bill Goetz, where he and Edie and Nedda and I had decided to have a cup of tea. The telephone rang and Bill answered it.

He said, "What!" He paused, looked in amazement at us, and went back to the telephone. "No! No! You must be joking! No, my name is William Goetz. You, you *do* know me. Oh, you *saw me* at the *press conference*, I see. Listen, we're only here for a couple— Please, now, you must give me a chance to explain. Now, really! That's going too far! I was *not* drunk. What do you mean, I was drunk when I made my speech at the press conference? I've never been— Are you out of your mind? Now, listen, I don't care whether you are an American. Hold on just a minute!"

He turned to us and said, "It's a drunken American reporter who says I was drunk at the news conference and that I've mortally insulted the Japanese and they've decided to boycott the picture. It sounds ridiculous to me."

He turned back to the telephone. "Listen, this is crazy and I don't believe a goddamn word you're saying! What! Who! What's your name? Marlon! You son of a bitch!"

And he hung up. Marlon wanted to keep us from feeling too smug. Only Marlon could have made such a hoax believable.

Bill kept on shaking his head slowly. "It never happened to me before. I'm supposed to be the smartest man in the business."

I had found as I grew to know Bill better that he was very much unlike the way he seemed. By that I mean he appeared to be a tough, cold-blooded businessman, but what he really was was a sensitive, decent, humorous friend. And when I say humorous I mean just about the funniest man I ever ran into. He could peer through those inch-thick horn-rimmed glasses and speak in his hacksaw voice and turn almost any situation into the hilarious.

Within a week we had a plan and we had found a location— Kyoto—where we would start shooting.

I had seen a smallish canal where men and boys were setting the bright colors in long panels of silk that had been dyed and stretched down the river. On the corner above the canal was a picturesque, little, darkish, bamboo-poled house; a pine tree stretched up above the fence.

This, we decided, would be Kelly's and Katsumi's Japanese house. We used it in the very first shot that was made—and cut toward the end of the picture in which Hana-ogi, the leading lady, is seen rushing down the side of the canal because she has heard of the double suicide of the Kellys.

She had to run in Japanese clog shoes and she was supposed to be highly excited, apprehensive, almost hysterically so. But she seemed completely lost.

We rehearsed it once. She shook so with nerves that I couldn't tell whether she was just unused to acting or so scared to death she would be unable to do anything. I tried it over and over again, and then we shot it. But it seemed to me she was burying her terror to keep it from me, and that's why the scene hadn't gone well. The episode left a seed of doubt deep within me about her. And even a tiny seed of doubt about your leading lady is not a very good thing to harbor, I have always found.

We went on shooting, however, and did fairly well that day. Marlon was in a few scenes, and Red Buttons. The next day, about noon, the head makeup man came to me.

"What's the matter?" I asked.

"Miiko Taka was forty-five minutes late this morning."

My heart sank. "What does that mean? Is she going to be like that? A silly amateur. If she is, we're cooked."

I decided to have a talk with her. When we broke for lunch, I said to Miiko, "Would you come to my suite at the Miyako Hotel after we stop shooting tonight?"

She said, "Yes. Is there something wrong?"

I said, "Nothing that can't be talked out."

"Fine," she said. "I'll be there."

When we were alone in my living room that evening, I emphasized to her how much she meant to the picture and how much every minute means when people are on location, how we depended upon her not only for her own behavior but for the morale of all the people around her.

I said, "You must never, never be late. *Never!* Not one minute. You must work harder than you've ever worked in your life. If there's anything wrong, I'll help you with it, or if it's a question of interpreting a scene, I'll help you or Marlon will help you. Everyone thinks you're marvelous, but you've got to become instantly professional. You must carry more than your end or we'll all collapse. You're our second star."

She didn't seem to change her expression, but in a very quiet voice she said, "You must never worry again. I will do everything you say. I will never be late. I will be reliable. I will carry my end."

And she did. She changed overnight from a willow wand to a rock.

Marlon's behavior, on the other hand, was a bit skittish, and I couldn't tell whether he was half kidding me or if he was really performing with his true feelings.

There was something he didn't seem to comprehend. I felt that the shots I was taking of him at this point didn't require too many actor-director discussions because they were semilong shots to show the location. The details of his performance wouldn't count that much. When we needed to discuss his motives, the subtleties of scenes, was when we got back to California for close-up sequences. Then it would matter a great deal. It would be crucial.

My chief concern now was simply to show the public as quickly as feasible that Marlon was in Japan. So all I had time to do was to stand Marlon in front of the camera, Japan behind him, and get out of the way. That was the most efficient way I could think of to deal with this complicated picture. If I started detailed characterization now, given how Marlon could talk, we might be there a year.

One day, on a sudden whim, I decided to show Marlon crossing a scene, running to go to the Matsubayashi quarters (as we were now calling our version of the Takarasuka Theatre and opera troupe). Just before we shot the scene, Marlon came to me.

"Should I be carrying a cigarette or not?" he asked.

I thought a second and said, "Well, it doesn't really matter, Marlon, and we have just so much daylight left."

He said, "But I mean, if he's in this emotional state, if he's feeling this disturbed, would he be smoking or wouldn't he?"

I said, "Follow your instincts, Marlon. They've got to be more considered than mine. The audience can't see the cigarette from this distance anyway, so it doesn't really matter. We won't cut into this scene. And this is a scene we will have to match in close-up in Hollywood, so you can have it either way."

He looked at me strangely and almost backed away to his position. We shot the scene. Marlon disappeared without a word, and I said, "All right, that's it," because it was the end of the day. But I was a bit disturbed by Marlon's attitude.

What I didn't realize until much later was that, God help me, Marlon had been testing me that day to see whether or not I was really paying strict attention to the direction of the picture. To Marlon, every gesture was important, and he expected help from a director or at least agreement on all the minute things. But I was doing broad strokes, sketching things in. I was going to perfect when perfecting time came. Right now I wanted to capture the beauty of the country, get good production shots of the stars in Japan, move fast, and save money.

A few mornings later I was coming down from my room at the Miyako Hotel when I saw little, chubby Truman Capote on tiptoe, registering at the desk of the hotel. I went over and squatted behind him, put my arms around his pudgy waist, lifted him up, walked him across the lobby, and dumped him out the front door. And, I must say, it wasn't all in good fun.

"Now, come on, Josh," he said. "I'm not going to write anything bad. I just want to talk the teeniest bit to Marlon on the condition of the world. You know how fancy he gets when he pontificates. He talks like an educated you-know-what. But really, Cecil Beaton's come with me. We just want to have a nice trip in Japan after my few words with Marlon—a few, that's all. Now, don't try to interfere with it, you hear, or I'll go after you, old friend."

I said, "Say anything you want about me, but you make fun of my picture and you'll regret it the rest of your fat midget life. And lay off Marlon, he's my star."

Nevertheless, I knew what Truman meant by Marlon's fanciness. I have sat in a room with Marlon, listening to him talk for hours, using four-syllable words when it would be just as effective to use one-syllable ones. In these moods of his, it is always "prevaricate," never just plain "lie"; "denigrate" instead of "run down." Truman Capote finds these pretensions of Marlon's hilarious. To me, they're touching. I am positive that Marlon is sensitive about the fact that he only finished a few grades in high school, determined that the world see his brilliant mind at work. Of course, in the end he only convinces himself, for it is the naive side of Marlon that thinks elaborate words are more of a sign of an education than short ones.

I rushed to Marlon and had only a moment to warn him. I

said, "Don't let yourself be left alone with Truman. He's after you."

But Truman is dogged, ruthless, devious, and driven when he smells something sensational he can write about. And Marlon was his perfect pigeon. Truman went whimpering to him with a tale of the "big shots," the all-powerful bosses who were forbidding him to see Marlon, and after "inviting him over, too." Bill Goetz and I were easily made out to be the big, evil boss figures. The fact that he had *invited himself* was hidden under a pathetic flow of words.

Since Marlon automatically sides with any underdog, and I mean any, Truman made himself out the most put upon of the underprivileged. Marlon, who generally hates all press, invited Truman to a late dinner. When I heard about it, I warned Marlon again that Truman was out to ridicule him publicly. I even quoted some remarks Truman had made about him. But Marlon was implacable.

"I told him I'd buy him dinner and I never go back on my word."

I began to wonder if Marlon was seeing Truman because he really felt sorry for him or because he secretly wanted to make fun of me and Bill Goetz in print and, yes, maybe stick pins in the picture itself. Marlon could be tricky, too, in his quiet way, and he loved to upset autocratic applecarts.

Two nights later, it was reported to us, Truman spent most of the night talking to Marlon in his quarters.

The next day, both men were silent about their meeting, but I heard from Marlon's makeup man that Marlon had enjoyed the evening immensely.

Then Nedda, Bill, Edie, and I had dinner with Truman and Cecil Beaton. During cocktails, Truman took me to one side.

"Oh, you were so wrong about Marlon not being gossipy," he said. "No matter what you say, he talks. I couldn't stop him. His mother's drinking, his father, his uncles, aunts, cronies, everything. He talked his head off."

"I don't believe it, Truman," I said. "You must be leaving something out. He just doesn't reveal intimate or personal things."

"He did with me."

"Now, come on, Truman. How did you trick him into revealing secrets about his family, their drinking problems and all?"

Truman giggled. "I didn't trick him. We simply swapped stories. I made up stories about what lushes my family were, and believe me, I made them lurid, until he began to feel sorry for me and told me his to make me feel better. Fair exchange." He giggled again.

"Truman, please don't write this story. It's going to hurt him where he is tender. I can smell it. And it belittles the picture, too."

"Oh, don't feel sorry for Marlon, Josh. He doesn't feel sorry for you."

"What does that mean?"

"You'll find out." He giggled again and turned to join the others.

Truman left Japan and things got a bit easier—until one day when Bill came to me and said, "We can't afford to make that huge move by boat to Shikoku Island to shoot that bridge. The estimates have come in, and it will add hundreds of thousands of dollars to our cost."

I said, "Bill, you know what it was like to look for a bridge that size in Japan. There just aren't any."

He said, "They tell me there's one in the royal enclosure in the private garden that's closed to all except whatever royalty is visiting Kyoto. The only trouble is, nobody has ever photographed it. It's never allowed to be seen except by royal eyes."

"Then how are we going to see it?"

"Well, I've managed that. The problem is that if we like it, we'll have to figure out how to get permission to use it."

The next morning, he and I went with some Japanese dignitaries who led us through special secret gates of the royal gardens to the forbidden garden. And there, over a lake or lagoon, was our bridge: an ancient stone bridge with uprights carrying an endless wisteria vine. Of course, since it was winter, there were no leaves or flowers, but that was fine because that made the bridge itself all the more visible.

The officials said that the only way we might be granted the use of the bridge was if we gave a dinner for the head guardian of the emperor's palace and his staff. There was one must: Marlon Brando must be there.

Marlon agreed to go. He knew how important it was. If we could use that bridge, we could stay in Kyoto and get home maybe two weeks earlier.

We gave a formal dinner. Marlon sat next to the wife of the highest official, Miiko Taka next to one of the other officials, and Miyoshi Umeki next to another. James Garner, who was playing the role of the marine, Bailey, was there, and Ricardo Montalban—all of us.

I could not tell whether it was a festive or a nervous occasion because I was so nervous myself. All I know is that at the end Bill Goetz got up and made a little speech of thank you to the people of Japan which was translated by one of the interpreters of the royal palace. Then Bill introduced Marlon Brando.

As Marlon rose, I glanced around at the faces of the Japanese. They were stone-faced—on guard. Something about Brando challenged them. Marlon started to speak, and much to my shocked delight he was speaking in Japanese. He spoke not swiftly but calmly, securely. He had painstakingly memorized his words, working out the sound phonetically. He spoke about four or five minutes, all in Japanese, and then, thanking them in Japanese, he sat down.

He was a total smash; we got the bridge immediately. I will always be astounded at and grateful to Marlon for that effort.

I tried to tell him how I felt, but he intercepted my praise, changed the subject, and looked away.

I did not know it then, but it seems I had still not erased the doubt and mistrust he began feeling when I had told him it didn't matter whether he had a cigarette in his hand or not—that we were too far away to see it.

He was watching me, waiting for another slip, another indication that I was a slick lightweight. By this time, Brando seemed to have convinced himself that no one else in the universe had any talent at all. Or any judgment.

But we were not to lock horns, come to grips, until we got back to California.

In the sixteenth century in Italy, strolling players played permanently assigned parts—the young lover, the phony doctor, the old maid, and so forth. Stages were set up at street fairs, and the cast, quickly studying a new plot, began to act—making up their own dialogue, improvising their own stage business, extemporizing their songs. It was pure theatre, almost totally original. Commedia dell'arte. Marlon would have led them all.

He had "become" the character he was to portray. He stepped into the body of Lloyd Gruver and stayed. He walked like him, spoke with his accent, even found instant dialogue that fitted his way of talking. The metamorphosis was so striking that it became difficult to know what was Marlon and what Gruver.

He had insisted on playing the Air Force major with a gentle

Southern accent, although Michener's creation was not from the South. Brando knew that the race prejudice would come through nastier that way, and race prejudice was really the basis of our story.

As a model for his accent and speech, he used his memory of some Southern boys who had gone to military school with him. He cultivated their horseshit-and-honey charm. Being from Louisiana, I can spot a phony Southern accent at the first drawled breath: Marlon's was totally authentic, and so was his "small talk" and his Southern winning ways. I decided that since he had become the authority on Gruver, I would let him say anything he wanted during a scene, move wherever he wished. I alerted the proper crew members. He was my commedia dell'arte actor. He was going to give distinction to this picture. I knew it.

At my instruction, the cameraman, Elly Fredericks, lit the entire set so Marlon could move or sit anywhere—could even stand on his head—and be in proper light. The only people I had to worry about were Joe Curtis, my dialogue director, who had taught Marlon all his speeches, and Marshall Wolins, the script supervisor, who had to mark down accurately every take and describe exactly what was on it and how it might differ from the one before. To follow Marlon's improvisations must have been dizzying for both of them. Marlon began throwing in little Southernisms, little extra expressions, even other sentences, without asking anybody. He was doing all this ad-libbing because he was beginning to feel like the man he was playing.

That was especially hard on Marshall Wolins. "How am I going to put these wild variations down," he asked, "so the cutter can remember where they fit? He's even saying a completely different thing in the close-up than he said in the long shot!"

I said, "Well, we'll either use the close-up or the long shot, not both, so please let him say anything he wants. It's saving our picture. I truly believe it."

Marshall Wolins rolled his eyes upward in prayer and walked away. Joe Curtis consoled him and he consoled Joe. Both of them were responsible for the dialogue, but I was responsible for the picture.

But there were other complications. Red Buttons, hearing Marlon make his added comic remarks, and having spent all of his life on nightclub floors, began to take off with him. But I would cut each moment Red did so.

"Red, you're playing Kelly. You are never to be funny. You are serious. You stick to the script and play it straight. Marlon can be as funny as he wants, but not you. As Kelly, don't ever try to be comic again."

"I know, but—"

"But what?"

"Marlon is always going away from the script."

"We can cut Marlon's ad-libs if they're not great. You have a very appealing characterization, but by changing the attitude of your face and voice, you lose Kelly to a stand-up-comedian look."

To me, the role of Lloyd Gruver was not a very exciting or fully written part, even in the original novel by Michener, and so Marlon's ad-libs, his goofy flights of imagination, were giving the picture and Gruver infinitely more texture. The parts of Kelly and his wife Katsumi were special. When I first read their story, I turned to Paul Osborn and said, "Whoever plays these parts is going to win the Academy Award."

They are the kinds of roles that for some reason actors always fall for, then vote for. They are the underprivileged. Kelly hasn't the proper education—he's a kind of Air Force Dead End Kid. He and little Katsumi love each other so madly that when they are forced by the military to separate, they join in a double suicide. It's a cinch. Nuns win Academy Awards. Blind or deaf people win Academy Awards—or a girl with an operation on her neck, or a great lady whose lifelong lover died that year. The really great performances, such as I consider Marlon Brando gave in our picture, are taken for granted. He's a male sex symbol, so to hell with him.

But it's true about the sex symbol. I would suggest that any director who has any kind of trouble working with Brando, just call him too early for his scenes and ask him to wait over there with the girls. Then, and quickly, Marlon will become a pussycat. Marlon loves, beyond anything else, to flirt with the opposite sex—especially if their skin has some color—to tease, wheedle, make mock love, or just look. If he came to the set too early, I would introduce him to the group of Japanese girls who were having their kimonos photographed, and two hours later I'd find Marlon still sitting with them, smiling, not saying much, just looking blissful.

The scenes in *Sayonara* he seemed to love playing the most were those in which Gruver was watching the girls walk across the bridge from their sleeping quarters to the theatre while hoping to attract the attention of their star, Hana-ogi.

I had planned that for Hana-ogi's first crossing of the bridge she wear something startling. She had to wear pants, because the leading ladies of the opera company are generally seen in pants. But for a top I wanted her to wear something that was tight-fitting enough to show the contour of her breasts. We chose a white turtleneck sweater. And for her head a white Tyrolean hat with long pheasant feathers.

When Hana-ogi appeared at the bridge, she stopped, Gruver watching her, and stroked a white, twenty-four-foot long-tailed rooster that was handed her. Becoming conscious that she was watched, she looked up, saw Gruver, and moved impatiently away.

The rest of the scenes were simply a reworking of the same principle, with Gruver happily supplying the variations, always hoping to catch Hana-ogi's eye to make her laugh. We would see the girl crossing in a different costume, showing a time lapse. Gruver would be there—sometimes sitting on the edge of the bridge, sometimes standing on the rounded rock floor of the lake border, always waiting and always alone.

He was always in his uniform, of course, but for her each scene meant a different costume, a different headdress, different facial attitudes—until the climax when Hana-ogi comes by with her coterie and sees no one where Gruver usually stands. Cutting farther back into the park, Gruver can be seen watching her notice he is missing. It is a sexual moment, for then he knows, and only then, she's got a thing for him.

Marlon was almost soporifically happy during the shooting of all this. Where any kind of girl play is concerned, he knows exactly what the effect should be and plays it for all its sexuality.

Even offscreen I watched him performing, which I realized he was always doing. There are some people who feel that there is no Marlon Brando, that he is some devilish but pitiful ghost seeking a living body to inhabit.

It is my theory that when he feels lonely offscreen but is happy among friends and is talking his intellectual crotchet on some favorite subject, that these special times he does a complete slip. He has slipped into the body of some brilliant friend he admires and is in danger of disappearing inside of him permanently. Depending on his mood, Marlon plays dozens of different people all day long. Wise men feel that the true Marlon has been buried so deep that he has to be mined like gold.

One night during the Kyoto shooting we were all invited to a dinner at one of the beautifully decorated Japanese inns where geisha girls and maikos—young geishas—entertained us.

Geishas have been taught to make men feel at ease, make them forget the heavy problems of the day. Part of their technique is to start with a bit of warm saki. First, a geisha fills a cup for the man, and waits until he drinks it, then she fills it for herself but takes only a tiny drop, and then replenishes it for him—until the man loosens up visibly.

And then the childish love games start. Sometimes there are hand games—slapping back and forth like pat-a-cake. Or a coin is balanced on a piece of rice paper that has been glued with water to the rim of a tumbler. Each one takes turns burning a hole in the paper with a cigarette until the coin falls into the tumbler. The loser is the one to make the coin fall and must pay a forfeit.

Sometimes the fun is dancing or rhythmic exercise—bending or waving the arms to music. Whatever the game, it is always deliciously childish and as close to a trip back toward the womb as you can get for fifty yen. I am sure it is part of the technique of the geisha to bring out the boy in the man and make that boy have a good time.

And the boy of all boys for geishas is Marlon Brando. He could spend fifty years in a geisha house, and at the end of that time, I am sure he would be the same age as when he entered. It is a great joy of living to watch Marlon have sexual fun.

We were moving along well in Japan and were ready to shoot the puppet theatre, the Kabuki theatre, and the Matsubayashi show or all-girl opera. Bill Goetz started to carry out the financial arrangements that had been agreed to on our previous trip.

But the Shochiku Company, with which we had a contract signed by Mr. Otani, the president, and witnessed by several vice-presidents, declared that they were unable to go through with their agreement—that since we were there two months later than we thought originally we might be, and it was now the main season for all these companies of theirs, no performers could be released unless we paid ten times as much as they had first agreed upon.

Bill came to me, furious. "Do you know how much this will add to the cost of the picture?" he said. "It's impossible! We can't pay it. I think we should go back to America and do the whole thing there—get some dance director to round up some Japanese-looking people and build some goddamn Japanese scenery and shoot it in Hollywood. I'm not going to be taken by these people!"

I said, "But the main reason we came to Japan was because of the Japanese theatre. It's these shows that are the very core of *Sayonara*, particularly the all-girl opera company—and we've certainly got to have the puppets. They trigger the death of Kelly and Katsumi. We can't possibly do the puppets in Los Angeles. As for Kabuki, Bill, do you think a Hollywood Kabuki company can give anything of the fantastic effect of the real thing? It would be laughable. No one would come to see the picture."

He said, "You're right. But what can we do? Go into the Japanese legitimate theatre business? Produce these shows ourselves and then photograph them?"

We looked at each other. It was a thrilling challenge.

"Of course! That's exactly what we'll do," I said. "We'll hire a theatre, a choreographer, and a director—put together a Kabuki company, hire an all-girl company, stage all the dances with Japanese actors and dancers, use Japanese designers. It'll take effort, but that's what we've got to do!"

Bill said, "And we can do it cheaper than what it would cost to pay Otani the original terms!"

It was exciting, the kind of improvisation that makes motion pictures the best game there is. But there was one snag—the puppets. Without the puppets the climactic moment of our picture would be gone.

Bill said, "Maybe there's an amateur puppet company who could do it for us." Within twenty-four hours he called me. "I found the puppets! They're Communists, so they're not allowed to play in the big theatres, but they tour the provinces and they're willing to come to our special theatre and do it for us."

I said, "Do you have anything against working with Communists, Bill?"

He paused a moment and said, "Do you?"

I said, "Only if they have some objection to working with us."

Before the week was out we had a Japanese casting director, stage directors, costume designers—and the scenery was designed and being made. We had rented a geisha theatre to serve as the stage and background for both the puppets and the Kabuki. We had decided for our Kabuki sequence to stage and photograph a spectacular lion dance which I had remembered from an earlier trip. A male actor played the part of a lady geisha dancer who turned into a fierce lion, and went mad whirling his white mane.

Ricardo Montalban, as our Japanese Kabuki actor, was perfect for the part, because he is a fabulous dancer. He learned to play and dance the woman, and later the mad whirl of the lion's white mane which made a circle of twenty feet in diameter. The puppets were equally effective, and although the Shochiku Company owned the rights to the puppet play which Michener had written about, these clever Communist puppet masters altered the ending of the double-suicide story to make it their own and changed the lines to fit our story.

It worried me for a while that Japanese scholars would object that this was not part of the original puppet play, but no one has ever mentioned it and I suspect that no one has ever noticed it.

By the time we finished shooting our all-girl opera company, I was sure that in the struggle between the Shochiku Company and William Goetz we had won. And by a large margin. I hoped that Shochiku were gnashing their teeth at our success without them. But to our great surprise, they insisted on giving us a triumphant farewell party with much champagne, saki, dancing, geisha girls, cheering, and toasts. Maybe they'd heard the picture was good and wanted some credit for it. Anyway, we got on the plane with pale faces and aching heads.

Bill Goetz, at the recommendation of Ted Haworth, the scenic designer, had brought a Japanese architect to Hollywood to build Kelly's house, the interior plus the garden. This man had shipped an entire Japanese house, precut—every floorboard, shingle, tile, every rock for the garden, all the live plants, all the shoji screens for the interior, matting for all floors, every nail, tack, every piece of wire—all air freight from Japan. It was up and available for shooting after we were sent back to work.

And there was work to be done. To finish the picture, we almost had to start it over again. In Japan we had taken care of the trimmings, the backgrounds. The big scenes, the meat of the story, must be done now.

Red Buttons and Miyoshi Umeki had learned to play together naturally. As Bailey, James Garner, who had started out a bit overly comic, had become a wise marine. Ricardo Montalban had made himself an authentic Japanese actor. And Miiko Taka had blossomed into an exquisite star. She was the keystone of our picture—always on time, word perfect, completely professional, a leader not a follower—and gave Marlon the confidence he needed to play his complicated role. He quite openly adored her, and so did I.

But now we were going to work with some of the actors who had not gone to Japan: Kent Smith and Martha Scott, who played Marlon's fiancée's parents, General and Mrs. Webster, and Douglas Watson, who played the evil colonel.

The shooting in Hollywood was always efficient, sometimes better than that, and, according to Marlon's mood, brilliant or slightly less than brilliant—never worse than that. Everyone seemed to be stimulated and perhaps even inspired by Marlon's extraordinary ability.

But it was not all strawberry parfait. Marlon and I had two historic, out-and-out verbal battles, both of which I won at the last second, much to my surprise. There was another which nobody won because it got so complicated that neither of us knew what the other was talking about.

The first conflict came when we had set up the camera inside the shoji screen hallway of Kelly's house, to which Gruver comes with Bailey. Because he has heard that Kelly's been shipped out, separating him from Katsumi, Gruver tears down the slats that have been nailed against the door, then, after taking off his shoes, goes to the sliding shoji screen which is the entrance to Kelly's bedroom.

We had already shot in Japan the scene preceding this: Gruver's arrival at the side of the canal where dozens of Japanese people are standing watching the house silently.

In rehearsal, Marlon went through the motions of getting into Kelly's hallway, took off his shoes, approached the bedroom, and quickly slid open the shoji screen.

I said, "Just a minute, Marlon. Don't you think you ought to tap on the screen before opening it?"

He turned to me in a fury and said, "Why should I?"

I said, "Because you're a Southerner. You put on a show of being a gentleman, at least, and I don't think any Southern man would burst into a bedroom without tapping on the door."

He said, "Why should I tap on the door when they're dead?"

"But you don't know they're dead."

He said, "Well, I'm a pretty big fool if I don't know it after the way those people looked out by the canal."

I said, "But they might only be guessing. You haven't talked to anyone, you haven't discussed it. There's a slight possibility that one of your friends might still be alive. It's a very delicate situation at best. I really think you ought to tap lightly on the door."

He said, "Well, I really think I ought not to—and I'm playing the part."

I said, "If you push it open, you'll be taking the suspense out of one of the biggest moments you have in the whole picture—and losing the chance to show that you have sensitivity, decency, breeding, that you have compassion."

He said, "I don't believe in courtesy. I'm finished with that. I've left home. I wouldn't do anything my parents told me to do."

I said, "But you'd do it for your own sake, wouldn't you? For your friend Kelly's sake?"

And finally, after a few more shouts, he said, "All right, I'll do it. But only on one condition—that we shoot it *two ways.*"

"All right," I said. "Okay with me. As long as I have this one take, I don't mind shooting it your way."

So he went back into position and I rolled the camera and called, "Action!" Marlon approached the house, called Kelly quietly through the slats, then tore the slats away, helped by Garner, then came into the lower hallway, looking for some sign, listening for something to give him a cue, pushed off his shoes with his feet, and then in his socks approached the entrance with the closed shoji screen. He listened for a second, then he tapped on the screen and slid it open slowly, and went in. I said, "Cut."

He came out, taking off his coat as though getting ready for the next setup inside the room.

I said, "I thought you wanted to shoot it two ways."

He gave me a dirty look and said, "Forget it," and left. The tapping must have felt good to him.

The second contretemps was during the penultimate scene when Gruver goes backstage at the opera house to tell Hana-ogi that he is going to defy the Air Force, his father, all his family, tradition, everything, and, if she will have him, marry her. This was a scene that had been written almost as Marlon had dictated it, and we had studied and weighed it very carefully and then gone back to a lot of Paul's original scene.

Hana-ogi is in her bridal costume with her beautiful wide-draped headdress. She is just about to give it and her wig to the wig man when Gruver bursts into the wig room, impatient to see her. It was a scene that I found, in reading, very strong.

The day we shot the scene there were visitors on the set. Edie

Goetz had come and brought a friend. I called for a rehearsal. Marlon's entrance took me by surprise. He shouted at Hana-ogi as I imagine an angry gangster speaks to his moll. He was a brute, aggressively threatening this girl. Played this way, the whole scene became repulsive to me, as I was sure it would to an audience. I didn't want Hana-ogi to go with this uncouth, adolescent man. He wasn't reliable emotionally; he was not the adult we had thought he had become—far from it.

I stopped the rehearsal and went over to Marlon and tried to speak quietly to him so that none of the visitors or even the crew could hear.

I said, "Marlon, you're confusing me. I don't understand your attitude."

Marlon began to shout in the loudest, wildest voice I ever heard him use. "What the hell do you mean, I'm confusing you? Who do you think you are? I've got this thing worked out and I think it's great. And I'm going to play it this way."

I said, "If you do, it's going to be our ruin and yours, too."

He said, "I don't give a damn about you or the picture. I give a damn about myself. I've got to have one strong scene; they expect it of me."

"But it's not strong—it's loud," I said. "You're not helping yourself, or the man you've created. You're the one who's being hurt by playing it this way. You are throwing your whole performance in the ash can."

He said, "You don't know what you're talking about. I have instincts and I trust them more than I trust you. This is the right way to play it. I've had to do one tough scene in every picture I've made. They want it."

I said, "Well, this isn't the time to do it. Let's go back and do it someplace earlier."

And then he began to shout so loud, and I began to shout so loud that when I looked around, I saw everyone trying to avoid looking directly at us but also trying not to miss a word.

I said, "Let's go back to your dressing room."

We marched to the back of the set and over to a tiny, onstage portable dressing room made of thin Celotex. We went inside, continuing to shout. The argument grew until we were bellowing. Everything came out about what we had always felt about each other, what we felt about the script, why didn't I listen to him when he made suggestions for the dialogue?

I finally said, "You can't end the picture as an incomplete man. You can't end on this childish note."

He said, "What do you mean, childish?"

I said, "You're supposed to be an adult by this point—no longer an Air Force Boy Scout. But you're like a three-year-old. An adult can have the same strong feelings but he should be in control of them. Not hysterical. Speak with personal authority. Know what you feel. But don't yell your head off, because if you're yelling then you won't convince us that you speak with purpose."

Marlon, who was ready to say something louder to top me, suddenly made one of those miraculous changes of his from high to reverse without going through neutral.

He said, "I see what you mean."

He seemed to forget I was there. He walked past me and went onto the set. I had to run to catch up with him.

He said, "Roll 'em," and when I got to my place by the camera, he was already entering the wig room and playing with such calm authority, such virility, such inner passion, that I had nothing more I wanted to say. I just watched it go on film.

We only had four more days to shoot. By this time, everyone in the cast and crew were like firehorses who had smelled smoke. All of us were rushing to the end. Any half minute that went wrong was a nasty annoyance for everyone.

It was on one of those mornings that I came on the set and saw Marlon sitting in a chair, looking disconsolate, a sling around his neck supporting his right arm. With my true nose for panic, I rushed to him.

"Marlon, what happened?"

He got up quickly, apologetically, and said, "Now don't blame him. It wasn't his fault."

"Whose fault?" I shouted. "What happened?"

He said, "It was my stand-in. But don't blame him. He's a nice guy. We were just kidding around. We were just pretending to box and he was only going to take a fake crack at me—only he hit my arm. I don't think it's broken. I think maybe it's just out of joint. I can be in some scenes, don't worry about that. At least, I can say any lines offscreen if you want me to."

"Offscreen!" I yelled. He was in every other shot that was left, and he had to be there in order for us to finish the picture on time. I saw the electrician setting up for the scene that we had planned, and said, "Stop that lighting now because we may have to change this thing altogether. Don't make any more moves—anybody."

I went back to Marlon and said, "Marlon, it really does mean an awful lot to us to finish the picture."

He said, "Listen, I want to finish the picture as much as you do. But what can I do? It's happened, that's all."

I said, "Well, can you move your fingers?"

He said, "Oh, sure, I can move my fingers," and he moved his fingers gingerly.

I said, "Oh, that's not so bad then."

He said, "The only thing is, I *can't* do *this,*" with which he clenched his fist and lifted it in the air and slapped his bulging biceps. "Can't possibly!" he said.

And I realized I was the victim of another Brandoism. He knew that this would scare me more than anything in the world and he had planned it all night long.

We had a big farewell party. I had brought Japanese cigarette boxes for everyone, with their names carved into the lids. Marlon came over and I told him how pleased I was with his Gruver, and he said he really hadn't thought it would be a good picture at first but now he felt it might be.

After weeks of cutting and scoring, we previewed the picture in San Francisco, and Paul Osborn flew out to see it. I was a little worried about Osborn's reaction when he discovered that Marlon was speaking half Osborn and half Brando. But he was entranced. "It's the best picture I ever worked on."

It was only after he slept on it that he realized how many lines there were in the picture that he hadn't written. In a delayed reaction, he was angry that Marlon had ignored his lines and made up his own. But I assured Paul that the original Gruver was rather dull and pompous, and Marlon in his quest for humor had corn-poned it up. Paul agreed that this made it forgivable.

I had spent a great deal of time on this picture trying to show as much about the Eastern mind to Westerners and the Western mind to Easterners as I possibly could. I was not out for a propaganda picture; I simply tried to illuminate. And I was amazed that I had got a bit of what I wanted.

Sayonara received every kind of notice there was—marvelous to just wonderful, but mostly enormously enthusiastic—and was one of the all-time box-office champions. Billy Wilkerson of *The Hollywood Reporter* wrote a front-page editorial after he had seen it and very carefully stated that it was the best picture he had ever seen in his life.

I think Marlon will agree with me that Billy did what I have done all my life: he let his enthusiam get the better of his self-control.

Truman's *Sayonara* piece came out in *The New Yorker* soon after we had finished shooting. It was just as bitchy as I had feared: it made us all into idiots.

Marlon was quoted about me, and in hoping to prove what a corny director I was, described a shot in which he had clowned outrageously for the kids in front of Kelly's house. He said he did every stupid thing he could think of to see if I would fall for it.

And I had, simply because I found his antics funny, and left them in the picture whether they proved I could direct or not.

But the main part of Truman's piece was a cruel analysis of Marlon—every unfortunate detail, including his alcoholic mother and Marlon's various pretensions. Truman left nothing out.

I called Marlon about *The New Yorker* piece and found he'd already read it. He was livid.

"That little bastard told me he wouldn't say any of the things I asked him not to and he printed them all. I'll kill him!" he shouted to me over the phone.

"It's too late, Marlon. You should have killed him before you invited him to dinner."

Months after the picture had been released, I could hardly believe my eyes when I saw a letter in my mail with the name Marlon Brando up in the left-hand corner of the envelope. I naturally thought it was a hoax. But I opened it and it was from Marlon all right, single-spaced and three and a fraction pages long.

He told how he had talked to and heard from several Oriental friends who congratulated him on the first breakthrough film about the Oriental. They were treated on the screen as equals in every way with the "superior" white race. It was the first time in movie history that an Oriental had been treated as a first-class citizen in a Western story. Marlon was so amazed, relieved, and delighted that he had to tell me how proud he was.

And then he continued. He said there were several times in the shooting of the picture when he thought I was a blithering idiot to make certain suggestions to him about what to do in a scene. Now that he had seen the picture on the screen and with an audience, he decided I was right on all counts.

The letter had no fancy words or phrases, no pretensions. He said it all simply. And all of it simply made me feel good.

INGLORIOUS
TECHNICOLOR

ACCORDING TO all rules of logic, they were in the picture because I wanted them there. Untrue! I hated them and will always hate them, but since I instigated them, I found myself powerless to do anything about them in the end but suffer. What am I talking about? Those garish color changes that upset the whole chemistry of the movie of *South Pacific*.

It started with the fact that I have long hated Technicolor film, especially for outdoor scenes. To me, it makes natural tints look like an old-fashioned chromo: the sky is too blue, the trees too green, the earth too brown, and flowers—my God, their colors must have been invented by a decorator of birthday cakes. So, I was nervous about shooting *South Pacific* in tropical surroundings near a tropical sea. What would the color look like?

It was only after talking to Eliot Elisofon, the great still photographer, that I began to feel some hope. He had been color consultant for John Huston on *Moulin Rouge*, and I remembered his reincarnations of Toulouse-Lautrec's chartreuse washes and pink footlights.

"If you photograph *South Pacific* in straight picture-postcard Technicolor, you should be shot," Elisofon said to me.

"What else can I do?" I asked.

"Anything! Use filters, overexposure, shoot through a Navajo blanket or a Spanish shawl. Anything! Just don't make it look as though you could turn it over and find written, 'Having wonderful time in colorful Tahiti—wish you were here.' "

Naturally, I believed him, because I wanted to so very much, but I wanted a great picture, too. I'd never been able to experiment with color because of the strict code of conservative cameramen. Jimmy Wong Howe had broken down and let me use a faint rose filter for the community sing in *Picnic*, but Milton Krasner wouldn't let me use a simple fog filter in *Bus Stop*. Ellsworth Fredericks did produce some startling lighting in *Sayonara*, but Japan was oddly colored to start with and *Sayonara* was photographed in the gray of winter.

So I was grateful to Elisofon for the push. I took what I thought was his advice and thereby made one of the major mistakes in my career.

He only told me what to do. He never warned me that there was an enemy lying in wait for me. The enemy's name is Panic. Studios feel that experiments cost money and should be forbidden. Not being warned, I plunged on.

I went to Leon Shamroy, my cameraman for *South Pacific* and a man I had known since my first year in California. He was grouchy, cynical, hated actors ("I'm ready for the bastards") and producers ("Here come the idiots"). Only he used stronger words. But underneath he was the well-known pussycat.

To me he said, "What's this cocksucking idea you've got about color?"

I tried to picture for him the visual effect of the stage show of *South Pacific:* the whole stage changes color before and during every song. The orchestra begins its introduction and the normally lighted sky dims slowly almost to blackness, side spots and floodlights give golden outlines to the character singing, a tiny pin spot concentrates on the singer's face. A mood has been created that allows spectators to concentrate on the words and music and the emotion of the singer's performance. At the end of the song the whole stage builds back to normal light and the play continues in realistic lighting.

"And what the fuck do you expect me to do about that? You can't take light away from a real sky just because the music starts —and you can't make a cut and change lighting because people will think it's four hours later. What the hell do you want to change things for, anyway?"

I said, "Well, Leon, I really don't know. I just felt somehow that to see the same vivid Technicolor blue in the sky, the same sun, the same beach, for the whole length of the picture might be a little overpowering and lacking in mood. I was just hoping we could treat the film in some daring way, but if you don't know how to do it, I'm sure I don't."

"Well, film is a realistic medium. It's up there on the screen. It's what it is. It demands reality. You're talking about fantasy."

Good God, why didn't I stop right there? Shammy's right, he's smart. Film is a realistic medium.

Then he continued: "And when you start screwing around with it, it's maddening to the viewer. They see the wheels going around, and start thinking about that and lose their concentration on the story."

But I could see he was thinking. I had caught him with a challenge.

"Wait a minute. I just remembered. There used to be an old bastard that did a great paint job on a moving filter," he said. "He knew how to sneak into another color without anyone figuring it out. We might get him to paint some for us and we'll make a few tests."

"What would one effect be? On the screen, that is."

He continued. "It would mean that when a song starts you could begin to wind the filter across the front of the lens, and gradually the film would take on that tint as though by voodoo. But you've got to be sure it's the right density or it'll drive people crazy."

In a few weeks Shamroy had got a couple of his filters painted and we were out on the back lot, shooting test scenes with them. One filter was very, very subtle and left an almost subliminal impression on the eye, whereas the other one had a bit more bite to it, and I must say that for the song "Bali Ha'i," which had magical implications, I felt that the second filter could be used. I asked Leon how he felt.

"Well, if it was me I'd shoot it two ways, with and without a filter. You never can tell about a thing like this. It might go wrong and kill the picture."

I went to Buddy Adler, our producer, and explained the situation and let him see the color tests. Buddy said at once, "I agree with Leon. I'd like you to shoot it two ways. We've got to protect this picture. It's a big one."

I left the color changes to Leon to perfect, and I went off to New York to complete the casting with Rodgers and Hammerstein who, along with George Skouras, owned the producing company called Magna.

I'd had trouble with Oscar and Dick about this movie before. Back in 1950, in the days of the second company of the stage play of *South Pacific*, Oscar had told me that he and Dick were forming a motion-picture producing company to produce pictures based on their stage productions. The first was to be *Oklahoma!* and the great Fred Zinnemann was going to direct it. The second, *South Pacific* possibly, with a director to be decided.

With great fanfare, *Oklahoma!* was filmed, and when it opened and did not skyrocket, Dick and Oscar spoke out openly of their dissatisfaction with the way it had been directed.

Shortly after that, I invited Fred Zinnemann for lunch and asked him to tell me about the cooperation he had received from Magna on *Oklahoma!*.

He said, "I didn't do a good job. It was my first musical and I was in awe of Dick and Oscar. But I shouldn't have been. After all, this was their first film production and I had had years of experience. I should have followed my instincts, not theirs."

I knew what he meant.

So when one day in 1957, eight years after I directed *South Pacific* on the stage, Oscar said to me, "I think you're the right person to direct the film *South Pacific*," I grew very cool and careful and answered, "Oh, do you? Really."

He said, "Yes, if you only had a film under your belt. It's going to be awfully hard to sell you to George Skouras when you're not known as a director of pictures."

"Oh, I understand that perfectly. Why don't you get John Ford?"

Now, I didn't direct *Picnic* in order to get the job of *South Pacific*, but still I now had *Picnic* under my belt. And I had followed that with another good film, *Bus Stop*. Both big hits. So when Oscar talked to George Skouras he had two film hit names to drop. And in addition I'd taken on *Sayonara*.

So I'd established my credits. Magna offered me the job of directing *South Pacific*, but the salary they had in mind was much less than I got for my first picture, *Picnic*.

I was determined but calm at my meeting with Oscar and Dick.

I said, "I know you both very well. I respect you as artists and businessmen and you know how much I care for you personally, but I want you to understand something. I won't make a step backward in my career for anybody or for any reason. I would love to direct *South Pacific* and I think I could do a good job—the best. But I have to have more than I got on my last picture or I'll be forced to take another film that's been offered to me. It would be an honor to direct *South Pacific*, but it's also a huge responsibility to put such a masterwork on the screen. So, I will only do it if I share in its profits. I'm sorry, but otherwise I will be forced to do something else."

And I left. To my surprise, they agreed, and along with my brilliant lawyer, Bill Fitelson, we came to a generous, profit-sharing setup. At last I might make up for the author's royalties I wasn't given on the play.

The casting, too, started off with certain problems.

First of all, none of us had settled exactly on whom we wanted to play Nellie Forbush. The list ran from Audrey Hepburn to Elizabeth Taylor, with a couple of side trips to Doris Day.

Everyone asked why we didn't just use Mary Martin. The answer is that Pinza was dead and the problem of finding another Emile de Becque to match Mary seemed hopeless. The only big star who was the right age for her was Vittorio De Sica, but he seemed to us too saturnine for Emile.

All three of us had seen Rossano Brazzi in *Summertime* with Katharine Hepburn, and each of us had the same idea. He might play Emile—if he could sing. Dick and Oscar said he had sung for them and they had approved of his voice. Knowing that, I agreed, and he was signed. I figured if his voice satisfied the experts, that was enough.

One day I got a call from Mike Todd. He said, "I think my wife, Elizabeth Taylor, should play the lead in *South Pacific.*"

I said, "I think so, too. But can she sing?"

"She's got a great voice."

I said, "Well, then, I'll arrange for her to meet Dick Rodgers," which I did.

Dick and I were in his office, which had a grand piano, when Elizabeth and Mike arrived. She was twenty-four, thin, and extremely beautiful. She had even been out-of-doors and was slightly freckle-faced. She was so right and ready for all-American Nellie Forbush, she looked to me like our God-given answer. Mike left us, and then Dick said, "Elizabeth, do you think you could hit a few notes for me?"

She gulped, swallowed, and looked terrified, and said, "I'll try."

Dick played some chords and waited. She didn't make a

sound. Then he played some more and she grabbed onto her courage and rather hoarsely forced out a few breathy notes. She tried one more time, and then the room was filled with embarrassing silence.

She said, "Josh, will you take me down to a taxi?"

She grabbed my arm and we got to the elevator and went down to the main floor. As we stepped out into the vast and busy lobby, she spied the waiting Mike Todd across the crowd, and she belted out in full, marvelous voice, "I'm in love, I'm in love, I'm in love, I'm in love, I'm in love with a wonderful guy!"

I couldn't believe it. She was singing—really singing.

I said to her, "What happened?"

She said, very simply, "Dick Rodgers happened. He scared me to death with his stern face. I couldn't sing a note."

When they left, I went back up to Dick and said, "She can sing. She sang in the lobby. I don't know whether she can sing well enough to do the songs herself, but certainly she can sing —and she could be dubbed."

Dick closed his eyes and winced, which he always does when he's meditating, and then said, "We can't dub the character of Nellie Forbush—not in this picture. Absolutely impossible!"

That finished that. The ideal girl was gone. Losing her, to me, was a disaster, and as I think back it was worse than that.

Later on, I was in Hollywood on *Sayonara* business, and Roz Russell gave Nedda and me a party in the beautiful yellow-and-white room in her house on Beverly Drive. Dean Martin was there, and Frank Sinatra—quite a few musical people. Among them was Doris Day.

I never had felt she was right for the part: I had the feeling that she would make Nellie into Doris Day, and that the public would know in advance exactly what her performance would be like. The world had memorized her. I wanted a surprise.

But, having lost Elizabeth Taylor, I couldn't ignore any talented prospect.

Dean Martin was singing, leaning on the piano, and Frank Sinatra and several other stars sang a chorus or two. It was a very cozy party. Then someone said, "Doris, sing a chorus of something."

I urged her as well. I thought if I could see her be spontaneous, joyous, the unrehearsed, basic Doris Day, she might change my mind.

"Oh, no," she said, suddenly very tight and drawn in. "No, no. I never sing at parties."

Everybody began urging her.

She said, "No, I don't feel like singing."

And deep in my silent heart I said, And I don't feel you'll ever be Nellie Forbush either.

I searched the agencies as well as the Hollywood parties to get another idea for Nellie. There just didn't seem to be anyone good enough to sing the part who was also young enough to play it against the older man, Rossano Brazzi.

Then Mitzi Gaynor came at me with an almost irresistible offer. "I know you won't think I can play Nellie," she said, "but may I test and try to prove that I can?"

We tested her twice, and Dick Rodgers was so careful that he spent several thousand extra dollars and had her redo the test and sing "I'm in Love with a Wonderful Guy" at a slower tempo and in a different key. I don't know what that did for him, but still, it was worth it because it made him decide she could do it.

When it was announced, everybody had a different reaction to Mitzi. Some said, "Oh, absolutely not. Oh, my God, I can't stand her." Others said, "She'd be charming and young—she'd be lovely."

Arthur Hornblow said the most astute thing, it seemed to me. He said, in his rather professorial manner, "Oh, she's very good. Excellent, in fact. Very vivacious and charming—and full of sex, too. Of course, she has to be policed."

"Policed? I haven't heard that expression since the army when we used to police the area by picking up cigarette butts."

"That's exactly it," he said. "You have to pick up her cigarette butts—smooth the too cute wrinkled nose, shrink the wide-wide smile, calm the rolling eyes. You have to take away the things she does that get in the way of the things she ought to do. Mitzi gives you too much for your money. You've got to get your exact worth, no more, and then she's great."

It certainly sounded worth it. We signed her.

As Bloody Mary, Juanita Hall had been unique in the original stage production. Now, eight years later, since age didn't matter in that role, there seemed to be no contest as to who would play Bloody Mary in the film. But Dick and Oscar were so gun-shy of this huge production after the comparative failure of *Oklahoma!*, so worried about the vocal side, that they would sign Juanita only with the proviso that Muriel Smith, the opera singer, do the actual singing.

That was a great blow to Juanita and to me. Not that Muriel Smith hadn't a beautiful voice—I had directed her as Bloody

Mary in the London company of *South Pacific*—but Juanita Hall had her own style of singing and it seemed a shame to miss its special quality in our picture. Still, they were experts on music and, more than that, my bosses, so in spite of my misgivings, I was forced to say okay.

While I was interviewing lines of beautiful girls for the role of Liat, the exquisite Tonkinese daughter of Bloody Mary, our casting director said to me, "There's an Oriental girl coming, but late because she's working in a bakery."

When she came, it was worth the wait. She was the most beautiful seventeen-year-old girl I had ever seen—France Nuyen. She couldn't speak a word of English, but I spoke enough French to persuade her to say a word or two aloud. I was thrilled. I felt she would surely be chosen. And she was.

Just before shooting started I got a message from Rodgers and Hammerstein that Rossano Brazzi was not to sing one note in the picture. I called Dick and Oscar and they told me that Brazzi had become so jubilant at being given the part that he went back to Italy boasting of his singing powers and had even made a record which someone thoughtful enough sent to Dick and Oscar. When they heard it, they were horrified and broke off all negotiations with him. They would talk only with the proviso that his voice could be dubbed by a great voice.

One of the mysteries of my life was how Dick and Oscar with their ear and their experience could have signed a man for a major singing role who couldn't carry a tune. He must have given them a giant snow job or maybe they had cotton in their ears when they auditioned him.

By this time I wondered, if Juanita Hall and Rossano Brazzi were going to be dubbed, why the hell couldn't Elizabeth Taylor? But it was too late to rock the boat.

Muriel Smith flew over from London for two days and recorded two Bloody Mary songs with her usual brilliance. Juanita listened to her with a Tonkinese poker face.

Since John Kerr had the part of Lieutenant Cable, we found a young singer who had a voice that sounded like his to interpret "Younger than Springtime" and "You've Got to Be Carefully Taught."

To Brazzi's continued unhappiness, the voice of Emile de Becque was to be done by Giorgio Tozzi, the distinguished Metropolitan basso. Every time Tozzi hit a particularly beautiful or effective note, I could see Rossano Brazzi roll his eyes heavenward or wince in pain. Fortunately, Tozzi did not see him. As a matter of fact, when Brazzi was around, he provided the closest I'd ever seen to fawning: "Thank you for being my voice."

Tozzi and Mitzi sang the duets, and Mitzi performed her songs impeccably—no policing necessary.

Each singer being dubbed was given a record of the song he was supposedly singing so that he could memorize not only the exact phrasing but also the breathing for the camera, for if that is not exact, it is immediately apparent that someone else is doing the singing. The camera picks up everything—every thought, every fleeting idea—so the singer cannot silently mouth the words: he must actually sing aloud along with the voice that has been recorded or the camera will know by the movement of his throat.

The recordings were sent on to Dick Rodgers and Oscar Hammerstein in New York for their approval, and I went on with my directorial plans.

Although I was to do the dances, as I had done in the original production, I knew they would have to be changed somewhat for the wide screen, so I asked that the studio hire LeRoy Prinz to help me. He was to go ahead of me to Hawaii and pick out some local people.

We had also planned that a large boar's tooth ceremony be added to the picture to give it a little more size, and Dorothy Jeakins was hired to do some primitive dance costumes for it.

We were to shoot most of the picture on the island of Kauai, one of the Hawaiian Islands.

Our children, Tom, seven, and Susan, six, were looking forward to being with us. The advance man had found us a slightly primitive but very comfortable house smack on a bay where the kids could build bonfires and ride in small boats, and even wade or swim. And Nedda's daughter's children, Kathy and Johanna, along with their mother, Ann Connolly, were joining us.

We took a new nurse with us. Joyce Compana was an easygoing, Mary Poppins type who simply walked in and took over to give us years of peace and comfort. The children liked her immediately.

We flew to the main island of Oahu in a body. On the first day I interviewed young, local American men who were trying out for the parts of Seabees and marines, and American Hawaiian girls who were the right age and looks for Navy nurses. They were every bit as good both vocally and visually as the originals.

I left LeRoy Prinz to work with both the nurses and the boys on impromptu dances for the rhythmic movement we had planned for "I'm Gonna Wash That Man Right Outa My Hair" and "There Is Nothin' Like a Dame."

My family and I flew on to the outer island of Kauai and got settled in our ramshackle, sea-stained house on a hidden bay. The kids were delighted, and made friends with the local Hawaiian boys and girls. Nedda's two granddaughters and our daughter Susan arranged for hula lessons from one of the older sisters of the family nearby.

The shooting of *South Pacific* on Kauai went comparatively smoothly. Mitzi was fun but a true professional, and Brazzi was reluctantly professional himself. John Kerr had memorized his songs so perfectly that he could act, think, and sing along with the recordings and make us believe, even while we were watching carefully, that it was his own voice we were hearing. France Nuyen had begun to learn a few words of English and was a vision of loveliness every time she appeared, though slightly sullen. Juanita Hall, of course, could play Bloody Mary backward, and was naively irresistible.

Within the first few days I had filmed, at a location bounded by huge black rocks we called the nurses' beach, "I'm Gonna Wash That Man Right Outa My Hair." It wasn't as exciting as it had been onstage since washing hair was, after all, no novelty to motion pictures, but we did it as well as we were able to under the circumstances.

When Oscar Hammerstein arrived to watch the shooting, the first thing he did was look at the rushes. He felt I had missed "I'm Gonna Wash That Man . . ." completely, and asked for it to be shot over.

I said, "I'll shoot it over Oscar but you won't like it any better because hair has been washed in films for years." I shot it over and he still didn't get the kick that he had onstage. I finally convinced him he never would.

"I'm in Love with a Wonderful Guy" was done on and off the top of a rowboat, with the real sea close in the background. The sea was so loud we had to turn up the sound of the playback for Mitzi to hear it and lip-synch it, but she had rehearsed so carefully that we were through with it after two takes.

When we moved up to shoot the opening scene at Emile de Becque's plantation house, everything went well until Brazzi had to be photographed singing "Some Enchanted Evening" to the playback of Giorgio Tozzi's voice. The moment the song started I could tell that he was resisting it. It was too emasculating to this Italian that he should be forced to sing to another man's voice. Whether he did so deliberately or not, he kept making mistakes, and Ken Darby, the vocal director, would say, "No, I'm sorry, Rossano, you've bumbled it again."

Suddenly, Rossano burst into a fury of Italianate English: "Diss goddamn cheap shit voice, I cannot sing to it."

This was a real danger signal and I decided to take over. I sent everyone out of earshot, and then I turned to Rossano and said, "Rossano, we are on an island in the middle of the Pacific with an enormous company and stupendous daily expenses. You are costing the picture money. If you can't sing to Giorgio Tozzi's voice, which is a great voice, then we have to shut down and replace you with someone who can sing to his voice, because you know that Rodgers and Hammerstein are never going to let you sing the songs no matter how many times you deliberately miss matching the words. Now, you have a choice to make. You're either going to play Emile de Becque or you're not going to play him. But I'm not going to listen to one second more of your phony, childish temperament. Do it and do it well, or don't do it at all. I'll give you one-half minute to make up your mind."

He made a quick adjustment. He grunted a bit, patted me on the back, and said, "Let's go. Anything you say."

Up to this time, Shammy and I had been shooting several color changes, but we had always covered ourselves and the picture by shooting the same scene again without using a filter. It took a bit more time, shooting it two ways, but both of us felt safer.

Buddy Adler, who had been watching the rushes in California, suddenly took a plane and appeared on the set without warning. I should have guessed something was up.

While Shammy was lighting the next shot, Buddy took me aside and said, "I've got great news for you, Josh. You don't have to shoot two ways anymore. Only shoot your color change. The lab can cut out the color if you don't want it later. I've gone into it thoroughly."

I called Shammy over, who said, "Don't you think it's safer to do what we're doing?"

And Buddy said, "No safer, according to the lab, and you know it's much more expensive. It doubles the expense of the whole location while those scenes are being shot. You don't want to be responsible for that, Shammy."

"I don't want to be responsible for anything. You make the decisions." And he left us to continue his lighting.

Buddy said, "Take my word for it, those filter colors can be made to disappear. So here's the dope from all of us: shoot it one way. I'll see you at chow."

As he left, I watched him with a funny feeling that I had just had my head cut off with a sharp razor—so sharp it seemed painless.

What he hadn't told me and what was my ultimate downfall was that the leaching process would take at least three months. I was too stupid or too ignorant to ask him how long it would take, so I told Shamroy that I must listen to them. They had given in on the color; I must give in on saving expenses. The dice were cast, but I wasn't to see until much later that they had turned up snake eyes.

One Sunday when I didn't have to shoot and could sleep late, I woke to wild shouts of excitement. I looked out of my window to see my whole family gathered around seven-year-old Tom, who had just returned from a fishing expedition five hundred yards out in the bay with his little Hawaiian friend. While they were out in a rowboat, there had been a run of sunfish; in half an hour Tom had caught fifty-five. He was holding them up on strings, proudly. After he was photographed, he gave them to the cook and decided that it was such a record he was never going to try to beat it, and he considered giving up fishing for good. He wanted to retire as a champion.

John de Cuir, our set designer, had built a stage in a park with a beautiful tropical background for the outdoor auditorium of the Thanksgiving show-within-the-show in which Nellie Forbush, in a baggy sailor suit, sang "Honey Bun" and clowned with Luther Billis (wonderfully played by Ray Walston), who was in a grass skirt with coconut breasts. In the movie we could do what we could never do in the theatre: show the audience of marines and sailors watching the Thanksgiving show.

I found myself, at dawn, facing about twenty thousand marines and sailors seated on the ground in rows; they had been brought from their quarters by boat and truck that morning and were to be taken back that evening. They were rigorously disciplined and far too neat.

The big problem was that these poor guys were being asked to react to a show that wasn't there, because we were not going to shoot the show itself until we were back in Hollywood. After the first shot of their taking their seats, I could sense that they were confused and a bit restless, so I borrowed the technique we used during the first night of shooting the crowd in *Picnic,* and sent Mitzi out to talk to them while the cameramen laboriously set up for the next shot. The prime essence for making movies is patience.

Mitzi eventually ran out of stories, and then it was up to me. I told them every goddamned story I knew—everything that might interest them about *South Pacific,* particularly what kind of entertainment they were pretending to watch, and then bits of Hollywood gossip. But I, too, ran dry. I could not squeeze out one more word that wouldn't bore them as much as it was boring me. But in the end we got the massive shots we needed of them standing, cheering, mostly just applauding or laughing, and then of them leaving the outdoor auditorium. It was such a dreary day for them that I doubt if many of them ever saw the picture and realized what a thrilling scene they had contributed to our picture.

All through this shooting, the most colorful figure I think I ever worked with was Leon Shamroy. He was my constant companion, adversary, friend, adviser, and generally the focal point of our entire group. His obscenities flowed freely on every subject. He had invented the color change and he had worked it out carefully. He was the past master of anything to do with the camera. But he knew far more than that. I will always be grateful to him for making that experience a humane one for me. Dick Rodgers never left New York, so when Oscar Hammerstein got too nervous I could always talk with Shammy and use his particular language to help me blow off strain. We dubbed his language Shamroviana. It was a great way to let off steam.

Ben Kadish was another rock. He was the first assistant director and he planned every day's shooting.

Movie companies always want to save money, and Magna was saving a fortune by having Navy and Marine cooperation. These great organizations supplied personnel landing craft, trucks, jeeps, uniforms, firearms gratis. But one piece of Navy equipment cost Magna thousands and thousands of dollars. It was a Navy cutter, a single piece of small craft that was used to carry Lieutenant Cable and Billis from the main island to the nearby romantic island of Bali Ha'i where the French planters had put all their young women when they heard the GIs were coming. For the trip of that cutter to the island we had built a scene for which we had hired over three hundred extras. Dorothy Jeakins had dressed them in native costume with the aid of dozens of dressers. John de Cuir had built exotic houses on stilts with tapa cloth awnings and huge, carved Polynesian faces such as are seen on Easter Island. All of this had been assembled on a special beach with five or six strange, pointed mountain peaks in the background—the cones of dead volcanoes. The years had eroded all the earth that had once formed these peaks, but the lava inside these cones had hardened to steel-like firmness and remained to form the fantastic twisted spires which gave a mystic, fairy-tale quality to the scene, adding to the feeling of spectacle we had come so far to get.

We filled the beach with action. The extras covered a quarter of a mile along the water and in it, and practiced throwing leis and bunches of flowers as a festive welcome to the Navy boat.

We were to shoot the scene over the backs of Billis and Cable, shirtless and sunburned from the trip across. The camera was placed, with me beside it, in the aft of the cutter: the very point of view of the sailor who was steering.

I gave the command to roll the camera and shouted by electric megaphone for the action to start all along the beach. Flower leis began to be tossed, girls danced, young brown boys and girls swam toward us, smoke came from the tapa cloth huts and from dozens of bonfires. Little children in tiny native skirts ran among the crowd, flying kites.

The sailor assigned to us started the motor of our cutter and we began moving toward the colorful shore. I thought, It's so great and we're going to get it on the first take. But, oh, my God! how much wishful thinking that was!

After the cutter had moved about fifteen feet, the motor conked out and we found ourselves rocking gently on the waves as though we were in a tub.

I shouted to stop the action, and one of the mechanics came out to fix the motor. He looked a bit worried so I asked him the trouble.

"I tried to fix it all last night. The Navy sent us a lousy cutter, that's all. They couldn't use it, so they could spare it, I guess."

He started adjusting wires and rods and gauges. Half an hour later he looked up and said, "You better send for a Navy mechanic. I can't make this piece of junk work."

While hundreds of people waited, a Navy mechanic from a

station miles away finally arrived. By the end of the day he turned to me. "Why don't you make the Navy give you a good cutter? They've got plenty. This one's kaput."

That, of course, meant we had to send everyone home and try the shot over the next day. Leon Shamroy summed it up for us: "I learned early. Never trust a fucking boat."

The next morning we got the shot, with a new cutter, on the first take. And hundreds of natives got two days' pay instead of one.

The entire location trip and the timing of the start of the picture had been planned to fit the two days when actual war games would take place on a remote beach on the other side of our island. All forms of transport covered the beach; troop ships were close to shore; and there were thousands of men in battle dress marching, forming, running back and forth on the beach. We had to shoot our action quickly during those two days and yet keep out of their way. We needed ten or twelve short scenes at that war games beach, and we got good and sneaky at "shoot and run." The men in the background were simply that. They had been commanded not to look at us while we were shooting. With their help, we were able to give the impression that our cast was in the center of a great operation—Operation Alligator, James Michener had called it.

When we finished this war sequence we were ready to fly back to California.

On our way back, we had to stop for two days in Honolulu to shoot a certain Oahu mountain with a hole in it—needed for a scene in which Emile and Cable are hiding on the enemy island.

Nedda, the children, and I were escorted by our bellhops to our suite on the twentieth floor of our Honolulu hotel. As I was pointing out to the bellboy which bag should go to which room, I looked through the vast living room and onto the balcony, and saw six-year-old Susan climbing up over the balustrade and leaning far out to see the view.

I dropped to my knees and in a sick voice said, "Look—Nedda—Susan—balcony." I closed my eyes. Oh, my God, shades of Bill Holden!

Nedda's voice cooed as she slowly moved on her knees toward Sue. "Sue, darling—sweetest, darling Sue—come back in, darling. Come back here, darling. Susan. Susan, darling." And then a quick grab. "Susan, you silly little fool, how dare you!"

We did not unpack our bags. We just moved to the ground floor.

Back in our lovely house in Beverly Hills, the days moved very swiftly toward finishing the picture. Most of it had been done. We still had two major sequences—the show-within-the-show which we called the Thanksgiving show, and the elaborate boar's tooth ceremony which LeRoy Prinz had been rehearsing for several weeks.

Since we had worked out all the clowning and the formations in the original New York staging, it was very simple to put the routines together again for the Thanksgiving show, but the boar's tooth ceremony was so elaborate that it took much longer than we expected.

It was done in a forest of bamboo copied after one we had seen on the island of Kauai. The black dancers who had been chosen by LeRoy were dressed in Dorothy Jeakins's extraordinary combinations of light blue and white which contrasted vividly with their skins. LeRoy had worked out an interesting dance which was climaxed by Archie Savage, a black dancer from the original New York company of *South Pacific*, dancing on red-hot coals which were buried in a pit. The flaming coals may have been phony but the effect was real.

It took us four full days and thousands of dollars to film the huge ceremony. We photographed angle upon angle of naked feet dancing, heads whirling in the air, close-ups of elaborate blue makeup. And when it was put together, we threw the whole thing on the cutting-room floor because it obviously was an expensive, ostentatious, and bloody bore, because if as one critic said, "The story of *South Pacific* is pure as a lily," then the boar's tooth ceremony was gilding the lily.

I finished up the bits and pieces of *South Pacific*, put it all together in a semirough cut, left instructions as to what else was to be done with it, including that the lab should keep the color down, and then I went to New York to direct *Blue Denim*.

I will always wonder whether my decision to do *Blue Denim* was not the worst decision I ever made in my life. Deep down I knew that I should have stayed in California and watched every inch of the cutting and every bit of the color changes, but I also trusted my cutter, Bill Reynolds, who was also my friend.

The next few months I was so absorbed in *Blue Denim* that I didn't fly back to check as much as I would have liked to on the way *South Pacific* was going. The first time I saw it was in

Hartford, Connecticut, when it was previewed in front of an audience for the first time.

As Bea Lillie once said, "You could have knocked me over with a fender!" I was never more shocked by anything in my entire life. I didn't dream the color would screech the way it did. Leon Shamroy had assured me it would be subtle. There was nothing subtle about the way the color changed. Shamroy had not been allowed into the lab to check on it.

Panicked, I went to George Skouras and said, "Please, let me take it back and get this color removed in the lab. If you don't, you're going to have a very poor picture."

Oh, no. Impossible. It was too late. They had sold previews starting ten days from that minute. There was no time to change anything unless those sold-out previews were canceled.

I said, "But you can't play around with a famous story like this. It must be carefully presented to the public."

"It's your fault. You made it cost too much money," said Skouras, "so I've got to get that money back."

And that's what happens when the money men are in charge of pictures. And they can buffalo even powerful men like Rodgers and Hammerstein. The creators are swept aside. It's too late to perfect.

It would have taken three months in the lab to make the color come out right, but Oscar and Dick would not force Skouras to give up those precious benefits. Return all that money? Impossible.

I wanted (and still want) to carry a sandwich board in front of every line at the box office, saying, I DIRECTED IT AND I DON'T LIKE THE COLOR EITHER!

The ghastly part of this story is that *South Pacific* turned out to be the most financially successful thing I ever did in my life. It made more money than all the rest of my pictures and plays put together. Unfortunately, that doesn't make me feel any better about it.

And I didn't really believe it was a big success until years later when I went to England and discovered the film of *South Pacific* had been playing at the old Dominion Theatre in the West End for five consecutive years; *in that theatre alone* the picture had taken in enough pounds, shillings, and pence to pay off *the entire production* cost. The English loved it, and as it was. The English have such dreary weather that the color seemed to give them a lift.

When I was interviewed there by the press, I tried to apologize for the color changes, and one of the reporters said, "But Mr. Logan, the *color* was what we *liked.* "

But my biggest surprise came later when I went to Palm Springs to talk about *Camelot* music with Fritz Loewe, who said, "I'm so glad you're doing *Camelot,* Josh. Alan and I were so careful about choosing a director that we ran all the films that were made from the big musicals, and found they all were directed as photographed stage plays. The only one done with flair and imagination was *South Pacific.* That's when we went to Jack Warner and said, 'Josh Logan must do *Camelot.* ' "

Now I ask you, should I have used those color changes? The answer is no.

THEATRICAL SIGNALS

QUITE OFTEN in the putting together of a play, an inside joke or story is told to emphasize a point. Once it has been used for effect the catch-line or -phrase is often repeated whenever necessary for further emphasis. Phrases like "Hold your hats, boys, here we go again!" and "That's when the shit hit the fan," or "There's always gotta be one wise guy in the crowd" are the punch lines of famous stories. Stories that most Americans recognize.

But some stories are private or are made private by being adopted by two people who want to use it as a shortcut.

"Your father should have such a sickness" is my favorite.

During *Mr. President*, Irving Berlin used to excite himself by using that catchphrase to mean enthusiastic and total approval. If I asked him how he liked the way Nanette Fabray was singing a song, for instance, Irving would brighten perceptibly and say, "Nanette? Your father should have such a sickness." He said it about the scenery, about Robert Ryan as President—all of which he obviously loved.

One day, during the Boston tryout, when he and I were walking in the Public Garden, I said, "Irving, what does it mean, 'Your father should have such a sickness'?"

He said, "Oh, I thought everyone knew that old Jewish joke: There was a solicitous Jewish mother whose beautiful daughter was seeing a young man every night in the parlor. 'What's he like,' she quizzed the girl. 'Mother, I think he's sick. He interrupts a kiss or a hug and runs to the bathroom: five and six times a night.' The mother went quickly to the young man. 'What's all this rushing to the bathroom?' 'It's your daughter,' he said. 'She's so soft, so voluptuous, so tempting that I get into a state when I get too near her and I have to run to the bathroom and—you know—relieve myself sexually, if I'm not being too specific.' Then getting her daughter alone the mother said, 'Five or six times a night! Your father should have such a sickness!' "

And ever since then your father should have such a sickness is the strongest approval we can get.

*　*　*

The most painful as well as the most elusive phrase in theatrical parlance is what to say to an actor or actress after you have just seen one in a ghastly play. You have gone backstage, you have found the number of the room, knocked on the door, and your friend has opened the door and is looking expectantly for a compliment.

Here is where the fainthearted collapse and start burbling: "Oh, it was wonderful, and the play's wonderful and you're wonderful, and your dressing room's wonderful." Somehow, everyone in the room knows it's total defeat, a rout.

The strong-willed saves face by saying something noncommittal. But what? It is impossible to use the words "very good" without offending, because it's not enough, although some actors grab onto any vestige of a compliment and respond, "I knew you'd love it."

After some lengthy discussions with high intellects of the theatre, we have come to the conclusion that there is only one thing safe to say to a good friend who's a bad actor or a good actor who's in a bad play. But it must be said with great emphasis on the first word: "*What* a performance!" Or, for variation, "That's *some* evening!"

I used this frequently and with great effect, and thought I had the whole situation licked when all of a sudden my success with it came to an abrupt halt: *someone used it on me.*

*　*　*

The most satisfactory signal I ever heard was given to a French telephone operator.

Harold and Florence Rome, Nedda, and I had taken a limousine over two-thirds of France's roads looking for Marcel Pagnol, the author of *Fanny*, before we started work on the play. We had missed him several times and decided to give up and leave France. But that was almost impossible, because there was a nationwide telephone strike at the time.

The operator at the hotel told us that we could make no telephone calls whatsoever for any reason. Only calls about violent illness or death were acceptable, and no one was able even to try and fool the operator as there were monitors on every caller who spoke English and French. We sat in our room defeated.

But Florence Rome is a resourceful woman. She said, "I've got to call Jim Wise and let him know we're coming to Switzerland and how long we're staying, or we just don't dare go. I'm going to call right now."

We were terrified for fear she'd be cut off, and then we would all be cut off and never get hotel rooms, reservations, or whatever.

"Remember," I said, "you're supposed to make a call only if there's a death."

"Well, there *is* a death," she said.

Florence jumped up and went to the phone. "Hello, operator, I've got to talk to Switzerland, Geneva four three two. It's an emergency. . . . No, not sickness. Death . . . All right, I'll wait." She whispered to us, "I think she's putting me through. Hello, is this Switzerland? Jim? I hate to tell you but Maude Adams just died."

I let out a yelp and stuffed a sofa pillow in my mouth.

"Her body will arrive at Geneva Airport at eleven A.M. tomorrow, Air France, accompanied by two pallbearers. Please meet them at the airport and help get the body through customs. They need rooms at an inexpensive hotel for three days. And, call the Connaught Hotel in London and tell them the Logans are going to be there tomorrow night—after the funeral, of course. Stop weeping, Jim. I know you loved her, but she's gone. Just please see that the cortege is met with honor. Please stop crying, Jim." And she hung up.

"Was he really weeping?" Harold asked.

"Yes," said Florence. "He had to so he wouldn't laugh."

It was the most urgent and I must say the most efficient

telephone call I ever heard. We've used Maude Adams's funeral ever since to get past operators and cut through other difficulties.

* * *

One theatrical anecdote became an evil signal between Leland Hayward and me. We could use it in public with delicious satisfaction and no one had the tiniest idea of what we were saying.

It came from a story I heard about Tallulah Bankhead and Estelle Winwood. I don't remember who told it or what year it was or whether the story was accurate. All I know is that it is famous and went into my language.

The scene was a sunny backyard in Bedford Village, New York, many years ago. The time, nearly noon. A portable radio was on full blast. Both ladies were trying to live through the rigors of "the morning after." Tallulah was flopped back on a chaise longue, urging her craggy but still beautiful face up to the cleansing sun. Estelle, in equal pain, paced the garden paths like an infirm whippet. Both ladies, I might add, had been in this condition before. They had tried many experiments with life, both together and apart, actively joined many groups of borderline colors and sexes, and their indulgences had not always been limited to alcohol. But they had remained friends, which is rare in actresses.

The radio was shouting with the voice of an indignant announcer. "This unknown pervert," he said, "needn't think he'll get away with this! All those ransom notes, all that talk with the go-between by the cemetery wall, all those promises—and now we find the Lindbergh child was lying dead all along like a broken doll, dropped by the wicked man who built a ladder and stole him from his crib. But we shall see the end of this fiend! New Jersey is now crawling with state troopers armed with loaded guns. They will track down this beast. There will be no sleep till the culprit is *brought to justice in the electric chair . . .*"

At this point, Estelle looked up. "Tallulah," she said, "we're well out of this one."

The same day I heard the story, I was with Leland for a meeting of *Wish You Were Here*. While we were waiting for the others, he asked me if I had read the new play that a close friend of ours had written but had sent to a rival producer.

I didn't answer him directly. I simply told him the story of Tallulah and Estelle. When I got to the ending—"Tallulah, we're well out of this one"—he knew how I felt about our friend's play. He exploded in midair. And it took several minutes for him to pull himself together.

Several nights later, at the other end of the row of seats where Nedda and I sat in formal dress at the opening of an important play, I spotted Leland and Nancy. At the end of the disastrous first act, the curtain came down and the houselights came up full. The audience was rather silent, which is always to me a bad sign. A happy audience starts lively talk at once. I looked across the row of seats at Leland. He had been looking at me. He called out a word in a half-whisper, but perfectly audible to all. "Tallulah."

This got to be such a habit with us that we began to feel that our friends would guess it meant disapproval of the play, so we made an adjustment. Instead of "Tallulah," we simply aspirated the letter "T." It was not only completely puzzling to all, but it saved time.

* * *

Audiences very seldom give any indication of how they like or dislike a play. We who live by their approval would love to eavesdrop on a group in the lobby and try to get a hint of what should be repaired or shortened in a play, but if we try we are apt to hear something like, "I think it's awful, and was from the beginning." We begin trying to think of a way to rewrite but the talk continues. "Yes, it's awful. I tried for a while to be patient, but being a neighbor I can always hear them quarreling." They're never talking about the play but about a neighbor, a child, or a dog. Or if they talk about the play, you never hear it.

Dorothy Stickney, the wife of Howard Lindsay, the playwright, claims that she has heard only one clear-cut remark in a theatre lobby. She sidled up to a group in obvious discussion and she heard a woman say, "Don't look now, but the author's wife is right behind you, all ears." Those words have been turned into a constant signal, a warning not to try to hear opinions in a lobby. It's a waste of time. We use it to remind ourselves to listen to an audience's mass reaction, never to an individual.

* * *

When I was receiving the first showers of praise for my work in *Annie Get Your Gun,* Barton MacLane, the big, rough movie actor, came to town with his lovely wife, Charlotte, a girlhood friend of Nedda's. Of course we got them seats down front for *Annie*. At intermission, Nedda and I were waiting for them behind the last row near the entrance. The crowd was filling the aisles and foyer when Barton spotted us from way down in the second row. He was wild with enthusiasm and boomed across the theatre, loud enough to be heard by everyone, "Greatest fucking thing I ever saw!"

I started to duck my head when I heard a huge laugh from the whole crowd and even some applause.

Oscar Hammerstein, who had produced *Annie* with Dick Rodgers, loved that story so much that several months later he still remembered it. At the first intermission of *Finian's Rainbow* I was in the midst of a happy crowd; we had just seen an electrifying first act with a new choreographer, Michael Kidd, and a superb score by E. Y. Harburg and Burton Lane. Since Oscar and I are tall, we saw each other across the crowded lobby. He shouted across the intermission talk— "This is the greatest Barton MacLane thing I've ever seen." After that we used the words "Barton MacLane" whenever we wanted to be emphatic.

WITH AND
WITHOUT
A SONG

I DOUBT IF I ever experienced elsewhere the true strato-spheric joy I felt working with Sam Behrman. He had a skyrocket mind. And when he worked, he put his shoulders to the job, and if things got stuck, he pulled instead of pushed, and then if that towrope got snarled, he'd toss everything into the air to see if the knot would come loose by itself, and if it did not, he'd start again and I'd start with him.

The project was something we both loved, making a musical play, *Fanny*, out of Marcel Pagnol's theatre and film trilogy of Marseilles.

Our big job was to keep the salty patois feeling without chang-ing it to Americanese. The tough-minded César was always shouting in anger, *"Coquin de sort,"* which was outrageous and violent in French, but if literally translated into English, "Ras-cal of fate," became powder-puff talk, unusable. So we decided never to translate any cursing, just play out anger in some origi-nal, comic way. It seemed to work.

But the plot was a different thing. We had three stories to condense into one evening, or, rather, two and one-half, since the third, *César*, was flimsy and lacking in suspense.

The big problem was to find a great ending. In the three stories that Pagnol had written in sequence—*Marius, Fanny,* and *César*—the richest in character was *Marius,* the richest in plot was *Fanny,* and the most manufactured was *César.*

In the last of the trilogy, old Panisse was married to young Fanny and therefore (in a Catholic country) Marius and Fanny were prevented from ever getting together. Realizing this, Pagnol killed off old Panisse at the beginning of the last play, with much more story to tell but very little suspense. Then he manufactured some rather silly, unsuspenseful scenes, all leading to a final and awkward moment when Marius's father acts as a kind of deus ex machina cupid and pulls Marius and Fanny together —to nobody's surprise. We couldn't use that.

So, Sam and I decided from the very beginning that the play could last only *one fraction of a second longer than Panisse's death.* His being alive was the only suspense we had to hang on to, and it must be there until the very curtain.

But how could we solve all the rest that way—most especially, Fanny and Marius? We wrote several scenes and eventually decided on one in which the two old men, César and Panisse, ended the play, and the two young people, Marius and Fanny, did not appear at all. It worked fairly well but it was not conclusive. And we knew it wouldn't be satisfying to an audience.

Still we went ahead and finished the play, and Harold Rome wrote a superb score, one of the solid greats of all time. Ezio Pinza, tired of Hollywood and silly pictures, agreed to play César because Raimu, who played the role in the French pictures, reminded Pinza of his father. Walter Slezak was persuaded to play old Panisse, and we got two young people with beautiful voices for the young lovers, Florence Henderson and Bill Tabbert.

At first, all went well as far as rehearsals were concerned, but from the time it opened out of town, I felt there was something wrong. We had some bad dances, but that was easy: we got rid of them. We cut weak jokes. "Oh, the joys of evacuation," as Maugham said. Friends came by, as they always do, with opinions that weren't very helpful.

Most of *Fanny* was playing well, but I was still unhappy with the ending and so was Sam. More important, so was David Merrick. David was with me one night along with my secretary, Joe Curtis, in the Hotel Barclay in Philadelphia. We had three more nights to play before going to New York.

David said, "You got a great ending to *Mister Roberts*, and that fellow died just like Panisse. Why can't you get one for this play?"

"*Mister Roberts,*" I said. "Of course. *Mister Roberts.* But that was solved by a letter. We couldn't see Mister Roberts on that boat so we were forced to find out about his death through a letter. But we *see* Panisse. Why should—? Why couldn't Panisse *write a letter on his deathbed?* Dictate it to his old friend César. A letter to Marius asking him to marry Fanny! The audience will be sure of Marius's reply and Fanny's reaction. That's right! Joe, take this down. 'Dear Marius, will you do me the honor to marry my wife?' That should get a laugh, David."

David nodded soberly.

"Go on, Joe. 'She will be free soon and I recommend her very highly.' "

I went on to the end, " 'Hastily yours,' " and David sat there glumly and said, "Another laugh. It should work."

The next morning I took it to Sam. Sam said, "It's enchanting, but it must have five more big laughs."

He sat down and put them in the way you would put cloves into a Christmas orange. It was like a gift from the Magi. We took the new typed scene to Slezak and Pinza.

"No," Pinza said, "it won't work."

I put on every bit of pressure I could. I said, "But we have a flop, Ezio. It *might* work. Look, if it doesn't work in one night, we'll go back to the other ending."

He said, "It won't work."

Slezak shook his head, too. "No, it won't work. I know a lot about writing and the scene won't work."

I said, "Read it. Rehearse it. Just for tonight. And I promise it goes back the way it is now tomorrow night."

Our play hung on this thin thread.

So, they read the scene again, grumpily, giving me dirty looks every chance they could. Oh, God, what a painful effort it is to push across something at the last minute when the leading actors aren't excited about it. Someday I'm going to go to a director's heaven where you don't have to listen to surly actors sneering at good scenes.

I got my heavenly reward on earth that night. When the scene came, they started speaking it in low, grumbling tones. But the audience pounced like a marlin on the first line. It was a big laugh. This, of course, made the actors know that it was a good scene, so they both began playing it as if it were the best scene that had ever been written—and suddenly it was. The curtain came down to the biggest applause we had ever had.

I went backstage expecting them to say, "Well, we were wrong. It's good." But, oh, no! They said, "Sorry, Josh, it isn't as good as the last one, but do you want us to try it one more night?"

I tried to look worried and said, "Well, if you want to try it one more night it's okay with me."

It was soon their favorite scene. They never mentioned their doubts again. That scene had turned the trick.

Fanny opened in New York to enough good notices to give David Merrick a chance to publicize it into a smash.

I will always admire David Merrick. He is a realist. He is rough, even ruthless, but he keeps the bonfire alight. He doesn't let shows close the way his peers do. When he moved to Hollywood, it was a great loss to the New York theatre.

* * *

I had agreed that if Jack Warner would buy *Fanny* for pictures, I would direct and produce it, with the proviso that I could do it in Marseilles where it all happened. It needed a great screenplay. Not only was the plot of *Fanny* terribly long for a movie, but the emphasis in our musical play had been on the two old men, César and Panisse, because of our stars. For the movie, Warner wanted a four-cornered story to include Fanny and Marius, the two young lovers.

Julie Epstein, one of the truly gifted and experienced Hollywood screenwriters, read the material and refused. I couldn't believe my ears.

"My God, Julie, it's a classic! Why don't you want to do it?"

"Because I don't believe the boy would go to sea."

I said, "Perhaps a boy wouldn't go to sea readily now, but this is laid back in the days before the First World War when the sea still had an attraction for many young men."

We talked for hours, and eventually we struck upon the idea that the boy is not going to sea—he's getting away from his father. This evidently pressed the right button, and Julie accepted.

Jack Warner was delighted, and he said, "Now, let's understand one thing—I don't want a musical. I know I bought a musical, but musicals are losing money."

Julie said, "Thank God for that. I don't know how to write a musical, and besides, if you have all those songs, there won't be room for the young love story."

I didn't know how to feel about it. I agreed that the songs would take up a lot of dramatic time, but I loved Harold Rome's score more than almost any I had worked on. I had for years been planning to ask Maurice Chevalier to play Panisse, and I felt sure we could find a young girl who could sing and a boy who could act and sing. But painful as it is for me to look back on it now, I eventually agreed to do it as a straight dramatic picture with musical underscoring.

The moment I made that decision some casting chances opened up. Charles Boyer was willing to play César, but he had specified in his contract that he would neither sing nor mime lyrics to a dubbed voice. He had been embarrassed by that in times of yore.

And we had a promise, a verbal one, that Audrey Hepburn would play Fanny.

The film was to be made in March. I had three months to prepare for it.

Nedda and I, and Ben Kadish soon after us, left for Marseilles to look for locations. I was apprehensive about going to France to film a great French story.

Fanny was a minor classic in France. The three plays, *Marius,* *Fanny,* and *César,* are almost worshiped by the French, and Marcel Pagnol was one of the immortals of the Académie française. I'm sure the people of Marseilles read these three plays more often than any three chapters of the Bible.

From the first day we arrived in Paris I was subjected to belligerent press conferences.

"Why do you think you can do *Fanny?* Do you think you are better than Marcel Pagnol? Are your actors going to speak with a Marseilles accent?"

(The strong Marseilles accent, which has a Mediterranean flavor to it, strikes most Frenchmen as rich and hilarious.)

My only answer to that last was, "How can we use a Marseilles accent if we're doing it in English? How can we speak the translation of a language with an accent? We don't do Ibsen with a Norwegian accent or *Faust* with a German one."

They wrote this down very seriously, but shook their heads as though I were totally mad.

"Are you going to make just a sentimental thing, or will it have some of the bite and humor of Pagnol?"

That was an easy one. I said, "I am going to try to make *Fanny* exactly as Pagnol wrote it. I feel it is a story which is fascinating and funny no matter what language it's in. It will look French and seem French and be French to anyone speaking English. But fundamentally, it is a film not for France but for the world."

They didn't hear. They didn't even want to hear. I prayed that Warner Brothers would not show this film in France.

I met the casting directors, the scenic designers, and finally found a designer and a costume lady who seemed excellent.

Margot, the casting director, introduced me to Raymond Bussieres, who could speak enough English to play Marius's crazy friend, "The Admiral," who was forever, in his deranged mind, still on a ship.

For the part of Marius I was interested in the young man who had played the lead opposite Hayley Mills in *Tiger Bay*. He was German but he looked like Marius. He was dark, slender, and extremely handsome. More than that, he obviously was a fine actor. His name was Horst Buchholz. Horst flew to Paris with his beautiful bride, and after we talked a few moments, I knew he was right for the role. But when the rumor got around Paris that we were putting a German into a French part, I faced a group of angry reporters. When I produced Mr. Buchholz, they began to approve.

More difficult than all the casting was the *Malaisie* itself, the square-rigged sailing ship which must be the right size to sail out of Marseilles harbor and yet must look like a vessel equipped to go on a five-year expedition. We had looked at photographs of every square-rigged ship in the world. But all of them, without exception, were enormous training ships, infinitely too big to move through the head of the old port.

Ben Kadish ordered a man to fly to every port in the Mediterranean to see if he could find one that we hadn't considered. Several days later a call came from Palma. "There's one here in port. It's available, but you must use its captain." All of this was agreeable to us. The photographs were airmailed, and I started sleeping for the first time since I had been in Paris.

In the meantime, I had been flying regularly to London, then driving up to Stratford, trying to persuade Leslie Caron to play Fanny. She was terrified of the French. "They'll hate me," she said. "They'll absolutely despise me for walking in there and playing a role in English which is one of their holy cows."

Leslie Caron and Horst Buchholz in a love scene from *Fanny* in the Old Port of Marseilles. (Zinn Arthur)

The classic card game in *Fanny*. Left to right: Lionel Jeffries,
Salvatore Baccaloni, Maurice Chevalier, and Charles Boyer.
(Warner Brothers Pictures Distributing Corporation)

Marcel Pagnol and Josh looking over
an old port of Marseilles.

Irving Berlin singing the score of *Mr. President* to Leland Hayward, Josh, Russel Crouse, and Howard Lindsay.

The Logans in 1960 during the filming of *Fanny*.

"I know, but they won't see you," I said. "We'll show it all over the world, but not in France."

"Oh, they'll sneak around and see it, don't you worry. If you show it in Switzerland, they'll cross the border to attack it."

But when she read the script and heard about the cast—Boyer, Chevalier, Buchholz—she said yes. And just in time, because we had only three weeks to go, and her dresses had to be designed and made.

I had interviewed a dozen English actresses for the part of Honorine, Fanny's fishwife mother. I wanted someone as heavy and peasantlike as Alida Rouffe, the actress who had played the part in Pagnol's original. None of the English ladies were right. I began to believe there were no fat women left in the world. But we had to have someone or we couldn't start shooting. I agreed on an English actress, and we made costume tests of her.

But when I saw those tests and the way the actress pranced and preened, I realized that she could never play the part. I turned to Ben and said, "She'll ruin the picture. What am I to do?"

Ben said, "Pay her off. It's only fifteen thousand dollars."

"I know. But what will we do if we pay her off? Do you suppose that big fat woman whom we hired as Honorine's assistant could play it?"

We called that woman, Georgette Anys, the moment we got back to Paris. She was made by God for Fanny's mother. But she spoke only a few words of English. I asked her if she thought she could learn by rote.

She said, "I could do anything for a good part." She turned out to be peasant perfection.

We started shooting. Perhaps the biggest break for *Fanny*, and it began having blessings showered upon it, was the fact that Jack Cardiff, one of England's greatest cameramen, had decided to leave England and settle in Switzerland. He needed some quick cash and when we asked him to film *Fanny* he couldn't resist.

When we first arrived in Marseilles, one side of the port, the east side, looked just as it had when our story was laid. And that was, fortunately, the side topped by the great spire of Notre Dame de la Garde, the famous church to which all the sailors prayed.

But the west side of Marseilles's Old Port had been rebuilt during and after World War II with concrete blockhouses. The concrete bore no resemblance to César's and Panisse's old Marseilles.

Rino Mondellini, our designer, was going to construct a series of facades and attach them to the sidewalk surrounding the port to conceal that concrete area from the camera. The mayor had given us permission, but Rino's men had drilled only eighteen holes in the concrete of the sidewalk when the town rose up like an angry mob and stormed Town Hall. The mayor told us quickly that all promises were off. He couldn't buck the whole town.

There was nothing to do. We took down whatever poles had been erected for the facades, and as Rino looked at the eighteen holes in the sidewalk he said, "The most expensive golf course in the world."

But something had to be done about the unauthentic side of the port. I asked if it was possible for us to photograph the scenes from only one side. Not possible, everyone agreed. You can't photograph this whole story looking in one direction. It would be confusing geographically and awkward looking.

I said, "In *Sayonara* we used a scene in Hollywood shooting one way, and the same scene in Japan with the camera pointing the other way. Isn't there some other harbor around here we could use to photograph the west side, then come back to the Vieux Port for the east?"

"Yes," Rino said, "just down the way. Cassis."

We drove down to the endearing harbor with its picturesque buildings on both sides and decided on it immediately. We would play every scene two times—once in Marseilles while the cameras looked east and once in Cassis while the cameras looked west. Cut together, they would be one harbor.

Mike Romanoff, our assistant director, said, "And we must shoot it a third time looking north, for the interior of the bar will be built in the studio in Paris."

"But that's going to take months!"

"If it takes months," said Ben, "we'll take months. It's got to be right."

And that's the way we shot it.

In two or three days the Marseilles people who had been our enemies suddenly became our friends, which was inexplicable to us until one of them explained that they had seen our helicopter filming Marseilles and had decided we must love their beautiful city if we would go to the trouble to go up and photograph it from a helicopter. No one had ever done that before.

We didn't tell them that our helicopter was really looking for various other locations we might need outside of the harbor and down the shore. We would also use the helicopter to close in on Marius standing in the shrouds of the square-rigged ship, then to pull back to show the ship in full sail, off for its five-year voyage.

We made many passes with the helicopter camera to go from a high shot down to a close-up of the harbor, but the copter made the film too choppy to enjoy. So we finally used an airplane, which was steadier, to dive at the harbor—over which we eventually showed our titles.

Charles Boyer was not in the first day's shooting. He had stayed in Paris at his favorite hotel, the Crillon. He looked very nervous when he arrived at the set.

"What's the matter?" I asked.

He said. "You know the Berkeley. I always go there for lunch. I always talk to Pierre, who is the headwaiter, about my not sleeping because he does not sleep well either. Both of us have been insomniacs since we were twenty years old. This time, Pierre said, 'Mr. Boyer, I sleep! I have found the answer—acupuncture. I went to the Chinese doctor. He stuck pins in me and I sleep. Here is his address. You must go this afternoon. You will see, it will change your life.' I thanked Pierre and went to the Chinese man, a little apprehensive, I must admit. I took off my clothes. He stuck hundreds of pins all over me and when he was finished he said a few words to me about relaxing, and he gradually pulled the pins out of my body and told me to dress. I paid him and went back to the Crillon. I decided, when I saw my nice room, why not take a nap? Maybe I could drop off. I got out of my clothes again, lay down on the cool bed, and brushed my palms across my chest and abdomen to make the blood relax—and my hand hit a sharp pin. There was still one there. I pulled it out. I tried to sleep. Something was wrong. I felt around again. I found six of those damned pins that he had forgotten to take out. I will never go again. If I never sleep as long as I live, I will never go to an acupuncturist again. Now let's act."

Boyer, who was following in the footsteps of Raimu, was a bit nervous, but then, he's an actor, and I do think that, underneath, most actors feel they can do it as well as or better than the man before them.

The most spectacular moment, of course, was the actual sailing of the *Malaisie*, and how it got out of that harbor under full sail I will never know, but it did—with eight cameras photographing it.

Marcel Pagnol and his family came down to watch part of the shooting. He was happy to see what was going on.

Another thing that impressed the people of Marseilles was when we photographed Leslie's long climb to Notre Dame de la Garde. Photographing at varying heights was a way of displaying Marseilles at its most impressive; also, the sight of Fanny in her cheap, wide-brimmed straw hat was touching and lovely. She was going up to pray to the Virgin, as she had just discovered that she was to have Marius's child.

One thing that had worried me from the beginning of our shooting in Marseilles was finding a proper house to which Panisse could move after his marriage to Fanny.

Mike Romanoff, who incidentally was really Prince Michel Romanoff and whose passport bore the simple sobriquet "Michel of Russia," took a tour of Marseilles and came back with the news that he had found two houses. When I went up on the hill and saw them, I was shocked.

"They're too big," I said. "They look like palaces."

"That's all we can find, and at least from those houses you can see the city and the sea. We can really know we're near Marseilles, and it does show that Panisse has grown to be a rich man. Of course, I agree real Frenchmen don't move to big houses like this. They're too stingy."

But it was the only house we could find, so I had to shoot there.

I think if there is any artistic fault to the picture it is that we never found the proper house for Panisse, but we filmed it anyway.

The great fun was still to come—Cassis, where we shot our scenes in the western direction. Smack on the water's edge was a delicious outdoor restaurant that made the best salade Niçoise and served that nectar, cassis rosé. All of us gained weight happily.

I noticed a lot of ancient old ladies in black dresses gone a bit green with age. I decided to leave them exactly as they were and ask them if they would let us put the camera on them. This struck them as hilariously funny, but after we started rolling I gave them directions in my best French—look there, look here, look worried, cross yourselves, the priest is coming—and they gave me enough reaction in that short time and with that small amount of film to add tremendous reality and color to the scene. Professionals just couldn't have given the same effect.

Chevalier was at the height of his career and had a great part. He was happier than I had ever seen a man. We got along wonderfully. But one time, when he was particularly late, I found myself talking to him irritably. He turned away, hurt, and I realized I had gone too far. I didn't know how to apologize so I simply said, "You must forgive me, Maurice. I've had mental problems in my time. Sometimes when I get very upset I go too far."

It wasn't exactly the truth, as I really felt great, but I thought it might help excuse me.

Much to my surprise, he looked up at me. "You have mental problems? So have I. I understand perfectly. Let's forget it."

We were frantically looking for a place to live in Paris for the summer—someplace big enough for our whole family, when, at a dinner party, a friend of ours spoke to a lady whose husband had just died. "Would you like to rent your apartment this summer when you go to Biarritz? You have a very large apartment and the Logans have a family and two servants."

Surprisingly, the lady said yes. The large flat was on the Avenue d'Iéna and was probably the grandest place any one of us had ever lived in. There were six bedrooms and four bathrooms. The main living room had eighteenth-century Chinese wallpaper, and each piece of furniture was a signed work of art, with patina and of graceful design.

The owner said, "Please do not hide anything in closets. I want you to use everything—all the bibelots, all the ashtrays—and if you would be kind enough just to shove my clothes to the side in the closets you can use the closets as they are. Let's don't bother to have an inventory or anything. Just take it and I will be grateful to you."

I believe that Nedda and I and our children—and Carl, our butler, and his wife, Selma, our housekeeper, who had come over from Connecticut to take care of us, plus the French cook and French chauffeur and a couple of extra maids—had the best three months of our lives there. It was so beautiful, so well situated, and the children were so happy to be in it.

We gave parties constantly. It was just too easy. The cast got to count on us for a snack any time they needed one. It was Ring Lardner's wonderful story, *Liberty Hall*, only with a French accent.

Every morning, Thomas, our French driver, drove me to the studio in Boulogne where Rino Mondellini had built the bar on one of the huge sound stages. He had put the bar at the side of the stage, and through the beaded curtains he had built the Old Port with cutouts in the background. All of the bar scenes were filmed in this setting except the outside scenes we had shot on the edge of the Old Port itself.

Jack Warner had sent word that for safety's sake, if we ever had a chance to film two of the original songs with Chevalier singing them, we should try it. He was obviously beginning to think he'd made a mistake by not making *Fanny* a musical. I shot Chevalier singing to the assembled family around his dinner table the song "To My Wife." He did it charmingly. At first it seemed to fit the way it had when we did it on the stage, but when we cut it together with the dialogue before and after it, the song seemed out of place. It was a poor chemistry of mixed styles. I decided to tell Chevalier immediately that we weren't going to film the other song, that it just didn't work. He was personally very relieved: he wanted to do a straight dramatic part.

That was the night that Harold Rome and his wife Florence arrived in Paris to visit. We gave them a bang-up dinner. Harold played his songs from the play of *Fanny*. Most of us sang them, and as they bade us good night happily and went to their hotel, I closed the door.

"Nedda, I didn't have the heart to tell Harold that we cut Chevalier's song."

Fanny received several Academy Award nominations. I am extremely proud of it and feel it did what I hoped and prayed it would do: bring Pagnol's great work to the rest of the world. The performances and the backgrounds were superb. But that didn't make up for my sorrow about the superb score and lyrics that Harold Rome had written.

MEL BROOKS
OR NOT

"I'M GOING TO write a play called *Springtime for Hitler* as soon as this one's over," said Mel Brooks.

"You're what?" I said.

Charles Strouse and Lee Adams, the composer and lyricist, were as aghast as I was.

"*Springtime for Hitler!* You can't *say* things like that, Mel—the audience will throw stones at you."

"Well, that's what I'm going to do—and then I'm going to marry Anne Bancroft."

We decided that if funny-face Mel kept all of his mad dreams to himself, maybe he could finish the book of *All American*, which we were trying to do with him.

He had never really written a stage story before, but Lee and Charles and producer Ed Padula were willing to take a chance on him because he was so brilliant with dialogue. So they had given him a small book called *Professor Fodorski* and asked him to try to make it into a play. I had gotten into it almost by accident.

In 1961, my first night back from Europe after shooting and cutting the movie *Fanny* in France, I went with Nedda to see *Bye Bye Birdie*. Nedda and I were entranced. The songs were charming, melodious, and funny, and the staging by Gower Champion was impeccable.

When it was over and we were walking up the aisle, a man stepped out of the shadows with a pleasant, smiling face and said, "I'm the producer, Ed Padula. Did you like the show?"

I said, "I loved it. I loved it. Please find a show like that for me someday."

He broke into smiles and said, "I certainly will. I'll call you the moment I do."

And a few weeks later he called, and soon five of us were sitting around my studio on Old Long Ridge Road in Connecticut, where I had a lot of space and a piano. I liked the general idea of the script, although I felt it needed much more of a story and some new material. It was about an immigrant professor who came over to our Southwest and taught football with mathematical principles.

As we sat talking, I was conscious that two of the young men, Charles Strouse and Lee Adams, were cultivated and enthusiastic and comparatively contained, and that the third one was a bustling original. I didn't know then, of course, that he was going to turn out to be one of the most daring and famous funny men of our generation, but I did listen to his rather off-center remarks with great interest because there was obviously a huge brain behind that rather Easter Island face. It was my first view and taste of Mel Brooks. Gray-haired, smooth Ed Padula was a permissive referee.

We began discussing casting, and we mentioned all kinds of comic men who might possibly play Professor Fodorski. Suddenly, Mel Brooks jumped up and started a peroration. "You think this man should be *funny*, don't you? You think he should be a *comic* and have a funny nose and a funny face. Well, I don't feel that way at all. I think he should be a leading man, a handsome man like Charles Boyer, maybe, or Francis Lederer or Paul Lukas. He should be able to smooth-talk, too—charming talk that attracts ladies. He should be a *romantic leading man.*"

He paused for a second, and then added two very emphatic words. *"Or not,"* he said, and sat down.

It got so we began roaring with laughter any time Mel Brooks opened his mouth. It was no way to get a full afternoon's work done, but it was fun. And we did keep digging away at the plot and the score and the character of Fodorski.

Every once in a while on a lunch break Mel would bring up

again the play he was going to write next: *Springtime for Hitler.* And we would exchange grimaces, shake our heads, and say, "Please, Mel, we know you're only joking, but—"

"No," he would say, "I'm not joking. That's exactly what I'm going to write. A play about Hitler's young and idyllic love life."

And we would warn, "Please, Mel, you mustn't. Honestly, no audience is going to come to see a story about Hitler's love life. They'll just be embarrassed—they'll stay away in droves."

And they did stay away in droves—but from our play *All American.* They *came* in droves to see Mel's movie, *Springtime for Hitler,* which was, of course, later titled *The Producers.* It made us wonder later, when Mel wrote and directed hit after hit and became the comedy king of our time, whether Mel was hoarding all the brains in that room.

He could always get us laughing, too, with his promise, "And I'm going to marry Anne Bancroft."

"She wouldn't have you, Mel. You know that. You're just like the kid that presses his nose on the candy store windowpane. He can never get through it—never!"

He and Anne Bancroft have been married for years.

Anyway, it was obvious to us at the time that Mel Brooks had delusions of grandeur, but he was so funny and so willing to turn anything into a comic situation that he was irresistible to work with. The trouble is, he would never sit down to write a playable second act, and we got closer and closer to rehearsal time. Finally, in a moment of desperation, I called everybody together and we all more or less dictated the act, using Mel's general idea. We were happy with it but Mel never liked it. I had a simple solution. I told him to write another one, but he never got around to it.

But looking back, I think Mel would have fallen even further and faster with his second act than we did with our joint one. And I also believe that he learned a lot from *All American,* because from then on his sense of construction grew by leaps and bounds, till he now owns a big chunk of the movie industry.

All American got mixed notices but the audiences that came seemed to enjoy it, and certainly it had some of the most charming tunes ever written—"Once Upon a Time," a perennial standard, and "What a Country!" (which as of now is Amtrak's theme song). I will always remember the show as one of the pleasantest experiences of my life.

The real trouble with it was obvious. We never got as dramatic a scene on the stage as the one up in my sitting room at the Warwick Hotel, during our Philadelphia tryout.

The following episode seemed then and seems now to be Mel's idea of a practical joke. Nobody else could have conceived of such an outrageous, crazy nightmare except him. And yet it wasn't Mel. It happened exactly as I tell it to you now. This was no scene our play needed.

It was late at night in my suite at the Warwick Hotel. Joe Wishy, a young observer on a college theatre grant, was auditing our meeting, making notes for his thesis. All of us were commiserating with each other over the way *All American* wasn't going. Ray Bolger was our star, but somehow his public image seemed to have dimmed. We were batting around the idea of finding something stronger for Ray to do, when with no warning, the door was flung open, and a fat, scraggly-haired lady appeared in a diaphanous, baby-doll nightgown. Her pudgy knees showed below it, damp with sweat. Her bare feet were slightly smudged. Her fleshy arms were raised, and she was screaming.

She pointed a finger at Mel and screamed, "You have no talent!"

It was the first time I ever saw Mel unable to utter a sound.

Her screaming became higher pitched and further off-key. "You can't write a line! You can't tell a joke!" Mel's face fell open further. "You don't know what's funny! You can't smell what an audience listens to—you're a No Talent—you stink!"

It was Charles Strouse who recognized her as Miss Rita Almaviva, one of our many backers, and very rich. "Miss Almaviva," he said, "I think you're being unfair to Mel. He's—"

She spun around to Charles. "And *you* can't write a tune! Nobody can whistle anything you put on paper! You're going to end in the poorhouse—and you'll drag us all down there with you! You're a No Talent, too—you stink, you have stunk, and you will go on stinking! And besides, you're *Jewish!*"

Lee Adams tried the level-voice technique. "Miss Almaviva, my dear, why don't you let me take you back to your room?"

She leaned back and screamed at him, "You snot-nosed poet that can't rhyme! You ass without a hole! I always *knew* you were a vacuum, but no one would pay any attention to me and now look where we are now—in the bottomless pit of Calcutta!

"And stop writing this crap down, you white-faced owl." She was talking to Joe Wishy. He stopped writing quickly.

For a second, all of us were praying she would make some final gesture and leave, but that was not to be. She started going over each one of the men again, yelling imprecations, as vile as she could master at that moment. It was both ridiculous and pitiful to see her swishing around with her firm, round belly forcing her nightgown out in front. One of her pendulous breasts had snaked out from between the straps of her night-dress. It whirled with her.

Why she didn't attack me, I don't know. Perhaps she was afraid I was big enough to hit her over the head, which I had a great desire to do. I decided to run out of the room and get Ed Padula, who was on the floor below. But as I opened the door to my suite, I saw my wonderful man-of-all-work, Carl, who was staying at the hotel to help me through the tough problems of a Philadelphia tryout. He wore an overcoat over his pajamas, and he had put on slippers.

"Can I help you, Mr. Logan?" he asked in a calm voice betrayed by worried eyes.

"Maybe you can. Stay right where you are." I turned. Rita was now bouncing around the group, repeating everything she'd said twice before, growing even louder.

Nedda appeared from the bedroom, very sleepy but full of compassion. With outstretched arms she tried to comfort Rita, who threw her across the room, whereupon Nedda staggered back to the bedroom. Rita's passion rose, and we had no idea what to do with her.

Then with as much finesse as possible, Lee and Charles took her gently by the shoulders and led her toward the door. She pulled away from them as though they were trying to stick her with poison arrows. She picked up a sofa pillow and hit at them.

"Let go of me, you gangsters! You've got to be smart to get rid of me! You've got to have brains and talent—which you haven't got!" She swung the pillow wildly.

I opened the door and signaled Carl, who came in and with a delicate, reticent manner approached Miss Almaviva and said, "Could I help you to your room, ma'am?"

She whirled, startled that there was another person watching her.

"Yes, of course, I'll be with you right away," she said.

Carl went to the door and stood, waiting. She carefully gave everybody a final vicious look and hissed, "Good night, you shits —you talentless shits." She threw the pillow into the room. Then she turned and let Carl help her through the door. We could see the two of them disappearing down the hall—she staggering, with both breasts swinging free, and he steadying her with the slightest modest touch on her elbow. I closed the door slowly and turned.

Mel Brooks said, "Fine man you got there, Josh, fine man. Tell him I say he's okay. Give him a pat on the back and say, 'That's from Mel.'"

Joe Wishy looked up from his notes. "This is going to make an interesting chapter for my thesis. When it's cleaned up, that is."

But he wouldn't be able to decide any more than we could whether she had had a few drinks too many or was just unnerved by what the show was going through on the road. Either way, she had given me one of the most memorable evenings of my career.

THE PLAY
DOCTOR

I T'S DANGEROUS. It's walking on eggs and playing
with fire. It may even be dangerous to talk too much about.
Why? Because it's stepping on egos. It's playing God. It's
waving a schoolteacher's scolding finger at a brilliant adult who
knows he needs it but resents the hell out of it.

I'm talking about the hush-hush, undercover profession called
play doctoring. There are no rules, no textbooks for this kind of
doctorate. An intrepid practitioner must follow his nose, be
strict but humane, authoritative but modest. It's walking a tight-
rope over a sea of fire.

A show on the road is in trouble. There are no laughs at the
funny lines and there is unrest rather than bated breath during
the scenes of suspense, and they don't seem to care when the
curtain comes down.

What's the matter? The producer thinks one thing, the director another, while the author of the play thinks everything is
great. His beautiful play is on the boards. What more could the
world want? If it's a musical, the composer and lyricist blame
the book, and the book writer or librettist feels the disease is in
one or more of the songs. And all are at odds as to which member
of the cast is letting them down.

What to do about it? The show must open in New York in three or four weeks, and in the nightly hotel room meetings of those in charge there is discord—full agreement as to the fact that something is wrong but none as to what.

If only some God would come down from the sky and make fiery pronouncements. Or perhaps King Solomon could appear to tell you to cut the baby in half or at least do that to the second act. But in the absence of a mighty or at least wise man of fantasy, what about a real human being who could see the show and tell us what to do—how to fix this near hit, how to remove the "near" and substitute a "sure"?

That is the atmosphere in which the first play doctor was born. Not a real doctor, mind you, but a good friend or at least a friendly samaritan who has had spectacular success in the past year or so as a director or author on Broadway.

Mike Nichols! What this play needs is Mike Nichols! Michael Bennett! Neil Simon! Or, further back, Jerry Robbins! Gadge Kazan! George Abbott! George Kaufman, Abe Burrows. Moss Hart. And even earlier, George M. Cohan, Arthur Hopkins, Winthrop Ames, Winchell Smith. And, I'm sure, in the previous century, Dion Boucicault or Joseph Jefferson. And could it be that in the eighteenth century David Garrick lent a hand to a friend, or Marlowe or even Shakespeare, or way back to Sophocles. Do you suppose Aristophanes put in a few laughs in a friend's play, or did a friend put a few laughs in his?

I cannot talk for any of them. I can only tell of the play doctoring period in the life of Josh Logan. After directing *Annie Get Your Gun, Mister Roberts, South Pacific,* and *Picnic,* I was fair game for the needy or moribund play. There developed a comic —half-cynical—expression in Boston, Philadelphia, Wilmington, Baltimore, Washington, and the outlying tryout towns. "What this show needs is Josh Logan."

To be honest, I was flattered. I was so personally entranced by the magic phrase, "We need you," that in spite of my wife, who felt I was overextending myself, I couldn't seem to help it. I almost always said, "Yes, I'll come." I was so happy and proud of my success that I became, at least for a time, Lord Bountiful or, rather, Dr. Bountiful. If I could save an ailing play with a few Band-Aids or a slight cut with a scalpel, it would make me feel kind, strong, even potent. I always paid my own way— railroad, taxis, hotels—and after the performance I was always asked to sit with a group of the creators while I told my reactions. Some were accepted; sometimes Dr. Bountiful fell on his ass.

What I hadn't realized at first was that I would also be climbing sheer rock palisades, and egos are the highest palisades God ever made. How would you like it if you had put your heart's blood into the writing of a play, perhaps working for a year or more, and then some successful son of a bitch comes down from New York and tells you to eliminate the first scene or have the girl kiss the boy rather than the reverse? It's like a stab in the groin rather than an appendectomy, even though you know in your soul it's what you need and must do. But does that prevent you from hating him for a moment, especially because he's right and because he saw it in a flash and you haven't seen it in a year?

I have grown to believe that when a person writes or works on a play, he subconsciously allows cataracts to form over his eyes. Sometimes an audience cures the cataracts. Often I am asked whether it is worth playing before an out-of-town audience before opening in New York. Is there anything you can learn? My reply: "Everything."

A play isn't a play without an audience. Unless in some way you please or intrigue an audience, you won't have one.

Vivien Leigh told me that she learned more during her silent moments as Sabrina in *The Skin of Our Teeth* than when she was actually playing a scene. Most of the time she had to lie about on a couch far downstage while the others continued the major portions of the play. From her place of vantage she was able to hear the audience comment. Since the British public, according to her, thoroughly hated the play, she was constantly hearing choice bits of criticism.

At one matinee, two ladies were watching the play when one of them turned to the other and said, "Are you going to take tea at the interval?"

The other replied furiously, "No! Don't let's give them one penny more!"

Once when I was lecturing to a roomful of students at Harvard, a young student asked, "Mr. Logan, why is it always such a good idea to please an audience? Don't you make yourself less important when you do that? Isn't an artist only an artist when he pleases himself?"

I found a yell pushing up through me. "But that's masturbation!" This, of course, got a huge laugh and cracking applause. But I went on to say, "If you want only to please yourself, then stay in your room. To me, theatre means actor and audience, it is lover and loved."

Once, during tryouts of *Mister Roberts*, I realized the play was not doing as well as it should. The audience reactions were not clear-cut; they were muddled in some way. I went out to look for a vacant seat and sat among the audience. There I discovered something about my direction of that play that absolutely astounded me. I had made a ghastly series of staging mistakes.

Whenever I had felt a strong, funny line coming up, I had made the actor pause a fraction of a second before speaking the important words. On this particular night it was disastrous because there was a man—what I call "an audience guesser"—sitting four or five seats away from me who spoke aloud the line that was coming up, during that little fraction of a pause before the actor said it. Whereupon the audience around him laughed, and then when the actor said the same line onstage, there was no laugh in that section of the theatre. All these people did was turn to him, smile and nod, meaning, "You guessed it."

Here was my precious play plummeting on to its destruction like a truck rolling downhill. There seemed to be no way of stopping it. For instance, onstage Roberts was saying, "Doc, that new hospital over there hasn't got nurses, has it?"

DOC

Nurses? It didn't have yesterday.
Pause

AUDIENCE GUESSER

It has today.
Laugh

PULVER

It has today.
No laugh.

I was infuriated, mostly at myself, but I was taking it out on him. I gave him a dirty look which he couldn't see, and then went on listening to the play.

Pulver was saying, "A little breeze came up and I took a big deep breath and I said to myself, 'Pulver, boy—' "

AUDIENCE GUESSER

There's women on that island.

PULVER

There's women on that island.

And again, the laugh came not where it was supposed to but just before.

This went on all through the evening. I was infuriated but mesmerized. I really was surprised at how well he was able to guess.

My frenzy deepened. But finally toward the end I had my inning.

When Roberts, on his way to be on another ship, is handed some "jungle juice" by the crew and it is poured around into tin canteen cups, he lifts his to the men in a gestured toast and they lift theirs toward him, and at that silent point my friend in the audience said, "To the greatest crew in the U.S. Navy."

And this was the first time he was wrong, as I had directed it so that nobody onstage said anything. They all just drank a wordless libation. Victory. I fooled him. The blood gushed into my head. I was uncontrollable. I leaned forward to the man and said, "Fuck you, you son of a bitch," and then I was pulled by my assistant past the people nearby who looked up at this madman, startled. I stumbled backstage, panting with frustration and fury.

Of course, the next morning at rehearsal I took all those pauses out and have never had that problem again.

* * *

Playwrighting is not only my profession, it's my tennis, my golf. Solving a play is a dangerous but exhilarating game, even when it's someone else's game. As my enthusiastic pal, Irving Berlin, says, "I cannot resist a story conference."

My variegated play doctoring saga started off with my friend, José Ferrer. The two of us had soared to pink heights with *Charley's Aunt.* We both had a trust in and warmth for each other that were forged and annealed in the hot fire of our first smash hit.

A few years later, in 1946, Ferrer called me. "Josh," he said over the phone, "I'm in trouble. We're in Boston with *Cyrano de Bergerac* and it's a disaster. The production's beautiful. The cast is great, and we're playing the Brian Hooker version, so you know that part's all right."

"Who's directing?"

"An old friend, Mel Ferrer. He was my leading man in *Strange Fruit.*"

"But can he direct?" I asked.

"I don't know. I love the guy so much that I never thought

about it. Please come. You're the only son of a bitch in the world I trust, and this is my biggest chance."

Soon I was standing at the rail behind the orchestra seats not two feet from Mel Ferrer, who seemed entranced by the performance on the stage. And I noticed that sometimes he laughed when the audience didn't, which was my first clue.

It wasn't a hard show to watch. Certainly, no audience ever saw a more spectacular performance than Joe Ferrer's in the sword duel, during which he fought and at the same time improvised and recited aloud a rhymed ballad in alexandrine verse. Joe's tonal ability, combined with his natural grace and athletic dexterity, made this scene unique in all productions of *Cyrano*, I am sure. Even Coquelin, who originated the part, had played it with a crowd to conceal his lack of prowess with the sword, and Walter Hampden's extras were equally diversionary.

I turned to congratulate Mel, and he waved his hand in a deprecatory manner as though he staged this kind of thing every day.

The second act takes place in the confectioner's shop of Ragueneau. Cyrano, who the night before fought one hundred men single-handedly at a great gate of Paris, is pursuing his love, the beautiful Roxanne. He is too ashamed of his monstrous nose to admit that it is *he himself* who loves her. He lies and says her silent lover is one of the cadets de Gascogne. Her heart leaps up and she joyfully and hopefully guesses it is the handsome Christian. Cyrano, cut to the quick that she would prefer the stupid Christian to himself, takes his courage in hand and refrains from revealing the truth.

As she leaves, Roxanne turns to Cyrano and in full admiration says, "One hundred men against one! What courage."

Cyrano then turns front and speaks one of Rostand's classic lines. To himself he says, ruefully, referring to his own bravery in not revealing his love for her, "I have done better since."

I was waiting for that line, as it is so flamboyant, so Rostand. But I could only see Cyrano turn and speak front or rather seem to speak. His words were drowned out by a platoon of the cadets de Gascogne who crossed by the window behind him, talking full voice. The scene had no finality, no point. I was shocked and naturally thought it a mistake. I turned to Mel.

"The cadets came on too soon," I said. "I missed the line."

"Of course you did," Mel said, suppressing a smile. "I had a terrible time thinking of something that would cover up that corny line."

I was horrified. "Corny! Corny! You're talking about a master. Rostand constructed a whole scene carefully to build to that line, and you blot it out with sound! My God, what are you doing? You know what I believe? You think this play is old-fashioned, ridiculous, beyond contempt!"

"Of course I do," he said. "Everyone with taste feels that way."

"Then don't direct Rostand, goddamn it. Stay away from him. He's done very well without your taste. Besides, maybe a little bad taste is good theatre!"

Fixing *Cyrano* was simply a matter of directing it with respect for the text. I urged Joe to take over quickly and direct it himself, eliminating all of Mel's diversionary touches. This he did, to great acclaim. He even then put it on the screen with award-winning results. But Joe told me that I was the crucial diagnostician of his *Cyrano de Bergerac.*

* * *

Unfortunately, one time I was asked by Norris Houghton, my former colleague from both Princeton and the University Players, to come to Philadelphia to see his production of Melville's *Billy Budd.*

It was only Philadelphia, but I was loath to go. Although I had known Norrie for years, we had never exchanged many ideas with each other on the theatre. But when I refused, my sister called me in a fury. "You'd go to Boston or anywhere to help some unknown, but if a friend wants you, you won't go. Norrie is desperate. You've got to go down there and help him."

So I went and sat through a performance in Philadelphia. The first problem was the physical production of *Billy Budd.* The long first scene was played on a deck with a wrinkled and wiggly cyclorama behind it. It was so distracting I could scarcely hear the play. Then there was an endless wait between scenes while stagehands noisily changed the set. The second scene was a fine, solid set in a large room belowdecks. At the end of the play I met Norrie alone at a bar across the street.

"What do you think, honestly?" he asked.

"Honestly," I said, "it has merit, but if you don't want to lose money you ought to close it Saturday."

His cheek flinched. "What's your second thought?"

I said, "Open on the second set—it's solid and convincing. Put all the information the play needs to reveal in that believable room belowdecks. Use the deck set with its wiggle only at the last minute when you have to, and then so Billy Budd doesn't get lost, let him *do* something semispectacular—run up a mast, fire a gun, behave as a brave sailor should—something to make him stand out vividly as the first act curtain comes down."

I went on and gave him notes for the rest of the play, which he wrote down, and then I went home. He called me the next day to say they had taken all the suggestions but one, and they worked well. The first act without a change was great.

"What's the one you *didn't* take?"

"Well, Josh, we weren't stupid enough to listen to your advice about closing the play, which was your first suggestion."

"Nobody ever does," I replied.

The play went on to be a distinguished success critically, which meant it never paid its costs back. But it was a worthy effort, although all I ever heard was that I told them to close it.

* * *

The King and I, which had been offered to me, was a classic and perennial success, but on the road it had its problems. I was called by Oscar Hammerstein partly because he had originally wanted me to direct and partly because he and Dick Rodgers were truly puzzled about certain reactions. To me it was in almost perfect shape when I saw it in New Haven. I suggested that at a certain point they cut some transitional scenes of Mrs. Anna and go immediately to the king. They objected, but after I left, they decided I was right and made the change. But I must insist that it was a superb play even before I opened my mouth.

* * *

The Theatre Guild had agreed to put on a play by Henry Denker called *Time Limit!* It was a semimystery play of the Korean War about an officer in the Army who had been brainwashed by the enemy and had become a traitor in the eyes of his compatriots. The Guild wanted me to direct or at least coproduce. Therefore I was in on the original casting, which included two fine actors, Arthur Kennedy and Richard Kiley.

When I saw it out of town, Kiley, the suspected traitor, had been directed to read his cold-blooded, unsympathetic lines in a two-faced, stuttering manner, making it clear to the audience that he had his fingers crossed while lying and was really innocent underneath. To me, this killed the point of the play, which was to convince the audience that he was guilty as hell until his innocence was revealed in the last scene. So my chief contribution was to urge that he be played as the villain he was suspected of being until the big switch. I worked a bit with Kiley, an intelligent actor, and left town. The play became a hit, and, I believe, because it was now directed as Henry Denker wrote it: as a mystery play.

* * *

The most outrageous, unbelievable case of my doctoring a show was one I worked on without ever seeing or reading it. The play was an honorable failure, seemingly unsavable, and yet it eventually became a commercial and artistic hit. It was called *The Silver Whistle,* and again it starred José Ferrer.

Nedda and I were in Chicago with one of the replacements for *Mister Roberts.* Nedda had seen my play so many times that she decided to see *The Silver Whistle,* a new play at a nearby theatre. She loved Joe Ferrer and was praying he would have another hit. That night when I asked her about it, she said, "You know, I think you could easily make it into a hit."

I laughed and said, "Me? That's all I need, another problem to solve." But I was intrigued. "Why do you think I could fix it?"

"Because all it needs is a climactic ending, and that's your specialty."

She told me the plot. A younger man enters an old people's home and brings new life and hope to the inmates. They organize a bazaar at his instigation, and the police come to arrest him for selling things without a license. They arrest the old people, too, and José talks the police out of the arrest.

I thought about the matter, but I had no time then. Yet Nedda told Armina Marshall of the Theatre Guild she was sure I could find a new ending for the play. So a committee from the play came to our apartment one night in New York: Ferrer, Armina Marshall and her husband, Lawrence Langner, plus the author and the director. We discussed the play, and I said that according to Maxwell Anderson every play should have a lift at the end, one leading character should grow. So instead of Oliver's saving the old people from arrest, the old people should save Oliver, thus showing that he had imbued them with strength and Oliver can feel he's accomplished something in life. The committee agreed, thanked me, and left.

A week later I went to see the play for the first time, three nights before it was to open on Broadway. It was fine until the end. I grabbed Lawrence Langner and said, "Why didn't you let the old people save Oliver, as I said?"

He answered, "Because it's too late to rewrite and far too late for actors to learn new lines."

By now I was too involved to be put off.

"No new lines, Lawrence—just switch the exact lines that are there. *Let Ferrer say the old people's lines and vice versa.*"

"Good Lord," he said. "That might work. But I won't do it unless you put the change in yourself."

"But it's so easy to do—and I'm not the director."

"You put them in or else it stays as is."

By this time I was so sure my idea would give the play a lift that I agreed. The next morning I faced the cast and said, "I'm your surrogate director. You say Oliver's lines and he will say yours."

The cast seemed to understand the problem at once and since they all knew the other lines of the scene because they had been cued for weeks, they made the switch almost automatically. The scene jumped to vivid life.

That night it was the satisfying climax to the play. The audience howled and remained to applaud. The next night the play opened to the same enthusiasm from the public and the critics.

Two days later at a cocktail party, Ward Morehouse, the *New York World-Telegram* critic, asked me if I had had anything to do with the ending of *The Silver Whistle.* When I denied it, I asked why he asked.

"Because all during the play—which I was enjoying, mind you—I kept wondering, shall I or shall I not give this play a good notice, and then I made up my mind: if it has a good ending, I'll give it a rave and if it hasn't, I'll let it down easy. Well, it had a great ending, so I raved. Then someone whispered to me that you had worked on the ending."

"They must have been crazy. I'm far too busy."

"I know. That's why I really didn't believe it."

* * *

But, as I said, it's not all bouquets and medals. Doctoring plays can be very painful. In the first place, it's like the position of a nurse or a governess. It's not your baby, and no matter how fond you become of the infant or how satisfactory your application of first aid, you must leave and turn it back to the parent or surgeon in charge. It's frustrating because you have become familiar enough with the subject to feel you're one of the original writers. You must feel that way in order to work with it successfully. Then the time comes for the umbilical cord to be cut. It sometimes takes days to get over that severance. You call to find out if your suggestions have worked. They don't want to talk by this time; they're pretending you were never there. Your wife is disgusted. "Forget it, you'll never be acknowledged enough or even thanked enough for you. I'm sorry you got into this." Wives sometimes are quite smart.

But Dr. Bountiful finally met his Waterloo—not a professional defeat, just a personal one, but it cured him of fixing other people's plays for good—and if not for good, forever.

Leland Hayward, who had evidently begun to believe I could do anything, insisted that I come to Philadelphia in 1948 to see his production of *Anne of the Thousand Days,* starring Rex Harrison and Joyce Redman, a historical play about Anne Boleyn and Henry the Eighth by Maxwell Anderson, my scholarly friend from *Knickerbocker Holiday.*

I had been quoting Anderson for years, and singing his and Kurt Weill's "September Song." Perhaps people could say I was his disciple. But I wasn't sure he would want me to come down for this one.

Leland had given me the script to read and my feelings were split down the middle. I was fascinated by Max's telling of the realistic story of the king and his second wife. It was full of excitement, suspense, bawdy sixteenth-century humor, and heraldry. But Max had chosen an awkward form for telling Anne's own personal reactions.

The play opened in the Tower in a small set on the side of the stage, with Anne in a dungeon waiting for the executioner. The story of her flirtatious affair with Henry, of his defiance of the Catholic Church, their marriage, their baby girl, and his resultant displeasure with Anne—all this exciting drama was played on the full stage as flashbacks in Anne's mind.

Starting with the prologue, there must have been ten times when the suspenseful story was interrupted to go back to the Tower for another one of Anne's, or, rather, Max Anderson's, poetic narrations.

I didn't see how on earth it could be done without endless stage waits. In the theatre, one minute of blackout seems to an audience like half an hour. But there would be far more than a minute's lapse each time, as Anne had to be onstage at the ending of every scene in the main story in full costume and hairdress, not to mention earrings and necklace—and yet in her Tower scenes she was supposed to be in a skimpy muslin shift, hair pulled back, with bare throat and hands. Generally, an experienced playwright—and God knows Max had written dozens of plays—would have let Anne exit from the main story in time to make her change for the Tower scenes, and have a minute or two of action by others to give time for it.

I asked Leland what he was going to do about it, and he said, "Max has written a lot of movies lately and he says they do these instantaneous changes in pictures, so why not on the stage?"

"But the cutter does that. Of course, it's instantaneous, because it's all shot on different days and then put together. I think you better ask Max to write you some cover scenes for Anne's changes."

Leland said, "I'll handle it, Josh. I'll just tell Max to fix it."

That's all I knew until he called me to come see it. Bretaigne Windust, my friend and the director at the time, was having trouble getting Max to rewrite. "Maybe he'd listen to you, Josh. Kurt Weill is down here giving Max moral support, as well as Max's young wife, Mab, who's a pain in the ass."

I took a train to Philadelphia and saw the play that night. Rex Harrison gave a tour de force performance as Henry, and Joyce Redman was equally spectacular as Anne, except she soliloquized so much that I kept waiting for the entire audience to start communal snoring. But the main story was really powerful and hot as fire.

Every ten or fifteen minutes, however, a tank of cold water seemed to hit us all as the lights blacked out. In the darkness, we could just make out a stagehand tiptoeing from the wings in white shirt-sleeves, hoping to be invisible. He carefully placed a stool a few feet onstage where the Tower was. Then we could see him tiptoe back, and after a ghastly pause, Anne tiptoed in and sat. A spotlight hit her, and as though Max Anderson pressed a button, Anne began soliloquizing. This lasted six or seven minutes before another blackout, and the whole megillah started over again, only backward. We had to pretend we couldn't see Anne, in the dark, exiting with her hand starting to open her back zipper, then the stagehand on cat feet grabbing the stool and sneaking it offstage.

Another endless wait in the dark before the lights came up full on the main set, with Anne onstage in a new costume and puffing slightly, and the story took off where it had been left and the whole audience woke up and started having fun again.

The next time the blackout happened and the stagehand stumbled out in the dark with that stool, I could hear the audience moaning a bit at the thought of another long wait. And so on, through the evening. But the curtain came down to tremendous applause, especially for Rex, and I had the feeling that if she hadn't had to go through those stage waits, Joyce Redman would have been hailed as loudly as he.

I didn't want to go to the hotel room conference, but Leland found me in Rex's dressing room.

As I walked into the conference room, I felt as if I were going before a tribunal. It was filled with seated people, all watching me tensely. I laughed to try and ease things, but they still stared blankly.

"It's a great show, Max. I must congratulate you. The story is as vibrant and modern as anything today."

Max smiled a bit and said, "But?"

There were soft chuckles all over the room. Rex Harrison was there, Leland, Windy, Mab, Kurt Weill with Lotte Lenya, his wife, and John Wharton, Max's lawyer.

I said, "I'm sure I don't need to tell you that there's something very wrong with the evening."

"There are too many soliloquies." It was Max talking again, with a chip on his shoulder. A short, baby-faced, smoking woman brushed past me. It was Mab.

"You said it, Max, I didn't," I said, trying to be funny.

"I knew you'd want them cut," snarled Max.

"How did you know?"

"Because everybody says that. Can't you think of something different that's wrong?"

"There isn't anything else that's wrong. It's a great show, as the audience tells you. Except when they're bored by all those blackouts for her costume changes and by all those endless words that they feel they've heard a few minutes before."

"That's not true. Every word is different. I've checked them," snapped Mab, still pacing.

"Then I think you should explain that to the audience, Mab."

No one spoke for a moment. Then Leland said, "Which one shall we cut—which soliloquy, I mean?"

I thought for a second. "Outside of the prologue soliloquy in the Tower to show Anne's eventual fate, do you need any of them?"

There was a gasp from the whole room, and I continued. "If you could part with all those words, Max, you could have one of the biggest hits to ever come along."

"That's the most ridiculous, commercial thing I've ever heard," said Mab in a kind of screech. "Max is a poet, not a hack. This play will be in every library in the country."

"Then why doesn't he print all those soliloquies in a little book and distribute it—but leave the rest on the stage where audiences can cheer it?"

"Josh," said Max, finally, "thank you for coming. Your reaction has convinced me of one thing. I will never cut one word of one soliloquy. Even if it means closing the play."

"Hear, hear," said Kurt Weill, John Wharton, and Mab, but no one else.

"Then I better get the hell out of here. I'm sorry, because mostly it's a great evening. And Rex, you and the cast gave me a big thrill. Max, thank you for all you've done for me in the past. I have the greatest respect for you and I wish you well. Good-bye, everybody."

I turned and left.

In the next weeks all kinds of rumors came from Philadelphia. Two soliloquies were cut. The next night they went back in and two others were cut. It sounded confused, but it showed me that at least they were trying.

By the time the show got to New York, the rumors were abundant and varied. It was great. It was terrible. Max was fighting with Leland. Leland was sulking.

Leland insisted I come to the opening.

"Why should I? I've seen it."

"Listen, you bastard, I've been fighting the third world war because of you. Max isn't speaking to me. He isn't even going to be there, he's so mad. Kurt Weill is sitting in for him."

Nedda and I went dressed to kill or be killed. The curtain went up and the air seemed to have cleared. The actors had confidence and verve. The laughs rolled right up to the balcony. After Anne's prologue in the Tower there were *no more* soliloquies. Scene followed scene. The story was powerful and it was played surely, deftly. The cast knew they were in a hit and the audience seemed to know it was witnessing one. The applause went on and on.

When I went backstage, John Wharton saw me and said, "We've got Max Anderson on the phone. Come talk to him."

"Hello, Max, this is Josh. I guess someone has told you you have a smash. Congratulations."

Max's own voice seemed a little strained. "I couldn't watch it,

Josh. Those cuts hurt too much. But if it did the trick, I'm relieved. And many thanks for speaking your mind."

Back on the stage, where dozens of enthusiasts had collected, I saw Leland and his wife, Nancy. "There's Kurt Weill. He's Max's proxy. Go tell him how you feel."

"Kurt," I said, excitedly, "Max has a big hit. I really loved it. Isn't it wonderful! I'm so happy for Max."

I stopped talking, because I saw a dark look, and he said in an emotional voice, "Max and I don't believe in the boom-boom-boom school of theatre the way you do, Josh."

"What's the boom-boom-boom school, Kurt?"

"We believe an audience doesn't have to sit forward in their seats the whole evening. Once in a while they like to sit back and relax."

I felt my throat tighten to hold back the roaring anger that came from my guts. Leland grabbed my arm as though he thought I might hit Kurt. I spoke hoarsely but with all the force I could muster without exploding.

"If you've got them leaning forward, don't ever let them sit back and relax. Keep them leaning toward you, hold them there, tie them there. I never heard of the boom-boom-boom school of theatre before you said it, but I believe in it now. If it means never bore an audience, than I say boom-boom-boom forever! And as for those soliloquies—"

Leland used full force and pulled me away from him into the crowd. Still trembling with rage, I took Nedda home to a sleepless night.

And that did it. That was the last time I ever tried to fix someone else's play. I put Dr. Bountiful out to pasture. It wasn't because I felt I failed. It was just too painful to help someone else and have to suffer for it.

* * *

I soon found that fixing plays was reciprocal. Other play doctors answered my own telephone calls and readily came to my aid. Howard Lindsay and Oscar Hammerstein each came out of town to diagnose the illness of *Fanny*. Oscar simply said, "It's okay if you get a good ending," and that's all I needed. That remark helped make it a hit. Earlier, Sam Behrman and Maxwell Anderson had advised on *The Wisteria Trees*. I certainly collected as much or more than I paid out. In the theatre we help each other.

There are several echoes that deserve recalling. When I was in Philadelphia with *All American* we were nearly a hit, and yet there was something wrong with the glue we were using to stick the whole thing together. Besides, what we were trying to stick was so fragile it wouldn't stay stuck. I tried everything I could think up. But no use.

A phrase went around town, started by a friend or perhaps a foe:

"What this show needs is Josh Logan."

MR. AND MRS.
PRESIDENT

S OME SHOWS, at first sight, seem to be dogs and turn
out to be great. Others, at first sight, seem to be great and
—*Mr. President* was one of the latter. What could possibly go wrong with directing a book by Howard Lindsay and
Russel Crouse and a score by Irving Berlin? I said yes as quickly
as I had said yes to *Miss Liberty* years before. I was saved from
that one by a change in schedule. But nothing saved me from
Mr. President.

I don't know why I had to hurry. When I went into it there
was no book and not a single song. Howard and Russel came to
my apartment and told me a story they had in mind. It was so
sketchy I really couldn't judge it but I knew that they were
devoted craftsmen and would work hard on it. Hadn't they
written *Life with Father* and won the Pulitzer Prize with *State of
the Union?* Besides Howard Lindsay had always been my adviser
and friend. He spoke my language, or, rather, I tried to speak
his. His knowledge of stagecraft and playwrighting was beyond
compare. I would not always call his writing poetic or necessarily eloquent, but it was never less than dramatic, accurate, and
beautifully professional.

Although I had never worked with his partner, Russel (Buck)

Crouse, I knew of him from friends. He had the reputation of being the Saint of Forty-fifth Street. Everyone loved him and always urged him to do his special turn at a party. He would act out in full-body pantomime the letters "M is for the many smiles you gave me, O is for . . ." et cetera. M was formed by standing in a far straddle and pointing his arms down in a V to form with his legs the M.

Each letter was a similar contortion, until the spectacular climax—"Put them all together, they spell Mother"—on which, in order to finish on time with the music, he jumped, bent double, semaphored his arms, and rolled about frantically to spell the whole word in the two bars of music left. It was always a smashing success and most endearing. From the moment I saw this flamboyant, show-off humor, I wanted to work with him, and here at last was my chance.

Of course Berlin was kind of a compelling force with me. He excited me so that I would have committed a minor crime to work with him again. It had been a long time since *Annie Get Your Gun*. And my pal Leland was producing. I *had* to do it.

And the trouble started almost from that minute.

Lindsay and Crouse had promised us all a first version of the book of *Mr. President* by a certain date, but long before that, Leland called and said that the date had to be set back because of the very serious illness of Russel Crouse. Buck had to have an operation that would keep him from working for at least a month.

Howard Lindsay, too, had been ill, but I had no idea he wasn't in good enough shape for another show.

Irving Berlin was the driving force for us all. He had and has an energy that the years do not lessen, and the idea of doing another show was so important to him that he gave a vigor to the whole venture.

Whatever illnesses caused Berlin to have depressed times in his life, they never seemed apparent around a show. I knew he didn't sleep well. But in our meetings he was the most exciting thing in the room, talking with the optimism and defiance of a kid.

With Lindsay, Crouse, and Berlin behind it, *Mr. President* had caused excitement in the public's mind even before the play was ever written: the requests for tickets and benefits started early. The Kennedy Foundation wanted the opening night in Washington as their benefit, and they promised a beautiful formal party at the British embassy afterward for the cast and the writers. It was going to be a big occasion no matter what happened.

The hitch was that people kept saying how much they were looking forward to a satire on President Kennedy and his family. And this wasn't one. It was based on a plot which Howard and Buck had originally started as a straight play, a play to show that we waste our political talents, that we throw Presidents in the ash can once they have been in the office, or put them out to pasture as we would a horse too old to run. It was meant to be a serious but homespun play with comedy spillovers.

I think that when it was turned into a musical something happened to those two men and to their play. They never quite believed in it as much as they had in the original, and yet they were seduced by the thought of the musical hit which Berlin would surely bring them.

The first draft of the book was overlong. Leland and I figured that the very best thing would be to try to get them to pare it down to playable length. I thought they would be agreeable to that as they were considered the deans of professional stage behavior.

To break the ice, I told them the Emlyn Williams theory of cutting—cut every unnecessary adjective, use the shortest verb form, cut dependent clauses—and they laughed and seemed most agreeable to it. We had our first session together and I should have known from it that we were in for a total disaster. I doubt if I have ever been attacked as I was that day—mostly by Buck Crouse, who took me so by surprise that I didn't know how to react.

I had always heard that he was an old dear, a pussycat. "Dear Buck, saintly, darling, wonderful, generous Buck—sweet, thoughtful, dear, adorable, cuddly, cozy Buck." But I was never able to find where those adjectives applied. If I were to mention the deletion of one word or one phrase, much less a sentence, I was attacked as though I were an enemy coming across a trench with a bayonet aimed at Buck's heart.

I kept expecting Howard Lindsay to defend me, as we were old pals, but he simply looked fatigued and turned his face away.

We were evidently going to keep every syllable, every adjective, even though with all of them there was not a chance of our getting the play on the stage in one evening, even without the songs. Both of them agreed it was much too long, and yet Buck was defending things that I knew he couldn't possibly care about. Therefore, I began to feel it was something personal.

"Am I offensive to you in some way?" I asked.

"When you try to make these cuts, you are."

"But what are we going to do?"

He said, "We'll have to do something else. You can't take the meat from the bones or we'll have nothing."

I said, "I really think that's a slight exaggeration, Buck. I think we're taking very little meat from the bones. We're cutting gristle. It's just a question of not seeming to repeat."

He said, "There's not a repetitious word in this scene. We're playwrights. It's been beautifully worked out by the two of us. We never repeat."

At that moment, I should have got on a plane for anywhere and left the Saint of Forty-fifth Street. Or else I should have said to Leland, "Don't put on the play, at least not right now, because I know there's not the slightest chance of success if the authors' attitude continues this way."

What I could not understand was Howard Lindsay, the man I looked up to above all men in the theatre. How could he sit in the same room and not speak up in the script's behalf? But, of course, he and Buck had in the past twenty years grown very close, very powerful, and very rich.

I was unhappy and frustrated, but I closed my eyes to it, because I was so anxious to work with Berlin again that I thought perhaps (and this was the most foolish decision of them all) that the music might save the show. If anyone else had said that, I would have shot him down.

At our next meeting, I urged Buck and Howard to cut the play by themselves. But Howard said, "No, we need an editor," and so, God help me, I tried a second time.

Again, the moment I opened my mouth to suggest that a phrase be made shorter, the knife edge of Buck Crouse's voice cut into me. I decided to fight back. I got up and let both of them have it.

"I'm not going to stand for this," I said. "We're all three in this and we have got to get the script cut or the show will run until two A.M. Something has to be done and you've both got to do it. I can't keep on listening to Buck's insults."

And for the rest of that session, at least, things went a bit better. But Buck went on voting no to anything I voted yes to. I was sick about it, but Leland urged me to hold my temper.

It was uncomfortable for Leland to feel that any of his friends were not getting along with each other, so he just plain avoided the subject. I was disheartened by his attitude as well. I didn't want to be the one who caused trouble, who made the boat rock, or worse who made waves.

Berlin, of course, was far away from it all. He lived in a spider web of song and music, with dreams of the cheering public and visions of people lining up at the box office. He concentrated on our advance sale, which was already beginning to be well over two million.

If people say that Berlin is interested in money, they are most assuredly right. Money represents to him the kind of contact with the public that makes his work universal. That contact must be total or it's no fun at all for him. It's the insurmountable challenge he gives himself when he wakes up in the morning to win the world. All he cares about really is not action but reaction—what *you* thought when you heard this phrase of his music, how *you* felt about a line of lyric, did *you* laugh, or wasn't it funny?

I certainly loved most of his score, particularly "It Gets Lonely in the White House," in which the President bemoans the mood of the country, the change that takes place when he makes a decision that is not popular. It was a song that could only be written by a man of great experience, and I found it most effective.

I persuaded Lindsay and Crouse to write a sequence in which the President made a round-the-world trip ending in Moscow, which gave Peter Gennaro, who was doing the dances, a chance to give some variety to the show by switching to various foreign people dancing and singing as the trip was made.

Robert Ryan came east and sang for Berlin, and agreed to play the President. He accepted without reading the script, as did Nanette Fabray, who played the President's wife. All of us had agreed to do the show because of the people behind it.

I am stressing this point because I believe it is the most dangerous thing one can do in the theatre: to go with big names no matter what. Love the property itself, the story, love how it is written—or else, for Christ's sake, don't do it. Stay away from it. Run from it.

I think, given my colleagues, that one of the things I did that was a mistake was in the staging of the play. I put bits of Berlin's music under some of the scenes. I was trying to add emotion to what I thought was a pretty cold-blooded scene. And it worked, as it had in *South Pacific.* But the moment I started doing this I got another yelp from Russel Crouse.

"That music is under dialogue," he said. "Dialogue should be said without music."

I said, "Why? Who made that rule? It was very successful in *South Pacific.*"

"This isn't *South Pacific,*" he said. "This is *Mr. President,* and we don't want any music under our dialogue. It spoils the jokes."

But I had already planned the music with Jay Blackton, who wrote it and was having it orchestrated. When we finally had a run-through before leaving for Boston, we invited several friends and family to see it. It went really excitingly, much better than I expected.

At the end of the play, Max Gordon rushed on the stage, called the company together, and said, "You are in one of the masterpieces of the theatre. Congratulations!"

I went to Max and asked him about the music under the scenes. He called it great.

Everyone was elated except Russel, who said to me, "That music killed the whole evening. If it wasn't there it would have been a hit." Eventually, he brought Howard over to me, and Howard said, "Josh, you know we're comedy writers, and we can't have things fighting us."

I said, "Howard, I'll get the music cut down so it doesn't fight, and then anything you both find is bad for your lines, I will take out. It will take me a little time, but I promise to do it."

And most of the music was out by the time we opened in Boston, or at least by the end of the first week. To me, the warmth of the show had disappeared. I felt the music supported the love story and the very thin plot. But I wasn't going to fight for it. I was supposed to be the director of their play; if they didn't want underlying music, they had the right to object.

The play got about the worst notices I've ever read in Boston. Elliot Norton, who had always been the wise old man of Tremont Street as far as I was concerned, hated the dialogue with a passion and took a special swipe at Berlin's music. The second week we were in Boston he invited me on his television show, and we had a spirited if not rancorous argument about Berlin's music. He said it was corny, old-fashioned, dreadful, tuneless, and I said it would last longer than he would last. I don't think the television show sold any tickets, but it gave me a lot of satisfaction and it made Berlin hysterically happy.

Thinking we had dodged the most damaging blows, we opened copies of *Time* and *Newsweek* to find an attack on the show that was beyond anything that had been said before. The fact that it was going to be seen by the President and the First Lady on the opening night in Washington gave the funeral pyre added fuel.

We approached Washington on tiptoe with tender feet, and well we might. The audience came in as though to the premiere of Sophocles' latest tragedy.

Up in the box where President Kennedy was to be seated was an orthopedic black leather chair, specially designed to support his ailing back; only now it was just a chair without the President's back. Sometimes it rocked a bit by itself, giving the eerie sensation of being occupied. Beautiful Jackie Kennedy sat beside the empty chair, and the rumor went around that the President was coming later because he had some problems with Cuba. All the rest of the Kennedys were there, as well as the diplomatic set and the staff of the White House and the various embassies —and as many Washington hostesses as could get in.

I had decided to sit down front for the historic occasion, as I remembered how thrilled I had been watching President Roosevelt when he had come to *Knickerbocker Holiday*. His presence had turned a flop into a hit. Maybe the Kennedys would do that for us.

But from the word go we were off on a gloomy evening. There was literally no laughter at all. Every time a joke was launched from the stage, the audience, like an audience at a tennis match, looked to the First Lady to see if she was laughing, and then turned back to the play, stony-faced. As Irving Berlin said, "They didn't come to *see* a show, they came to *be* a show."

At the end of the first act, a Kennedy sister who was sitting in front of me turned to her companion and said, "Well, thank God it isn't about us. That's what I was afraid of."

But I have a feeling that was what the rest of the audience was sorry about.

There could not have been any more painful experience than the first act of *Mr. President* that evening unless it was the second act. That act had an extra visitor. President Kennedy visited his orthopedic chair. If the audience had watched his wife during the first act, they never really noticed that there was a stage during the second act.

The curtain came down to token applause, and we all trudged

over to the British embassy. It was de rigueur; we had to go. I was in a numbed state of aggravated stupidity. The whole evening had been so gruesome, so humiliating, that all I wanted was to have everything come to an end, especially the party.

But that evening, I had to pretend to people that I was glad to meet them and glad they liked the show, when I knew they hadn't. I seated Nedda with a group of people she knew and then looked for a place for myself. There was a vacant seat at a table where a fascinating old lady was sitting. She was Alice Roosevelt Longworth, Teddy Roosevelt's daughter, who had a reputation for lively if peppery conversation.

I decided I wanted to meet her more than anyone else in the world, so I simply walked over and sat down close to her. Within a second we were introduced, and she leaned forward, so as not to be overheard, not quite knowing who I was, and, howling with laughter, said, "Did you see that *terrible show this evening?*"

And I said, blushing a bit, "Yes, I did."

"Don't you agree with me about how awful it was?"

I said, "It was, this evening, the most terrible show I have ever seen."

She started to laugh again, and she pointed over her shoulder to the man next to her who was, much to my surprise, Russel Crouse, and loudly whispered to me, "*He* thinks it was marvelous. He *loved* it. Can you imagine?"

She threw her head back again, emitting cascades of laughter. She was suddenly quite beautiful to me.

Then I noticed a man signaling me on the other side of the table. He was pointing covertly to my left. I didn't know him and I didn't know what the signal meant until I looked over my shoulder and straight into the face of Jack Kennedy. Amazingly enough, he was looking intently at me. I was so startled that for the first time in my life I couldn't think of a word to say.

The President spoke. "Are you the director of this show?"

"Yes, sir, I am. My name is Joshua Logan."

He said, "Yes, yes, I know. I wanted to talk to you. You know, in the show you have the President's plane landing in Moscow. I don't think that's right. We haven't got the proper relations for that. It would have to land in some neutral place like—I don't know—Copenhagen or Stockholm or Oslo, something like that. I think in that way the President would be able to talk far more easily to the people than he could at the Moscow airport . . ."

His voice began to fade away from me, like a failing radio, for I began to think of something so vivid that I couldn't hear anything else. I was saying to myself, You've always had some son of a bitch fixing your show—making suggestions for the first or second act—since you started in the theatre at nineteen. But this is the first time that that son of a bitch was the President of the United States.

But the President wasn't the only one in Washington who wanted to fix the show. Mrs. Robert S. McNamara, the wife of the Secretary of Defense and later head of the World Bank, wrote Nedda a long letter because she thought "a wife would have influence on a husband." The letter gave us gratis an entirely new plot with an ending Mrs. McNamara "figured out herself." Nedda decided just to write Mrs. McNamara a note of thanks for being so brilliant, and proceeded to forget the whole thing.

Several days after the opening Nedda and I had tea with a good friend in Washington, Florence Mahoney. Ted Sorensen joined us. He was a close adviser to the President and wrote most of his important speeches. We talked about *Mr. President* and Sorensen said he didn't mind it until the end. The President ought to say something more provocative in that last scene. He ought to have an inspiring speech. I asked him to make a suggestion and then I said, "Why don't you write the scene yourself. You know how Presidents should speak. If you feel our President should say something, give him some of your eloquence to say." Sorensen demurred modestly, but I insisted and finally he agreed to try. I was sure he'd forget about it, but in about a week his speech arrived. It was a speech for Bob Ryan to say that took up two pages of single-spaced typing. I suppose if it were spoken by Ted's personal star, John Kennedy, it would have sounded fine—but in our play it would have sounded like propaganda. I showed it to Leland and we agreed that this was as far as it should go.

The Washington opening had to be the worst night that *Mr. President* faced. The second worst night was the opening in New York. The first-nighters were so prepared by the press and by the talk that they came knowing they were going to see a dog. All they wanted was to be the first to go out and tell their friends how bad it was.

We had worked on the show somewhat, but only somewhat. Howard and Buck had rewritten, with great deliberation and misgivings, tiny portions of it, but Leland and I were sure nothing made any real difference because the idea was wrong in the first place as well as the title.

The audience came prepared to see one kind of show and saw something else. They expected to hear wisecracks and innuendos about all the Kennedys, but they saw a homespun story of an ordinary man and woman. It wasn't political satire but a bread-and-butter story of people in high places. For the people in the audience, it was very much like heading for a well-known steak house ready to eat a juicy, beautifully cooked steak, and finding that they had made a mistake and had gone to a fish house instead. Somehow, no matter how great the fish may be, it's not steak.

I do not believe that *Mr. President* was as bad as its reputation has left it. It just was ill-timed, ill-placed, and the only real mistake was ours. We should have known it.

The advance sale of two million dollars dwindled until *Mr. President* scarcely paid off its costs. How? Because theatre party ladies, who book far in advance, try to find out when the show opens in New York whether it is a hit or a flop. If it's a flop they start postponing each of their theatre parties until after the time they think it will announce its closing. Then they will have their money refunded and none of their clients will have to go to a bad show. In this kind of backbiting backgammon, the theatre owner is always outplayed and the ladies always win. The theatre and the show lose the advance. When the theatre party ladies began their deadly postponements, *Mr. President* received a deathblow—and became one of the major disappointments of the American theatre.

I caught a final glimpse of Berlin before he went back to his home in the Catskills. I tried to suggest that perhaps we could get the rights to *Sayonara* and make a musical of it. His face was a dark blue-purple and it seemed to be shriveled. His lips were tight.

"No," he said, "they don't want you and me to do anything now, those people," and he turned slowly away, and I knew he was under a spell of his lifelong personal agony—the pain of defeat, of total rejection, of wondering whether he had ever been good. He was back in the dark shadows he came from in the first place. How could a man who had hit such heights plunge into such inky doubt?

Not long afterward, both Howard Lindsay and Russel Crouse died—and it was only then that we learned that both had been victims of terminal illnesses long before *Mr. President* was first written.

Then I knew the reason for all their inconsistent behavior. I hadn't really been dealing with either one of them, only a fraction of each of them.

Howard left wonderful Dorothy Stickney, his wife, and Buck left lovely Anna Erskine and two brilliant and attractive children—who were living testimony to the great and lustrous years of Lindsay and Crouse.

FINDING
CAMELOT

WHEN I SAW *Camelot* on Broadway I was terribly disappointed except for the final scene when Arthur sends the little boy back to remind the world of the vision, the legend, of Camelot.

While other people raved about Richard Burton, I found him distracted, almost absentminded, as though he were thinking about a pretty girl he'd met while playing the part of Arthur. Recently, theatrical people devised a phrase which described Burton's performance accurately. He was "phoning it in." However, his quiet Welsh singing voice was charming to listen to.

Julie Andrews, who had made such a tremendous impression on the stage in *My Fair Lady*, was greeted ecstatically by critics and public alike. But to me, lovely and beautiful as she was, and with a perfect mellow soprano voice, she was never a dangerous Guenevere. The queen in my memory of the saga was a true femme fatale: shadowed, threatening, romantic, a pre-Raphaelite portrait. Because of her, Arthur lost England. Julie Andrews was just not that kind of world-shaking figure. She was cozy and little girlish and adorable. When I heard her sing "Lusty Month of May"—the word "lusty" had nothing to do with the ingenue way she sang or with the cute way her courtiers danced. Somehow, it all looked like the yearly maypole dance at Mansfield Female College back in Louisiana.

And what about Lancelot? Come to think of it, what *about* Lancelot? It's probably the most difficult part to play—that is, to play sympathetically—of any young man's part that has ever been written in English. In the first place, according to Alan Jay Lerner, T. H. White's Lancelot is French and has come across the Channel to espouse Arthur's passionate cause. He happens to be a holy young man who is able to perform miracles, including bringing back to life one of the knights he has killed in jousting. He does this by praying. And shortly thereafter he readily goes to bed with Arthur's wife. Lancelot is, so to speak, a holy cad. All of this makes him very difficult to play.

The role was played on the stage by Robert Goulet, a young, handsome, and rough-hewn singer with such leather lungs and such a true voice that he brought the house down after every number. But he was not, at least to me, ascetic enough to suggest the holy or spiritual, and his lustiness was that of a red-blooded American boy. Only his name suggested the French background Alan Lerner demanded.

I was not overwhelmed by the look of the stage production either. It suggested every crusader movie I'd ever seen, with Gothic arches and banners of rampant lions on red and white and gold. Oh, yes, lots and lots of gold.

I was quite surprised when the huge picture was offered to me, and I confess I was at first a bit disappointed. I thought, Oh, if only I could have got a great, surefire story instead of one so flawed, so difficult to pull together.

But when I read Alan Lerner's new scenario for the picture version, I was thrilled and suddenly wanted to do it with a passion.

My agent, Irving Paul Lazar, said, "Now, Josh, Jack Warner will not even discuss your doing it unless you'll go out there and talk to him. You know what he's worried about. He wants you to shoot *every frame of the whole picture on Warner Brothers' back lot.* Remember, you lost *My Fair Lady.*"

"I know," I said. "He was crazy for me to direct *My Fair Lady* until I said, 'Sure, Jack, I'll do it, but I do hope we can shoot some of it in England.'" I never heard from Jack Warner again, and before I knew it George Cukor was doing the picture—on the back lot.

So now, standing in front of Jack Warner at his desk, I said,

"Mr. Warner, I'd love to do this picture—any way and any-where you want it done."

He said, "Get this clear. If you can do it on the back lot and the stages of Warner Brothers here in Burbank, and by that I mean *every foot of it*, you can do it. Otherwise, get on a plane and fly back to New York."

I said, "I swear to you that I'll do it all here."

And I signed for the job.

"But," I said, "we must get a great cast, Mr. Warner, since we have no outdoor spectacle. Otherwise, we haven't got a chance."

"What about Julie Andrews?" he said. "She's gonna cost us an arm and a leg, but I think we can get her."

I said, "No. She was never right for Guenevere. Get a great actress, a beautiful one, a girl who can sing, a ravishing bitch."

"Okay, but what about Burton? We need some names."

I said, "Please, let me think about it for a while. Let me fly to England and look around. After all, *Camelot* is a big name in itself. You don't need such superstars, do you?"

I called home, and my sixteen-year-old son Tom told me he was going to wake up early the next morning to be the first in line to see a new English picture called *Morgan!* I said, "Why, Tom?"

"I like the sound of it. And besides, from the reviews that David Warner must be great."

I don't know why I said it but I did. "Well, if you see a Guenevere, let me know."

The next day, young Tom was on the phone. "Dad, I've found your Guenevere. The minute you get back here, go to the Sutton Theatre and see her. Her name is Vanessa Redgrave, and she's acres of beautiful, Dad."

With Bob Solo of Warner's, I flew to New York the next day, and we took a taxi to the theatre and saw *Morgan*. Certainly, there could have been no more exotically beautiful or more perfect piece of casting for Guenevere than Vanessa Redgrave. Bob called the agents and I called Jack Warner to have it run for him, and Bob and I flew on to London that night.

Vanessa was playing out of town in Brighton in *The Prime of Miss Jean Brodie*, but that Sunday night she came up to London to meet us at Claridge's. She brought two small records she had made of folk songs: "Where Have All the Flowers Gone?" was one of them, I remember. She was so extraordinary to look at that I was entranced. She had read the script, she loved Alan's writing of Guenevere, and there was just the question of how to handle *The Prime of Miss Jean Brodie*. If it opened to good notices, she was under contract to stay with it for six months. If it did not, she could be available to come to us immediately.

I saw another person that night, with reluctance. I had been warned about him by a fellow director. "Don't take him—he's very unreliable. He drinks and he's hard to handle."

My friend was talking about the Irish actor, Richard Harris, who walked in with a jaunty cap on and a wicked Hibernian smile.

He said, "I didn't come here to ask to play the part of Arthur, you know."

"You didn't?" I said, taken aback.

"No, I came here to ask if I could *test* for it. Would you run some film on me?"

I was intrigued immediately by his realistic approach. "Of course, we'll give you a test," I said. "Do you sing, by chance?"

He said, "Well, there *is* a problem there. Would it hurt the picture much if Arthur sang very well? Because, you see, I sing *very* well."

It was said jokingly, but he made his point. We scheduled a test in a week, where he turned out to be as commanding and humorous as I hoped he might be as Arthur. He had memorized quite a few scenes and played them with verve, excitement, and truth, and he also sang two songs extremely well. I knew in my heart he'd get the part, but we had no Lancelot, and no matter where I went I couldn't seem to find one.

An actor friend of mine introduced me to a young man who had flown up to England with him from Italy: Franco Nero. I had never seen or heard of him. He had a thick, bristling beard since he was playing a cowboy in a spaghetti Western outside of Rome. I could scarcely see anything of his face but his blue eyes which made me think he had a softer, more poetic side to him. After much halting English and voluble Italian, he reluctantly pulled out a photograph of himself without the beard: he had the fine face of a Burne-Jones knight, a match for my Rossetti queen.

I told him that an accent would be acceptable, but he would have to play in English. He said he could speak English—not perfectly—but would I listen? He stood in this hotel room, two feet from me, and through his spiky beard, he recited Romeo's speech to Juliet on the balcony. Also the speech at the end of the play when Romeo discovers Juliet dead. Then he said, "You ask John Huston about me. He says if I learn English I'll become a star."

I didn't dare allow myself to be completely sold, much as I wanted a Lancelot. I didn't know anything about his singing, and I didn't really know enough about his acting. True, he was the right size—broad and high enough for muscular. He would look well with Vanessa, and he would look like the kind of rugged knight Arthur might choose for the Round Table.

Back in Hollywood, I put Franco Nero—now beardless and in costume—through his paces in a test. The result was that we decided on him but insisted he come back to America immediately after his picture to study English.

So all was going well but there was a major fly in our ointment. Vanessa Redgrave had opened in *The Prime of Miss Jean Brodie* in London to rave reviews; the play was a box-office smash which meant she would by contract have to play in it for six months. We could not start the production as early as we planned. I explained that reluctantly to Jack Warner and he said, "Well, can't we get somebody else?"

I said, "No, Jack. It was hard enough to get her."

Meantime, I was meeting with a young man, twenty-nine-year-old John Truscott, who had been summoned from London to do the costumes and scenery. He was Australian, but he had designed the London company of *Camelot*. It had been a beautiful production, but to me just as faithfully medieval as the New York company. Here again were all the clichés of Gothic architecture, illuminated manuscript headdress, endless red and gold banners and rampant lions embroidered on everything.

John Truscott had brought me his sketches of the costumes from his London production, and I looked at them carefully. Beautiful as they were, I must have revealed some sense of disappointment because he said to me, "I can tell you don't like them. Why?"

And then I said, "Must every medieval picture look the same? Here we are, talking about Camelot, which existed at a time of no proven date, no excavations, no artifacts. We don't know if it was close to the Danish and Scandinavian invasions of England or whether it was close to the Roman days of the aqueducts and arches, or whether it was a combination of the two. Couldn't we get something rough-hewn, transitory, something special and unique? Make people notice the Camelot look?"

And John said, "Of course we could if I designed every inch of the production and we built a period of our own."

"Would you be willing to do that?"

"Of course," he said, "but they'll never let me."

"Start in drawing and we'll see."

He started and ended by designing every trinket, every bibelot that was on Arthur's desk, to indicate that Arthur was a Renaissance man of his day with a passion for all knowledge: architectural gadgets, mathematical measures, measuring clips, skeletons of strange animals. Pretty soon, everybody in the art department began feeling the fever and contributing to the Camelot look. All the costumes were redesigned, roughened in texture, reconceived—all the props, boots, shoes, chairs, tables, cups, chain mail. We decided, John and I, not to use the color red once in the entire film, just because it was used so often in medieval pageant pictures.

We called a meeting of department heads one day to discuss where the Camelot horsemen could ride to carry the word to the surrounding country. I was open to any suggestion: the picture needed some action, both for excitement and to provide the background for a musical montage to the tune of "Camelot."

I improvised various episodes: the runners might pass through a small city square where there was a boxing match taking place, or perhaps they would ride past a church from which a young bride and groom were emerging.

John suddenly jumped up, and in a long, soaring, poetic harangue that lasted several minutes and absolutely stunned everyone, he improvised what that young bride's bouquet must be made of. It would have no leaves—only wheat and blue cornflowers and small bits of thistle, plus peppergrass, Queen Anne's lace, and that, that, and the other—until finally I said, "John—" and he looked around at the astonished crew and said, "Oh, my God, what am I doing? Go on with what you were thinking." And sat down.

My only regret was that I never saw John's bouquet.

But his dedication and priestlike passion contributed more to the final film of *Camelot* than anything else.

Meanwhile, John searched the library for pictures. He handed me a book of Spanish castles, and when I saw with a start my old love, the castle of Coca, facing me, I yelled with excitement.

"That's the castle Nedda and I saw back in 1949 when we were touring Spain. We drank wine and ate cheese right below it. It's the most romantic castle in the world."

I took the photographs over to Jack Warner's office and said to him, "Now, I just want to show you something for your own pleasure, Jack. This is what Camelot *could* look like if we weren't stuck with your goddamned back lot. I'm not asking you to change your mind. I promised you that I'd make everything here, but I just want you to see what you're missing."

He looked at the picture and said, "Yes, it's beautiful, all right. I have to admit that. But you son of a bitch—I—"

I said, "I know. I promised. And I'm going to keep that promise."

One day Jack Warner called me into his office. He looked very worried. "Do we really have to wait for that tall Communist dame until November?"

"Yes, Jack, if we're going to use her, we certainly do."

"Isn't there anything you can do to shoot around her?"

"Yes, a few more weeks—I could manage a bit."

He said, "Our fiscal year commences the end of August. If you could start shooting a few days before that, our accountant says we could save quite a few million dollars."

I thought for a moment and said, "I could start in August, and easily. It would add something thrilling to the picture. But I couldn't do it unless you weigh and balance carefully. You want to save millions by making the fiscal year. You also want to save money by shooting on the back lot."

"Right!"

"Well, I'll swap you. Let me take the company to Spain in August and shoot Lancelot's quest at those great castles—and Arthur's and Lancelot's joust in front of Camelot castle and all the rides through the countryside. It's the only way I can possibly start in August, Jack, and fill up the time legitimately. It's the only way."

He forced a smile and said, "You did it, didn't you?"

I said, "I didn't do it, Jack. The fiscal year seems to have wanted a beautiful picture, too. But both you and I won, Jack —both of us won."

"Okay," he said. "Go ahead. Go ahead. Let's start in time for the fiscal year and to hell with that dame. We'll shoot around her in Spain and make a greater picture than if she was available."

And that's the way we got to Spain, and that's also the exact moment I fell in love with *Camelot*, with a love that I have never had for any other thing I've ever done. I saw a detailed vision of it and I knew John Truscott saw it, too: that this could be the most beautiful picture ever made.

Perhaps you are saying, Why go to Spain to shoot medieval castles that are supposed to be in England? The answer is very simple. The castles in England are either in ruins or have modern additions, whereas Spain is filled with entire castles that were built in the Middle Ages. That is why we know the phrase "castles in Spain."

John and I made a preliminary trip to Spain to find exact locations. There are seven thousand castles recorded there now. Many of them, of course, are worse ruins than England's, but a great many are not. And some are built on starkly dramatic rock mountains or ledges, and look down on lakes or valleys. I won't put any of these castles up against the Gothic Rheims or Chartres or Sainte-Chapelle, but if you are stirred by solid, rough-hewn, crenellated, authentic castles, go to Spain.

We went, and we spent several weeks in Madrid, making daily excursions to the countryside. We had to find twelve powerful, dangerous-looking castles for Lancelot to conquer in his quest to be worthy of the Round Table. But more important, we had to find the main castle of Camelot which would be the central focus of the story. And since the story began, flashed back to, and ended in France with Arthur in the midst of his final fight with Lancelot's forces, we had to find a dramatic-looking background for Lancelot's castle, Joyous Gard. And we found it: the elegant Alcazar in Segovia on a high rock.

I had little trouble convincing everyone that the castle at Coca was the best possible castle for Arthur's Camelot. It was majestic, and there was a valley below which we could plant or decorate as we chose. We could put in medieval roads, a bridge, and trees. The castle itself was on a high mound—covered with brown grass, of course, but that we could take care of with the proper green spray paint.

All the musical details had been organized by Al Newman and Ken Darby, who had done *Bus Stop* and *South Pacific* with me.

Since Frederick Loewe, the composer, lived in Palm Springs, only an hour and a half from Los Angeles, I went down to see him.

I asked him how he felt about the *Camelot* music and which cuts he would approve of. He said, "Just don't let them cut the comedy songs. For instance, be sure to let Guenevere sing 'Take Me to the Fair' because it's full of bitchy vitality and excitement. Otherwise, it will be all slow ballads."

I asked him for two changes in interpretation. I said, "Is it possible that 'The Lusty Month of May' could be sung at a slightly slower tempo?" I was thinking that Vanessa could act it better if she didn't have to go popping along like Julie Andrews.

Fritz thought for a while and said, "Oh, you mean dirty."

I said, "Yes. Lusty. Sexy. The lyric is languorous, sensual. Does it have to have such a sprightly beat?"

"No," he said. "That's a good idea—you want a 'Dirty Month of May'—and Vanessa Redgrave will be very good at it."

I then asked about a much more difficult problem that I had with the music—in fact, with the whole climax. At the end of the story when everyone in the court is conscious of Camelot's doom, there is a bright song that had been done in the theatre as an almost comic song: "What Do the Simple Folk Do?" In the second and third choruses the lyrics say that the simple folk whistle or dance or sing.

I asked Fritz if it would be all right if instead of playing it all the way through as though Arthur and Guenevere were having fun, we could play it as though they were simply pretending happiness, whistling in the dark to cover their true feelings. Could they almost break down and weep as they are singing the song, and then pull themselves back into the gaiety to cover their emotional break?

Fritz thoroughly approved. "Oh, yes! Oh, yes! If you can do that, it should be marvelous."

Franco had been fitted to armor that John Truscott had designed, made out of a kind of rubber mixture. It was like no armor I had ever seen before. Truscott had found a way of making it look original, different, and yet practical.

I met our stunt man, Tap Canutt, and Joe, his brother, sons of the great Yakima Canutt, the most famous stunt man of all time. They instructed me as to what could be done with horses when knights in armor rode them. They planned to go with me to Spain to do the stunts for Richard and Franco.

Tap was full of technical explanations of various ways that Lancelot could best the owners of the unfriendly castles. Hand-to-hand combat, horseback jousting, high falls, and other dangerous feats.

Richard Harris arrived in Hollywood, full of excitement. He had learned the songs, and went over them now with Al Newman and Ken Darby. His voice was good. Franco Nero, however, learned to mouth the songs to another man's voice.

Vanessa was still far away, playing *The Prime of Miss Jean Brodie*—and sometimes writing letters. I got one that nearly threw me off my office chair. She said, "I've got a wonderful idea, Josh. Why don't I wear one costume the entire time? Never, never change. Wouldn't it be terribly chic and original?"

I didn't dare show that letter to John Truscott, but I wrote Vanessa back. "Darling, don't you think that for sanitation's sake alone, since the picture takes place over a space of about twenty-five years, people might be a little worried about that one costume? Not only would it by rights be in tatters, but wouldn't it have an extra medieval pungency that we wouldn't particularly care to think about?"

I learned later that the best thing to do was just to read her letters, answer them sweetly, and forget her ideas.

Franco, Al Newman, and I had conferred on the fact that Lancelot's first song, "C'est Moi," could commence on the parapet of his castle, Joyous Gard, and then cut to various backgrounds as he progressed to Camelot. Above all, the song would give us the exterior beauty of the medieval structures and the Spanish landscape.

Six days before the fatal fiscal day arrived, the company took off for principal shooting in Spain.

In Madrid, Nedda and I took an apartment with Tom and Susan at a hotel called The Richmond.

My biggest personal problem was food. I defy any director of films to go to Spain and not have a conundrum with food, because the Spanish eat dinner at eleven or eleven-thirty at night, and there is practically no restaurant which opens at an early hour. Since movie directors get up at five o'clock in the morning to shoot or look for locations, eleven-thirty is a bit late for dinner.

So, we tried to cook dinner in the hotel room on a one-burner stove so I could go to sleep early and get up early. As the meal could be only a one-course affair, I decided I should eat exclusively from cans. But in Spain the only available canned food that seemed like a full meal was (ugh) canned spaghetti. I think that if I had to live on a desert island and eat canned spaghetti, I would just as soon throw away the spaghetti and swallow the can.

When we first entered the lobby of The Richmond Hotel, we discovered a diminutive person behind the desk—a child who was probably left in charge while his elders were away. With a high, piping voice, and in Spanish, he took our names, et cetera, and we were shown to our rooms by another child, a boy of eight or nine.

Nedda kept saying, "Surely there are older ones. They're running a hotel."

But, instead, each day they seemed to grow younger, and often I had to lean way over the desk to find someone.

Nedda said to me, "Do you realize that we're in a hotel run by babies? It's like being in the middle of a della Robbia."

Tom and Sue agreed to be part of *Camelot* and were fitted for costumes. Tom was going to be an eighth-century farm boy and Susan a goosegirl. The very first shot we made in the picture was of couriers riding through a town, with Tom plowing nearby and Susan being flustered with her gaggle of geese.

Naturally, all our Spanish shooting schedule was geared for scenery and action: the serious fight in the valley in which Lancelot knocks Arthur off his horse, the opening of the picture with Arthur standing on a smoke-filled battlefield with stunning Joyous Gard castle looming on the hill behind him and Merlin's face appearing in a hollow tree nearby, the end of the picture and one of the greatest scenes in musical comedy history, when Arthur discovers the young boy, Tom of Warwick, hiding, and realizes that someone will live to tell the world of Camelot. He sings to the boy:

> Each evening from December to December
> Before you drift to sleep upon your cot,
> Think back on all the tales that you remember
> Of Camelot . . .
> Don't let it be forgot
> That once there was a spot
> For one brief shining moment that was known
> As Camelot.

And then shouting, "Now, run, boy! Run, boy! Run!"

For this scene, Richard Kline, our cameraman, filled the valley below the Alcazar with a haze of smoke. A lighted window could be seen high in the castle; otherwise, all was desolation. Richard Harris and the boy were human and moving. The scene was worth the Spanish trip itself.

Of course, all of Lancelot's elaborate backgrounds for "C'est Moi" were filmed in their proper situation, along with a spectacular series of scenes with stunt men in armor as Lancelot won England castle by castle—a long sequence that was eventually cut.

After many shots of soldiers coming to Camelot, and of couriers riding through fields and towns, we finished our shooting in Spain and went back to Warner's dear old back lot.

Once a week Jack Warner would call me in and tell me I was behind schedule. I felt like doing something one of filmdom's great directors did under the same circumstances.

"How many pages am I behind?" he asked quietly.

"Twenty," was the reply.

The great director picked up the script and tore out twenty pages. "Now we're on schedule," he said.

Richard Harris was going to make a boyish, original Arthur. He had an approach to the young king that was stimulating to me: a wry, leprechaunish touch. It was his idea that when Arthur got the thought of the Round Table and its significance, he should get so excited he would leap from his chair and start running around the courtyard.

But Richard, at least in those days, needed a bit of grog in the afternoon to keep up his high spirits. It never interfered with his work—at least I couldn't detect it—but my heart stopped beating every time I saw him take a swig.

Harris would do anything for a laugh. He believed in high spirits. For one scene, after their marriage, we had planned for Guenevere to give Arthur a bath by scrubbing his back while he sat happily in an elaborately carved, ornamental copper bathtub raised on trestles with wheels. John Truscott had adapted it from one used by a Roman emperor. Richard had nothing to do in the scene but sit in ten inches of soapy water which would conceal his genitals.

When the scene was ready to be shot, and the water was heated to the proper temperature, Vanessa, with her embroidered washcloth designed by Truscott, was standing at the head of the tub, ready to scrub.

Richard was in a small prop room behind a long canvas curtain, taking off his clothes.

"Richard, we're ready," I called.

"I'm not. Not quite," he answered, I thought, with a little heavy breathing.

We waited a few more minutes.

"Richard, let's go! All you have to do is take off your clothes."

"That's what you think. I want to make this a great scene for Vanessa—memorable."

Still another wait.

"Are you ready yet?"

"Never readier!"

He popped through the curtain, stark naked and sporting a large erection protruding from his curly belly hair.

"I wanted to have something handmade for my queen," he said.

Everyone howled, particularly Vanessa. She was delighted, except she had to think of something to top him. It was all we could do to keep her from going to Richard, grabbing him by the handle, and leading him to the tub. Of course, the moment he lowered his turgid member into the coolish water, it suffered a sea change and we were able to film the scene with no trouble.

Jack Warner kept getting reports of Richard's actions and he also knew about the afternoon nips. I tried to reassure Jack that Richard was really great as Arthur and would never let him down—and while I was saying it, Easter came.

Nedda and I had a comfortable house on Beverly Drive across from Nedda's closest friend, Roz Russell. We decided to give an Easter luncheon for our kids and their friends. Pierre Olaf, the delightful Frenchman who was playing Lancelot's page, Dap, was going to bring the great Jean Renoir, and Richard Harris was coming as soon as he could take a shower.

But Richard didn't come out of that shower under his own power. He slipped and hit his head on a ledge and had to be taken to the hospital, where ten or twelve stitches were made on his upper forehead just below his hairline and back into his skull. He could not shoot for several days.

I got on the phone to our assistant directors to reschedule the next day's work. We had to shoot around Arthur, which was very difficult by now as the king was in almost every scene. We sent Richard flowers, liquor, and Easter eggs, plus a comic note of sympathy. But I needed a few notes of condolence myself. I was truly shaken by the problem of keeping the morale of the cast and crew from plunging.

The days passed and Richard didn't return. I kept trying to guess what was really the matter. I knew we could disguise the scar in various ways—with shadows, hair, makeup, careful angling. I called him, but only got a strange, noncommittal answer. Maybe tomorrow. Maybe the next day. Hope so. Miss you all.

He was away seven days, and suddenly he was back, bright as a cricket, Irish as ever, an adhesive patch on his forehead almost hidden by the lowered edge of his hairpiece.

"Richard," I said to him off in a corner, "I've got to know what's going on. Why has it been so long? Are you going to leave the picture? I think I deserve to know the truth."

"I nearly left. I nearly took a plane to England day before yesterday."

"Why?" I said. "Have you fallen out of love with Arthur? Have you stopped believing in me?"

"Of course not! Do you know what Jack Warner did? Without even talking to the doctor who sewed me up, he called me and ordered me to report for work that moment. When I said I had cut my forehead, he started yelling, 'You're a liar! You're trying to sabotage the picture! You're a lying, drunken crook! Get back to work or I'm going to sue you for everything you've got.'

" 'Mr. Warner,' I said, 'you will never see me on the set again until you come to my home personally, come inside and apologize, then invite me in a calm, modulated voice to please be good enough to come back to work.' And then I hung up and sat down to wait. Each day his secretary called, and I repeated my conditions. Meantime, I knew you and the cast must be sweating— but I was sweating, too."

Jack Warner had stubbornly waited, squirmed, cursed the Irish, and watched his mammoth picture treading water. Finally, there was nothing to do but try to save some of his thirteen million dollars by succumbing to Richard's demands. Realizing that he had brought this standoff challenge onto himself, he reluctantly went and awkwardly begged Richard Harris's pardon.

When I heard the story, I got a sinking feeling that Jack would be plotting revenge, but I was so happy to have Richard and normalcy back that I just put it out of my mind.

Although Vanessa Redgrave is maddeningly perverse as well as aggressive, she's a most beautiful and accomplished actress and a live, throbbing woman.

Although at first Vanessa Redgrave was determined to have only one costume, when she met John Truscott and saw his sketches, she was all at once in love with her clothes. She wanted to do her song "Take Me to the Fair" by changing scenes and costumes with every verse to show lapses of time. It was an exciting idea, and Truscott happily began designing more scenes and more costumes.

One day I took Vanessa to a room with a piano and a tape recorder so she could learn her songs. Franco Nero was in the next room, rehearsing. I introduced them and looked up, realizing that they were looking at each other and didn't know I was in the room. Franco invited her into his practice room where he had fruit and wine. So help me God, it occurred to me that moment, she's been looking for someone to have another baby with and here's this good-looking Italian. I think little Carlo is the eventual result of that meeting, and I'm positive they would agree.

Meantime, the sets and costumes were ready for "Take Me to the Fair," which she was to sing with each of the three knights separately.

We filmed the first sequence up on top of a crenellated balcony that overlooked the courtyard of Camelot. Vanessa did this scene while rolling a ball of yarn, the skein of which the knight held in his hands. The second verse was Vanessa in the armory, a sadistic lady and a sadistic armorer discussing violent sword play while examining steel blades.

The third was supposed to be filmed on the back lot with extras in the background while the third knight rocked Vanessa in a beautiful hammock. The rhythm of the hammock would keep time with the song she sang.

The next morning, just before we shot it, I called for another rehearsal. The playback accompaniment was turned on and Vanessa started to sing, but suddenly my mind seemed to have gone awry and my ears were not behaving properly, because Vanessa was singing in French. I listened again, and it was true. I stopped her.

"Vanessa, what on earth are you doing?"

"Isn't it marvelous!" she said. "I sat up all night making the translation. It's marvelously funny. It's hilarious."

I said, "I don't know what you're talking about. Why on earth are you singing this delightful song in a foreign language?"

"It's not a foreign language, it's French," said Vanessa. "We're making fun of Lancelot, aren't we? And he's French. Well, the whole idea is that by singing it in French we're making more of a joke of him."

"But how are you going to get the public to understand that? Are you going to carry a sign across your chest reading, 'I am singing in French in order to make a joke of Lancelot'? "

"Of course not. They'll *know*, " she said.

"They won't know, Vanessa. They never know anything that isn't spelled out. It's just impossible." I was beginning to sweat. "And besides, I'm not allowed to shoot it. It's illegal."

"How do you mean, illegal?"

"I mean, Mr. Warner bought this property, and at the same time bought the songs. They're already published, and if I shot it with French lyrics by someone else, Lerner and Loewe could sue Warner Brothers for a fortune. Jack Warner would spit blood."

"Oh, I don't believe that," she said. "I'm sure everybody would go along with a gentle spoof. Certainly, Alan Lerner can persuade Mr. Warner that it would be all right, because I'm going to sing it in French no matter what! What's Alan's number? I'll call him."

I gave her the number and she went to my portable dressing room where there was a telephone. When she came out she said, "The phone doesn't answer! He must have gone out. Can we wait?"

"No, no, darling, we've got to go on. I've got to shoot the scene, and I cannot shoot it in French. Please, darling, let's do one version in English, and then if you get Alan and he agrees, we'll shoot it again in French if you insist. But really, dear lady, you've got to believe me, French is the wrong idea. It would be totally confusing."

"Oh, Josh," she said, "I thought you had more imagination than that!"

But she did sit down and we got one version, and a lovely one, of Vanessa singing her verse in English.

Alan Lerner never did answer the phone, and for a fairly simple reason: I gave her the wrong number.

The enormous production went on in its huge, lumbering way, like a mammoth juggernaut about to crush us all. There were extensive night scenes of fighting in the courtyard on foot and on horseback. There was the great jousting match in carnival garb where Lancelot kills one of the knights and then miraculously brings him back to life. There were more scenes in the snow-filled woods, and eventually we reached the place in the script and schedule where we had about two weeks more work.

When we came to the set that morning, someone said, "Did you know we were finishing this afternoon?"

I said, "What are you talking about? We have two more weeks of work."

"Oh, no. You're finishing this afternoon. You better check."

I went to our company manager.

"Yes, that's right," he said. "Jack Warner's pulled the plug. He says you can't shoot any more after today—absolutely forbidden."

I said, "But doesn't Jack realize what we've got—"

"Oh, he knows. He just says he's not going to have this company shooting one more day. You've gone over schedule, and whatever you want you better take now or forever hold your peace."

It was unbelievable but there was no shaking Jack Warner. "Off with his head," says the Duchess in *Alice in Wonderland*. It made just as much sense.

I called Jack in his steam room in Palm Springs, and he wouldn't answer. I began to pile up in my mind all the various things that we still had to do—Arthur's speech at the Round Table about Guenevere and Lancelot, for instance—bits and pieces of Lancelot's miracle at the jousting match.

Alan Lerner came over to help and commiserate. He, too, was furious with Warner.

All of it was hysterical, but we kept on shooting until three or four in the morning. Finally I called a halt, deciding that if we missed anything we'd just have to come back.

But we never shot another foot. Jack wouldn't allow it. And we squeezed by. Since it did turn out to be the most beautiful picture I ever made, perhaps Jack was right. At least I had to thank him for giving me a chance to work on such a historically beautiful project.

A project which brought me a present from Alan Lerner—a picture of Jack Warner in a solid gold frame engraved with the words, "Fuck Him."

A LOAD
OF WAGON

IF I HAD done only *Camelot* with Alan Jay Lerner, I would have begun my story of him like this:

Alan Jay Lerner is a brilliant, youngish, middle-aged man with a cracking sense of humor and a passionate interest in life and all the living. He is a literate representative of Choate and Harvard, and he has retained a poetic gift over many years. He is one of our major talents and it was a privilege to work with him. Of course, I must add he was never on the set while I was shooting *Camelot*.

But . . .

But since in 1968 I also did a second picture, *Paint Your Wagon*, which Alan produced and this time actively, and which was based on his own play, with his lyrics in all the songs, I will have to alter my story. I have never quite recovered from that one—so I will begin again, like this:

It is my fantasy that Alan Jay Lerner was never conceived, or even born. He was pieced together by the great-great-great grandson of Dr. Frankenstein from a lot of disparate spare parts, with a big squirt of genius added to make it all stick together. His talent is prodigious, but that seems unimportant compared

211

to the fringe attributes that baffle—and sometimes madden—his friends and his business associates.

An extraspecial love potion must have been shot into him when he was first assembled, marked "Very attractive to ladies," because Alan has had seven wives. But don't believe the wag who said, "Poor Alan, no one ever explained to him that you could sleep with a girl without marrying her."

And I feel sure that his doctor creator did an early brain transplant into Alan from some financial genius, because Alan has always been able to raise money in fantastic amounts. A few years ago, for example, he got the Coca-Cola Company to put $900,000 into a script of the musical play, *1600 Pennsylvania Avenue*, probably the most unfortunate thing ever written by Alan Lerner and Leonard Bernstein. But it opened, and it was rumored Alan had to dig up a lot more money in order to close it.

Years ago, he started enlivening the periphery of big parties for me with his fascinating accounts of his doctor, a man who seemed to rule his life. The doctor could cure anything with special shots: colds, stomachache, sexual lethargy, depression, and general lassitude.

At one party I sought out Alan for his doctor's latest exploits. "Do you still go to that 'shot' doctor?" I asked.

"Of course. Oh, he's such a great man, Josh. You know, he doesn't believe in sleep. It's a waste of time, he says. So he gives you a shot that takes the place of sleep. He's got a great shot for sex and another to make you lose weight or gain. Oh, he's a phenomenon."

And he was. I soon learned that Alan's doctor was the sensational Dr. Max Jacobson, or Dr. Feelgood, as the slick magazines dubbed him. He later was deprived of his license to practice medicine, as many doctors felt his shots contained, among other things, the drug called "speed."

Alan told me that Max said he had given shots to Jack Kennedy in the White House.

When Alan and Burton Lane opened *On a Clear Day You Can See Forever* in Boston, Alan brought Max up and offered shots to the entire cast. Alan had evidently begun to think that shots could substitute for rehearsal and rewriting. As it turned out, shots couldn't help that show.

I have seldom been under the spell of another person, but there was a time during *Camelot* and the preparation of *Paint Your Wagon* when I admit to being under Alan's spell. He spoke brilliantly, was exciting to be with. He made me laugh and I found myself defending him no matter what he did, even when I suspected that he might be wrong.

Alan had chosen me for *Camelot* with no demands as to how he wanted it done—simply gave me carte blanche. He was around for the casting and visited the set once in a while. His job of writing had been completed before my work began. He had improved the stage play, I felt sure. His appearances during that picture were social.

But on *Paint Your Wagon* he was a permanent fixture—and to me, as it turned out, a stultifying one. He certainly had a right to be there: Paramount had made him the producer. It was just that throughout my directing career I seldom saw any of my producers, whereas on *Wagon* I saw Alan daily.

He had written the final screenplay from the free adaptation he had asked Paddy Chayefsky to write, and now as producer he was going to carry it off, come hell or Niagara Falls. And he obviously fancied himself in this new but lofty and powerful position—the little corporal of a nine-million-dollar Hollywood picture which was his own idea to begin with.

I was still working on *Camelot* when Alan asked me to do *Paint Your Wagon*. I hesitated then because I had not liked the father-and-daughter-in-the-Gold-Rush story of Alan's original play. I remembered dozing off several times during its "exciting parts." I tried to explain that to Alan, which only seemed to make him want me all the more. It seems he didn't like the stage version either. With me, he felt he could get something different.

"You're right about the plot," he said. "It was terrible. But Paddy Chayefsky's changing it. Please do it with me. I need you."

Those are probably the most persuasive three words in our language, so Nedda and I agreed to stay on in California after *Camelot*, rent another house as our lease was running out, and plan for the children to join us at vacation time.

Our mutual agent, Irving Paul Lazar, recommended with no reservations a unit manager named Tom Shaw. Irving had me go see Richard Brooks, the director, who had worked with Shaw for years. Richard told me how great and loyal Shaw was.

I moved over to Paramount to an office in the same suite as Alan's, and we began production by hiring Irving Lazar's wizard unit manager.

The second joint decision Alan and I made was to bring John Truscott, who had done the great costumes and scenery for *Camelot*, over from Warner Brothers. It was probably a major mistake, as John never cares about saving money. But his visual talent would give such quality to *Paint Your Wagon* we thought it was worth the chance.

Those first two decisions turned out to be disasters. Shaw was far from loyal to me. He left the picture before it was finished to go back to Richard Brooks. Truscott, I'm afraid, cost the picture several million dollars which did not show on the screen.

But all this was kid stuff compared to the personal hell I was still to go through. I watched good friends turn bad, bad friends reveal themselves. I watched my work as director held up to scorn, but more than that, I found myself, when working, feeling vaguely guilty and devoid of talent for the first time in my life.

The initial few days of conferences on the picture were fun: full of camaraderie, bawdy jokes, and excitement. We had several meetings in Robert Evans's office at Paramount. He was the studio executive in charge of our picture, and he was so flattering to Alan Lerner and me that I should have suspected something on the spot, but didn't, probably because of my childish appetite for praise.

Soon we were meeting with Charles Bluhdorn, the rich, wild, and space-age head of the great Gulf & Western conglomerate which had just bought Paramount. He talked about how *big* the picture was going to be and how we had to get the *biggest* stars to play in it. Bluhdorn's enthusiasm was so extravagant it was hard for any of us to match it.

Paint Your Wagon is the story of a group of lusty miners who gather in a valley during the Gold Rush of '48—of their lack of women and other privations. It centers on two miners who are partners and a woman who becomes the wife of both of them.

Since there was no final script yet, it was difficult to get stars to play in the movie, but Charlie Bluhdorn decided to go after Lee Marvin for the leading role of Ben Rumson. He came back announcing that Lee Marvin would play it for a million dollars without reading the script. It sounded like a holdup to me, but Bluhdorn was happy because they could pay Marvin the money at the rate of $100,000 a year over ten years, and in a way I didn't understand Bluhdorn would thus save $100,000.

We needed to have a girl star, of course, and another male name equal to Lee Marvin's for the part of "Pardner," Ben's name for the man with whom he shared his minings and wife.

Finally, Paddy Chayefsky arrived with a new script of his

own invention, but it was so overly detailed and at times so tangential that I for one could make no sense of it at all. The only new idea I really liked of his was the town collapsing in the end through greed. He deserved high marks for that.

Alan took Paddy's script and worked on it to develop a plot around the idea of two young men deciding to marry the same woman at the same time. It was a funny idea, but how would it be developed? That would be the trick. Still, I was all for it.

We set the time for shooting for early the next spring, which meant that we had to find our valley in the mountains before the winter snows came. It would be too late to wait for spring to find it. Our location men went exploring, and one of them announced, "I think we have your valley in Oregon."

We got there, but not before heavy snow had fallen; we looked at it from snowmobiles. No doubt about it, it was beautiful in winter, but we were going to shoot it in spring. We had to take the chance it would be right or wait another year. Then came the question of how the company would get to this valley from the town of Baker, two hours away, where there were living quarters. To spend four hours a day carrying an entire company back and forth is a very expensive venture. But someone said, "We'll fly 'em back and forth in helicopters. It won't take twenty minutes."

Much as I love location work, the decision to do the *entire* picture up there in that valley was made against my will. My reason was that it was a crazy expense. We certainly needed the valley for the wild, virgin forest and its rushing stream for panning gold, and we had to show the first miners pitching tents or sleeping in lean-tos. But the interiors could certainly be filmed back home on a set. Halfway through the picture, the town becomes a series of wooden storefronts, easily created on the Paramount back lot in Hollywood. This could save millions and look perfect.

John Truscott went on a loud rampage about realism and the truth of nature, and convinced Alan to agree with him. So, the full-grown storefront town was also to be built in that valley in Oregon, as well as the interiors. My attempts at economy went down the stream and got lost.

Alan rewrote the script and it was sent to Clint Eastwood, who had rather liked Paddy's first overwritten script. Now Clint sent word that he would not have anything to do with this terrible new script. He wanted out.

We were dependent on a big star for the part of Pardner, and we had sold ourselves that Clint was the only one for it. He was shooting a picture in England, so Alan and I flew there to see him. After a long evening conference in his room at which Alan and I spelled each other talking, Clint agreed to reconsider it, and one day later he accepted the new script, along with our promises of further changes.

We stopped back in New York for a while to do interviews for smaller parts. I saw an off-Broadway play, *Your Own Thing*, and laughed outrageously at a young man named Tom Ligon, who was playing Orson in the play. We got him to the office the next morning, and Alan and I both agreed he would be perfect as the innocent farm boy Lee Marvin would lead down the garden path.

The moment the last snow melted, the company started for Baker, Oregon, and hurried out to the valley to look at the greenery of spring. It was very beautiful, no question about it.

We needed masses of gold seekers, and were told that there would be no problem getting extras in this part of the country. All we had to do was put up signs in the small post offices saying that men with all shapes of beards were wanted to act in a new film being made by Paramount. And right they were. Bewhiskered hippies from all directions were soon tenting by the hundreds in the hills and woods around our location, ready to report for work with pay.

Nedda and I had rented a modest but attractive house on a main street in Baker and we had brought Carl and our new cook, Sheila. Of course we brought our children. I was all set to go to work.

The first shot scheduled was of a horse-drawn wagon carrying Clint Eastwood and his supposed younger brother along a high ledge. A rock formation would make the wheels slip and the wagon would be catapulted down the mountainside, knocking out Clint and killing his younger brother.

The day before the shooting, Alan, who was, I repeat, being a film producer for the very first time, called a meeting of the unit manager, the film editor, the cameraman, the first assistant, and me.

Alan said, "Now, the first shot you make is a carriage going down the side of a hill, but *I don't want you to photograph the carriage* at all. I want you to show what the carriage sees on its way down the hill."

I was startled and I said, "But, Alan, how will you know it's a carriage falling down a hill?"

He said, "We won't, until we see the wreckage at the bottom of the hill."

I said, "I was planning to put the camera on a sled and let it slide down—maybe twice—and that would give you the shot you want—but don't you think for safety's sake we ought to shoot a bit of the carriage catapulting downhill in case you want another cut? And to be sure that the audience knows where they are and what they're supposed to be seeing?"

This was the first time anyone had ever told me how to shoot the beginning of a picture or how to direct the beginning of a play. I was the director, and I felt I should be allowed to direct.

Alan said, "This is an order. You are not to shoot the carriage going down the hill at all. Just the point of view."

I answered as quietly as I could, "I think I should make that decision."

Alan's face grew dark and his hair seemed wirier. He said, "No. I'm the producer. I'm making the decision."

"But being the producer does not mean that you tell the story yourself. Otherwise, *you'd* be the director. Do you want to go out and shoot it yourself?"

"Oh, no, no, no!" he said. "I just want you to do what I tell you. I'm your producer." He seemed to be trembling.

I said, "I don't plan to do what you tell me, Alan, unless I think it's right. I really don't know how to do it any other way. That's the way I'll have to work this time—or else I'll have to ask you to let me off the picture."

I turned around, expecting corroboration from someone. I looked first at Tom Shaw, the unit manager, who was the most experienced moviemaker there outside of myself.

He said, "I think Alan's right. I think you should do what the producer says—whatever the producer says."

My heart sank. I said, "Tom, you've worked for years with Richard Brooks. Would Brooks have agreed to what Alan Lerner just demanded of me?"

"Oh, no," said Tom. "Not Brooks. He's a very independent fellow."

"Suppose Alan Lerner had told him how to shoot the first scene of the picture? What would he have done?"

"I'm afraid to tell you."

"Then why do you think I should listen?"

"Because you're two different people. Richard Brooks just wouldn't take it."

"And why should I?"

"Because I think Alan Lerner's right and I think you're wrong."

I began to think I was with Alice at the Mad Tea Party. The only eyes of sympathy I noticed were those of Jack Roe, the assistant cameraman, and Bill Fraker, the cameraman.

They lingered behind as the meeting was adjourned, and both men said, "Don't let 'em get you down—they're wrong." Then they hurried on with the rest so as not to be missed.

I decided that shooting it two ways wouldn't hurt. All they'd have to do was use his point-of-view shots for the final cut. But mine would be there in case they turned out to be needed.

I drove up by the side of the hill and saw the carriage sitting there. There was also the sled to which we were going to attach the camera. I arranged with Bill Fraker to have three or four other cameras covering the shot.

I had a bad night, but next morning after our helicopter trip everything was set. I said, "Roll 'em," and gave the signal for action. The carriage was pushed and it started down the hill. One of the wheels cracked as it passed our nearby camera, and it went on down and disappeared among the small pines at the base of the hill. Then, to get the carriage's point of view, we put the camera on the sled, turned the camera switch, gave the sled a push, until it skidded down the side of the hill, rocking once in a while with the holes and indentations, and eventually stopped among the little pine trees again.

Someone went down and retrieved the camera, and we tried that sliding shot again as cover.

Alan appeared in a flaming red linen blazer, a red-and-blue shirt, and a pair of bright yellow trousers with acid-green shoes, and walked about with a little smile that seemed to be asking approval of his dress. He nodded to me, and I went on down the hill to the next shot.

The company descended to the side of the river where the wrecked carriage and the two bodies were supposed to be. Enter Ben Rumson, the miner played by Lee Marvin. He checked to see whether the bodies were alive, and knelt down beside Clint Eastwood, who had stirred. And that is how the two men met. Within a few bits of dialogue they had agreed to become partners in the gold-mining business, and Pardner had his name.

The second day of shooting, Lee came on the set and I saw him looking about until he found the prop truck. He went over to the propman and whispered in his ear, and the man went into his truck and brought out a can of beer. Lee emptied the can.

We set up a scene around the newly dug grave of Pardner's brother. The body was lowered carefully on some straps which were held by pairs of miners on either side of the grave.

Lee, as Ben, delivered a speech over it in a delightfully sacrilegious, singsong voice. By the time he had rehearsed it twice and we had set up the camera and lights, Lee had finished two more cans of beer. His tongue was getting in the way of his diction.

Jack Roe suggested we break off for that day and attack the scene the next morning.

I had heard from a former producer that Lee drank, but I had also heard from the same source that he was a decent human being and made up for much of the time he lost, so it didn't worry me particularly on my way back to our little house in Baker. Only Alan worried me.

It was when I saw Nedda's face that I knew something awful had happened. She said, "Josh, Joyce Haber's column in this morning's *Los Angeles Times* says that you're being replaced on the picture by Richard Brooks."

I was stupefied, like a Zowie-Powie, Ka-lung-Ka-lung in a comic strip. It made no sense. Surely they would wait to make such a decision until they had seen at least one day's rushes!

I called my agent in California—Irving Lazar's associate, Milton Pickman.

Milton said, "Yes, there's some talk, but I can't seem to get to the root of it. From what I understand someone telephoned Richard Brooks yesterday and asked him to direct the picture. He refused because he wouldn't like to embarrass you while you're still on it."

I said, "Tell him he can embarrass me all he wants. I would like very much to get out of this fucking picture."

But Milton said, "Josh, you wait. Stay where you are. Go back to work tomorrow, and I'll find out all about it and come up there."

But that morning as I went to the set, I saw some executives from Paramount standing near the camera. My agent took me over to speak with them and they were very cordial.

"Please don't take this as anything peculiar, it's just that we would like to see how a big picture like this is getting started. Just go right on and shoot, and don't bother about us."

But I did bother about them. I bothered about the whole thing. Since I was still hired to shoot the picture, I continued as I had the day before, and since Lee was all right, we played the scene, and this time he was very amusing with his funeral speech. The scene itself ended with one pallbearer discovering gold in the grave and going crazy, whereupon the men holding the straps under the corpse pulled the strings taut, and the corpse shot up in the air like a flying mummy as they dove into the grave. I thought those Paramount guys couldn't have seen many more amusing scenes than that.

Getting back to Baker, I was conscious of the fact that everyone had gone to the first day's rushes. Nedda had seen them, and she had also seen Alan. When we got home, Nedda reported to me that Alan had said, "Oh, I do hope Josh wasn't upset by what appeared in Joyce Haber's column. I had absolutely nothing to do with it. I can't imagine how she got such a story. I never spoke to Richard Brooks. I've never even thought of Richard Brooks."

Nedda said, "You know what I think? He got someone else to make the call so he could deny it. He said it all so easily, so charmingly, that I had a feeling he had never told the truth a day in his life."

And I'm not sure that he ever did. I discovered that when he was cornered by some struggle with the truth or nervous about some decision, there was always a fingernail to eat or a bandage to pull from the ends of his raw fingers. He would pull off the little white cotton gloves he wore to cover those bandages and gnaw away with renewed enthusiasm.

That night, Nedda and I talked it all over, and I said, "Please get me out of this picture, Nedda. While I'm shooting tomorrow, call a lawyer and get me off this picture. I'm terribly unhappy. The fun's gone out of it, and when that happens I am in pain. I can't think anymore, or feel, or believe in what I'm doing."

She said she would go to Los Angeles and see a lawyer.

The next day's shooting went well, even though I was so distracted by what was going on behind the scenes that I couldn't quite focus on the scenes in front of me.

That evening, Nedda telephoned, "You're stuck, Josh. I went to the best lawyer in California, Deane Johnson of O'Melveny and Myers, and I was told that the producers can kick you out, they can do anything they want about your work, but *you can do nothing* except go to work every day."

It was such a depressing piece of news that I didn't know whether to try to go to bed and sleep it off, or stay up all night and talk about it on the telephone with Nedda, who was in a state of fury—or whether we should both get stinking drunk.

But the whole business dragged on and on with no explanation—nothing. No word of who it was who had asked to have me removed. All I knew was somebody had talked to Richard Brooks. I felt it had to have been Alan.

I directed the picture with joyless industry.

But I liked Lee Marvin enormously from the beginning. He did disappear from the set a few times after he had taken a nip or two early in the morning, but he was always back the next day fresher than ever—working hard, and full of really original ideas.

Clint Eastwood was much less talkative, but he was warm and decent. And certainly, Jean Seberg, cast as the woman in their lives, was lovable and beautiful.

Clint and Jean and I sometimes flew out in the small helicopter to the valley, but more often I flew out with Bill Fraker and Jack Roe. The two of them, my cameraman and first assistant, became my closest friends and strongest allies on the set. Not only did Bill Fraker have an artist's ability with a camera, but he had humor and humanity enough for ten men. He and Jack really pulled me through that vast enterprise. Friends are a powerful force.

One morning, Alan appeared on the set in a pink coat, green trousers, a red shirt, and striped shoes. It had become a habit, these wildly colored outfits, and the thing that seemed startling about it was not the colors but the fact that he changed colors three and four times a day.

That morning, as I was looking at the scene through the camera and working out the angles, Alan walked right out among the actors and started telling them how to read their lines and what to do. He seemed to have forgotten I was there.

In my experience, a director directs and a producer, if he wants a change made, goes to the director and suggests it.

The actors listened to what he had to say, rather confused, and I finally said to him, "Alan, do you want to direct the scene?"

He said, "Oh, no, no, no—I was just giving a few little hints here and there, to give them a little background. You carry on with whatever you were going to do, please." And he stepped over to the side, buttoned his coat, pulled his stomach in, and posed a bit as he watched me try to work.

I had lost track of what the scene was all about, and I asked them to go through it again in rehearsal, which they did—a bit fuzzily, as they were trying to remember what Alan's changes were. I explained the scene all over again the way I had planned it, and we shot it.

But I held myself in until Alan called another conference. At that conference, I said to him, "I don't want anyone to step in and talk to the actors—not you, Alan, or anyone else."

He said, "But I was just giving them some ideas."

I said, "But I'm directing the picture. You can tell me what the ideas are. I'll tell them to them. It just has to be done that way or we can't have a picture. It will fall apart right in front of your eyes."

I turned to the other people and said, "You understand, don't you?"

But Tom Shaw said, "No, I don't understand a bit. I think it's very nice of Alan to go in there and help you. You have a big job. If he has some ideas, he ought to give them."

I just looked at him steadily and thought he ought to have known John Ford. I bet they would have hit it off well.

Fortunately for me, eventually Alan had so many visitors to take care of on the set that he didn't spend much time with the actors.

The first group of visitors consisted of an old man with a potbelly, overaccentuated by his light blue knitted shirt and a general slightly greasy, untidy look about him. With him was a younger man and his wife who, I might add in passing, had the largest breasts I had ever seen in my life. Alan fussed among the three of them and was so solicitous of where they sat or stood so they could have a good view of the scene being shot that I wondered who they were.

Alan's secretary, a very pretty girl named Susan, came over to me and said, "A little bit later, Mr. Lerner would like you to meet his doctor and his doctor's son and daughter-in-law."

I said, "Could this be the famous Max Jacobson?"

"Yes, that's right," she said.

So this was the doctor I had heard about from Alan all those years, the one who cured every ill that Alan had ever had, except nailbite—who had even gone to the White House to give shots. I was fascinated, and while they were on the set I watched the three of them so much that I nearly forgot the scene I was directing. And I began to cherish them as they kept Alan's attention away from creative producing for a while at least.

My scene had finally got started when a helicopter came down right over it and landed not too far away. The motor sound was deafening. Fortunately, I was able to cut immediately, or else a lot of film would have been spoiled. We waited until the helicopter had quieted down, and I shot the scene. The moment it was over, I saw it was Karen, Alan's new wife, who had come in the helicopter.

The days inched on. I got up at four-thirty, took the helicopter an hour later, filmed all day, and flew back at night to eat and fall asleep. All I prayed for was that it would eventually end. All my life I had tried to discipline myself to be able to take anything that came along and keep working properly. Now I had finally been given the ultimate test. Although it seemed as though I had swallowed a bucket full of lead, I couldn't honestly say that I was in a mental depression, because I kept functioning and I even laughed once in a while. But I directed the picture very much as Old Dog Tray would have.

The picture was costing too much. I learned that what with the helicopters to the valley and back from Baker it was costing Paramount $80,000 a day just to be shooting in Oregon. Meanwhile, they were building an enormous gold-mining town farther up the river which was to be the completed town in the second half of the film. The town was being constructed over vast concrete cellars equipped with heavy machinery—levers, braces—designed by the special effects department to make the houses rock, sink, turn around, and in general collapse at the climax of the picture when Ben and his cohorts tunneled under the ground to get the gold that fell from the miners' pouches through the cracks of the floors of all the gambling casinos, whorehouses, and saloons.

I knew we were leaving when we finished shooting the collapse of the town, and so as each building crashed, my heart rejoiced. When the last building broke in two, we headed for Los Angeles.

Back in Hollywood we finished off a few more shots in the dance hall known as the Grizzly Bear, a mammoth set that had to be trucked to Los Angeles from Oregon. Then I was told by Paramount to make my director's cut as soon as possible. They needed to make releases quickly because the picture had cost much more than they anticipated. The figure was quoted at $19,000,000.

I worked with the cutter daily. I was getting toward the end of my cut of the picture when I was called into the office of Bernie Donnenfeld, one of the heads of the studio.

Bernie said, "How's your cut coming?"

I said, "Oh, it's nearly finished. I ought to be able to show it to Alan pretty soon, and we can go to work on it together."

He said, "That's what I want to tell you. He doesn't want that. He wants you to give it to him now, quickly, so that he can work on it alone. He's very anxious to do the cut by himself with no suggestions."

I said, "Why didn't he tell me?"

He said, "Well, you were allowed under your contract to have the director's cut."

"It doesn't make any difference what I'm allowed if he's going to take it over," I said. "I could have given it to him weeks ago and slept in my own bed in New York. It's finished. Tell him to take it—and good luck."

We left for home as soon as possible.

I didn't see the picture until it was previewed in Phoenix several months later. Alan had put in a lot of changes. He had started the picture with his favorite point-of-view shot of not showing the wagon going down the hill. He had given the songs he had written for the original show with Fritz Loewe a great deal of footage, which was to the good.

The audience in Phoenix was reacting rather better than I expected, despite the fact that the picture really should have been shortened a great deal. But as for me, I couldn't say anything about it. I just wanted to back away and disappear.

I went through the agony of the first night in New York, an enormous benefit. I knew that the reviews were going to be terrible, and when I heard from friends that the critics had attacked me, I decided not to read them. The less I remembered about that picture, the better. But I did learn later that in spite of all my misgivings, the picture did what Hollywood likes best: it made money.

Several weeks later, my son Tom, seventeen, and my daughter Susan, sixteen, who had been with us during quite a lot of the shooting and had grown fond of Lee Marvin, came storming into my room with a copy of the New York Daily News. They pointed to a column entitled "The Gossip Column," which consisted of a question written in by someone and an answer written by Robin Sloan, the columnist. Tom read it aloud, with fury. The question was something like: I understand that Lee Marvin argues with directors. Is that true?

And the answer: You only have to ask Josh Logan. Recently, on the set of Paint Your Wagon, Marvin objected to a reading which Logan had given him, and their voices raised higher and higher until Marvin went over and used Logan's boots like a dog uses a fire hydrant.

I have never been more surprised by anything in newsprint.

"Dad," said Susan, "it's not true! He never did such a thing, did he?"

"Of course not!" I said. "Don't you think I would have been bitching about it daily if he had?"

Tom said, "But I think you ought to write an answer and tell them it's not true. Please—for our sake. So I can tell my friends."

And here's the letter I wrote:

> Dear Mr. Sloan: In a recent column you accused Lee Marvin of treating my boots like a dog treats a fire hydrant. Lee Marvin is a very close friend of mine and we will stay friends for many years to come. It is true that we have had a few mild discussions, never any violent ones. Lee Marvin is a great southern gentleman who tips his hat whenever he meets ladies, and is very careful to call all older men "sir," in his delightful, antiquated way. Therefore, when he is sober it is absolutely impossible for him to have done such a thing, and when he is drunk, which he is once in a while I must admit, he is *really* drunk. He staggers and careens in such a way that he wouldn't have the aim.

The actual thirteenth-century Spanish castle of Coca in ruins in 1949.

Camelot. Lancelot (Franco Nero) riding away from the same castle (restored by the Spanish government). (Warner Brothers Pictures Distributing Corporation)

Camelot. Memory of love sequence during "If Ever I Should Leave You." Franco Nero and Vanessa Redgrave. (Warner Brothers Pictures Distributing Corporation)

King Arthur and Guenevere. (Warner Brothers Pictures
Distributing Corporation)

Susan Logan playing a
goosegirl and Tom Logan
a farm boy on the set
of *Camelot* in Spain.
(Warner Brothers
Pictures Distributing
Corporation)

"Don't let it be forgot
that once there was
a spot . . . Camelot."
Richard Harris as
King Arthur.
(Warner Brothers
Pictures Distributing
Corporation)

Paint Your Wagon. Clint Eastwood, Alan Jay Lerner, Jean Seberg, Josh, and Lee Marvin on the set in Oregon. (Paramount Pictures)

Josh directing *Paint Your Wagon* on a river in Oregon. (Paramount Pictures)

Paint Your Wagon. Lee Marvin rehearsing drunk scene. Joe Curtis (second left), dialogue director, watching. Marshall Wolins, script supervisor, on right. (Paramount Pictures)

The World of Suzie Wong. France Nuyen in rickshaw. William Shatner with suitcase. (Jos. Abeles Studio)

SEX, SI—
PORNO, NO

I WAS ONCE asked on television a rather direct question:
"Mr. Logan, why are you so interested in nudity?"
My answer was just as direct. I said, "Because I think sex or
physical love is the greatest force in nature, and nudity can be
a poetic way to show it."

Although all my friends expected me to be offended at being
publicly accused of too much interest in sex, I was delighted. In
the first place, I knew it would shock my mother, which was
recreation in itself. And to come down to facts, I do try to make
the physical side of all love scenes believable and palatable, and
I was delighted this television reporter had pointed it out.

Once, shortly before he died, Oscar Hammerstein said to me,
"There's only one important subject to write about. Sex." And
he was right. Sex is classic, at the roots of most dramatic conflict.

However, please note that I am talking about sex—*not* pornography. I avoid the latter as I avoid any dull subject.

The dictionary says that pornography is "obscene or licen-
tious." I say that sex is neither. It is beautiful. Beautiful, that is,
onstage when it has the precise emphasis demanded by the story
being told. But when it is forced into the plot, it grabs the

spotlight, and is offputting, unassimilated, and, therefore, offensive.

True sex stops before it gets to be pornography and, more important, pornography is not sexy. Love is dramatic action, while pornography is intermission.

To me, dirty motion pictures are neither exciting nor attractive, and never actually dirty because they are by their nature outside the viewer's personal experience at the moment.

Dorothy Parker, when asked once whether she read novels describing sexual intercourse or looked at lewd pictures, said, "Oh, no, it would be just as boring as looking at the blueprints of a friend's house. I'm excited only by my own blueprints."

But it's ridiculous to try to ban pornography or even censor it, and fruitless to arrest people who run stores that sell it. The moment so-called filth is banned and the newspaper's front page has a photograph of the mayor of the city waving his fist about "this disgraceful" area of town, that area becomes falsely attractive.

* * *

To be truly stimulating, a scene, at least to my mind, must have a bit of mystery, something that the mind is allowed to create itself, rather than having everything laid out in front of the eyes as on an operating table.

I learned that emphatically at an erotic show in Japan that took place in one of the large resort hotels. It had been going on for many years, every night of the week.

A group gathered in a smallish parlor in front of a scrim curtain that divided the stage from the audience. At first, it was impossible to see through the scrim, but after some appropriate music on the koto, the lights lowered in the auditorium and we could see dimly a beautiful woman in full kimono enter her bedroom, carrying a candle. She put the candle on the floor and proceeded to undress slowly, showing bits of her body here and there as the kimono slipped off her, and then she got into bed —or seemed to, as it was so very, very dim—and pulled the covers over her, leaving the candle alight.

After a few moments, the window shutters opened and a samurai soldier climbed in, dressed in armor and bristling with ancient weapons. He began ransacking the room for loot, and then he saw the girl lying in bed. He proceeded to undress, until he stood naked in front of the girl.

But somehow, with the dimness and the scrim, it didn't seem at all shocking.

The girl woke up. He grabbed her. She fought him off until, in a long kiss, she melted. Then they proceeded to go through the various phases of love. But it was quite different. In the first place, they were often in black shadow, and although the girl was resisting the man, we could see in quick flashes of candlelight that he was eventually winning her favor, and finally they were in a hot embrace and went into their act with mutual assent.

All through this, koto music was being played, and the whole thing appeared to be a disturbing fantasy. I wasn't terribly sure I'd seen it, or even what I had seen. The effect was so subtle that it became poetic, and right now I can only recall it with pleasure.

* * *

I grew up in stultifying Protestant morality and with the ever-present admonition, "Nice boys don't do things like that." We were never allowed to show any physical or emotional reaction to anything. "Nice boys don't cry." "Nice boys aren't curious about what's under girls' dresses." "Nice boys don't go to the bathroom, or at least they don't announce to everyone when they're going."

If I had listened to any of those admonitions, I could never have gone into the theatre, because everything that must be done in the theatre, I was taught not to do.

Evidently, I was the type to rebel very early and that early rebellion is probably one reason why some of my theatre work has been called "bold." Actually, it's more than bold, it's defiant. But I'm not the only bold one.

Perhaps the greatest sex I've seen on an American stage was with the Lunts in Bob Sherwood's *Reunion in Vienna*.

Two former lovers, deposed royalty, meet after many years at the Hotel Sacher in Vienna. Knowing Alfred is in the next room, Lynn stands in a draped velvet dress of white, a superb caryatid on the Acropolis, waiting to be discovered by her lover.

Alfred arrives in full white uniform covered with decorations. He sees Lynn and is thunderstruck by her unchanged perfection. He walks, almost prowls, slowly around the entire room, his eyes riveted on his love. Then he approaches her in slow wonderment, gets close to her, looks deep into her eyes, slaps her face hard, and kisses her passionately. I can still get excited thinking about it.

The second moment in that play that I will always remember with an erotic twinge was later in the plot. Lynn is on a chaise longue, as Alfred's hands are hovering over her, and nearby is a violinist Alfred has hired to accompany his love plan. Now the violinist leans over them, fiddling away erotically. Alfred talks, moves, gestures—always to accompanying figures on the violin. Finally, his hand swoops down to her ankle, then directly up her leg in the most intimate way, and the violin does a glissando, both movements coming to a simultaneous halt when the goal is reached.

Seeing such great artists give study to the erotic sides of a scene gave me the courage to try it myself. With the Lunts in my corner, I felt strong enough to express my true feelings about sex on the stage, to open all the closet doors.

* * *

The first play I did in which sex dictated most of my moves as a director was *Charley's Aunt.* Since it was an old Victorian farce with last century's mores, I tried to get a more contemporary feeling without changing its basic quality or form. This was made easier by casting physically attractive people as lovers. One really beautiful girl, Phyllis Avery, had exquisite full breasts, to which I frequently made reference in my direction. The audience never failed to howl with laughter when José Ferrer, dressed as the aunt in the black bombazine and white lace dress, with gray corkscrew curls sprouting from his temples, suddenly was frozen by something a few inches away: Phyllis's burgeoning bosom. His mouth hung open as his eyes devoured the delicious sight.

Sex, when unashamed, is hilarious. If it is a classic truth that the funniest thing on earth is an erection, certainly one that is being smuggled about under an old lady's bombazine is even funnier. Again, when you can make an audience imagine a picture, it's always wilder, sexier, more outrageous than actually seeing it.

* * *

After the war, I directed *Annie Get Your Gun,* in which I had Ethel Merman dancing at her initiation to the Indian tribe. At one point she found herself looking directly at the naked buttocks of the leading male dancer. Her reaction was such a look of delighted surprise that it brought equal delight from the audience.

* * *

When I was directing *Wish You Were Here* with its onstage swimming pool, one of our costume makers liked to regale our cast with stories of the old stars. She was a lady who had made the symmetricals for John Barrymore to wear in *Hamlet.* She explained that symmetricals were padded tights worn by leading men who didn't have perfectly formed legs. Layers of thickening were sewn inside to add the proper circumference to the calf or more muscle to the upper legs to simulate strength. And she sent the girls out of the room before she told the male members of the cast that Barrymore insisted that she sew a thick mass of material, plus a roll of cotton batting, inside the crotch of his tights to uphold his reputation as a matinee idol. This, she said, must always be her secret, as most people believed Barrymore to have been magnificently equipped. It became the cast's favorite story.

Her more current efforts came to light during a performance when one of the boys dove as planned from the board into the swimming pool, but on surfacing was met by a longish sponge that floated up before him. When he climbed out of the pool, he looked strangely concave between the legs and abdomen. A friend onstage handed him the sponge and said, "You lost your cock."

* * *

Those who think they saw *The World of Suzie Wong* because they saw the picture by the same name are pitifully misled. The picture, too, was laid in Hong Kong and the characters' names were the same or similar, but because of censorship, it was a pale and flabby affair when compared to Paul Osborn's strong and bawdy play. Paul used sex masterfully in the subplot of his play.

The main story is the romantic one of Robert, an artist who took a room in a Hong Kong whorehouse thinking it was a cheap hotel, and soon found himself in love with Suzie, the most beautiful girl and most sought-after prostitute in the city. But the subplot involves a man named Ben who stumbled into the whorehouse one day, drunk, complaining of Old Betsy, his wife. Suzie took Ben into a bedroom to give him solace and Ben came out renewed, for Suzie had taught him what his body was about.

He came back for more lessons every afternoon. And then, mysteriously, Ben stopped coming to see Suzie. A week passed, and Ben finally appeared with an explanation. On Suzie's day off, Ben, with no place to go, was sitting around home restlessly and happened to look over at his wife and *she didn't look so bad.* So, he took her to bed and gave her the treatment that Suzie had taught him. Old Betsy was so happy she wanted repeat performances. And, wonder of wonders, the awakened Old Betsy became attractive to Ben for the first time in his life.

The audience seemed exhilarated by the play's directness.

* * *

I want mystery, yes, but not timidity, so I decided long ago that there is a time when sex *should* be flaunted, when the bold move is more acceptable than the timid one. If an actor has something risqué to say, he must not simper, he must not apologize, or he will make the whole audience blush. He must speak out clearly and with confidence, and no one will be offended.

A LITTLE
REVENGE IS
BAD FOR
THE SOUL

BACK IN THE Methodist church in Mansfield, Louisiana, where I went to Sunday school every week, they preached that taking revenge is one of the worst sins a human being can commit, its punishment the eternally hot blast of hell.

But since that Methodist church's influence on me has eroded a bit and I have switched to the lovely if profane worship of the theatre, where violent rivalry warps us all, I have begun to feel that revenge is much closer to heaven than to hell. However, at one point in my life I got a perfect bull's-eye revenge on one of my best friends and it was no fun at all.

Once upon a time, before I directed the movie *Picnic* and all the movies that followed it, I made that very dramatic discovery.

It started with a certainty. It had been approved by everyone concerned that I was to direct the movie version of my big hit, *Mister Roberts*, just as soon as the movie sale was made. I considered this my play. I was not only its director but its coauthor and in actuality its coproducer. In fact, by contract, it could not be sold without me as director.

I had been preparing the screenplay off and on for five years; in fact, before Tom Heggen, my coauthor, died, we had discussed it thoroughly. I cut the play and substituted less censorable but equally effective language—and I had tried my changes with the road companies to be sure we hadn't lost a laugh or an effect. I knew the picture had to be shorter than the play, but I didn't want it to differ a whiff in spirit. Tom Heggen and I had worked carefully to make the stage version airtight enough to hold the emotion and the laughs. The script was now down to movie length, uncensorable, and ready to go. I felt comfortable.

The only blur on the horizon had been a disagreement I had had with Henry Fonda over the stage production he had toured across the country on the way to Los Angeles, where it was to be seen by prospective movie purchasers. When I flew to San Francisco to see the last performances before Los Angeles, I found that the famous Fonda understatement had infected the whole cast like a virus. The play had become strangely tame, and the rowdy sailors had all become Mister Robertses. I moved in and rehearsed the cast for a week to bring them closer to the original vitality I felt the play needed if it was going to attract the movie people.

But Fonda liked it the way it had been and seemed flattered by his imitators. My friend Leland Hayward, who had produced *Mister Roberts,* told me Hank had gone to him and said, "If that goddamned Logan directs the picture, I won't play it."

Fonda had been so definite that I was forced to find another Mister Roberts for the movie version. At that time (and spasmodically later on) I was a great admirer of Marlon Brando, and so I approached him. Marlon was under contract to do *The Egyptian* for Twentieth Century-Fox, but since he hated that screenplay and liked *Mister Roberts,* he told me not to worry: "You go ahead and make plans. I promise I'll do it. We'll make a deal, and I'll find my own way out of *The Egyptian.*"

With Brando, I was sure of having an important picture. Several members of the cast told me that Fonda thought he was too old to play the lead in the film of *Mister Roberts* anyway, and wanted to play Doc. That could mean the cloud between me and my old friend was clearing away. I was beginning to feel better. In fact, I had worked myself up until I was sitting on a soft pink cloud. Then someone lit a torch below it. The cloud melted and I hit earth with a thud.

I found myself in conference with my agent, Lew Wasserman.

Lew was wearing the agent's uniform: a black, conservative suit, a black tie, a sallow to gray-green face—and his somberest expression. He wasted no time making his point.

"You're a lucky man," he said, quietly. "He likes it."

"Who?" I asked.

"Ford."

"Ford likes what?"

"John Ford likes *Mister Roberts.* He's willing to direct the movie. Congratulations, Josh! It's the most important break you've had since I met you. John Ford is the greatest man's director in movie history. He guarantees you millions."

My heart started sinking, spinning through the floor, down through the earth below, and deep into the darkness below that.

"But I thought it was understood that—"

"You'd be good, too, Josh—I've said that right along. Ask anybody. But you can't throw away an opportunity like this. This man is a giant, and besides, Leland's told me to offer you a greater percentage of the picture if you'll agree to let Ford do it. A fourth of a John Ford picture, Josh. You can't get much more than that, man."

It was Leland. I felt it stab inside me. Leland wants to run the picture himself and he figures I'll steal the spotlight if I were connected with it. Oh, no, it couldn't be Leland—he's my friend. It's Hank Fonda. But he's my friend, too. But he refuses to do it with me, and I guess they're scared to do it without him. They're scared Brando will welsh. No, it's Ford. And Ford won't do it without Fonda. They're old pals. Oh, my God, what is it?

I knew Ford had come to see *Mister Roberts* awhile back but hadn't even bothered to look at the play. He waited in a nearby saloon until it was over. He only went backstage later to see Fonda for old times' sake. Fonda's dresser reported their meeting to me. When Fonda asked Ford if he had seen the play, Ford said, "Why should I look at that homosexual play?" That anecdote had traveled quickly through all the cast, and for a while John Ford was the most unpopular man at New York's Alvin Theatre.

I still don't know what he meant by that remark, as the whole emotion of the play is of men yearning for women.

I went to Leland and asked him if he was the one who wanted Ford. This embarrassed him painfully.

"Well, er, frankly, Josh, it's the money. Ford is money in the bank. He guarantees the success of the picture. Let's face it, you haven't directed a picture for seventeen years, since *I Met My Love Again,* and then you were only the codirector. You're a theatre director, the best there is, but can you guarantee how big a movie you'd bring in?"

I said, "Leland, you and I bought *Rear Window* by William Irish so that we could produce it and I could direct it as a kind of trial balloon for *Mister Roberts.* "

"I know, Josh, but Lew says Hitchcock wants to do *Rear Window.* We can sell it for more than we paid. And now, don't you see, we've got Ford. You'll own *one-fourth* of the picture if you'll just sit back and let the money pour into your hat."

"But he's never seen the play."

"I'll be there to protect your goddamn precious play. I'm gonna produce it myself, and you know goddamn well I'm not gonna let Ford twist it around and make a lot of changes."

If there was anywhere deeper for my heart to sink, it went. I knew that John Ford was not going to listen to Leland Hayward any more than he'd listen to a mosquito. He never listened to anyone.

Leland had told Marlon Brando how much we wanted him in *Mister Roberts.* But now he said that Ford and Fonda were a hot ticket, and besides, Darryl Zanuck had told him that Marlon couldn't possibly get out of doing *The Egyptian* for Twentieth Century-Fox, which was scheduled to shoot at the very same time as *Roberts.*

Leland said, "I guarantee Zanuck is telling me the truth."

Unfortunately, I believed him and I didn't call Brando. All the excitement I had felt, all the hope, left me. I was licked. I felt betrayed by the lot of them. And I *had* been, as it turned out. But so had Brando. He had ditched *The Egyptian* for *Mister Roberts,* which now ditched him. Marlon was furious. He felt Leland had double-crossed him.

It was a spaghetti bowl full of slippery double-crossers. Leland and his coterie must have got together and realized that it would take a colossus like John Ford to impress me enough to make me step out of the picture. I admit I was in awe of the name Ford. Why wouldn't I be, after *Stagecoach, How Green Was My Valley, The Grapes of Wrath,* and *The Quiet Man?*

My problem was that I didn't think his artistic level was as consistently high as everyone else seemed to. I admired his peaks but I found too many dusty valleys between them. But I still couldn't get around the fact that he was an enviable talent and an enormous name and that he probably would bring a lot of attention to the picture that I would not bring.

So, what could I do? What I did. Give in, of course.

I decided to close my eyes forever to *Mister Roberts* and to interest myself in working on something else. And that something else was, thank God, *Fanny.* I had a contract with producer David Merrick to write it with S. N. Behrman and then to stage it. I called David and said I was ready to go.

But during the next weeks I kept wondering what was happening to *Mister Roberts*, and picked up all the gossip I could. It was all bad. Leland had dropped my script and turned over the screenplay to John Patrick, a friend of mine and a well-known playwright, and told him to start from scratch. "Read the book and dramatize it as you would if it had been your idea." With all Leland had said about protecting the play, what was going on?

And what could I do about it? Nothing. For a while I felt very, very sorry for myself.

Work is salvation. Someone said it aeons ago and it's still true. I could have brooded over the loss of *Mister Roberts* for a long time, except I had the brilliant Sam Behrman and the play *Fanny* with Pinza and Slezak to help me blot it out.

Fanny had opened in Philadelphia when I began getting Dictaphone belts from Leland Hayward from Midway Island, reporting on the shooting of *Mister Roberts*, which they had started filming on a Navy ship and on the island itself where they all lived in the bachelor officers' quarters.

Leland seemed to be trying to make things seem better by quickly getting off the subjects I wanted to hear about.

He didn't tell me that the problem of the scenario had been turned over to Frank Nugent, a newspaper critic who had been brought out to write for Darryl Zanuck. A friend told me about it, and when I asked if Nugent could write, the friend said, "He was a critic and there's a nasty rumor that at the time Zanuck brought him out to write screenplays it was so that he wouldn't write bad reviews about Zanuck's movies."

I was kept in a cocoon until the shooting of *Mister Roberts* was finished. The movie was in rough cut when Leland sent for me via Jack Warner (he evidently couldn't face asking me himself) to look at the first run-through. It was nice to know that Warner had some doubts. I went to the Coast with a dual feeling, resentful at having been excluded in the first place and flattered that they had been forced to send for me.

The four stars were still hanging about the studio—Fonda, Jimmy Cagney, wonderful Jack Lemmon, who was just then becoming well known, and white-haired Bill Powell, on his way to retirement but still a very smooth actor.

The picture was run for me alone in a projection room. When it was over, I wanted to sneak out a side door and grab a plane and fly anywhere—to hell, maybe. But instead, I came out so Leland and I could look each other square in the face. His face was putty-gray with tinges of green; mine was purple, I'm sure. He couldn't seem to decide whether he wanted or didn't want to hear what I had to say. As for me, I wanted to get a gun and shoot him in the gut, and then drop the body on John Ford's front lawn. But that wouldn't take care of Ford himself and what about Frank Nugent, who deserved to be skinned alive at least? Nugent's writing was shocking. His was the shopworn Hollywood trick of taking dialogue that was good to begin with and switching it around a bit, just enough to make it seem like his own—and Nugent's dialogue was bad, bad.

Leland and his wife, Nancy, claimed they were ready to spend the evening with me and take anything I had to say. The first thing I told them was that I didn't think the picture could be saved. It was so shamefully inept all the way down the line— every big point missed or forgotten—that as a story it made no sense. The first and most important thing was the fact that onstage and in the novel it was a story that took place on a prisonlike ship with no liberty for anyone. And yet Ford had photographed these "prisoners" swimming, diving, cavorting every afternoon like happy kids at a boys' camp.

I said, "If they're in such a tragic mood that Roberts has to sell his birthright to get them a liberty, what the hell are they doing splashing water in each other's faces and howling like the Dead End Kids in the East River? And in Christ's name, what has Ford made Cagney do, play the captain like an old New England bumbler, without any hatred, without darkness, without threat? He's all Down East accent, and comic at that. Without a villain there's no threat—without threat there's no story. And Ward Bond playing tough Dowdy like a flabby cow, giving mother's milk at every close-up!"

As I went on, my voice raised a bit. "Instead of two palm trees being thrown overboard at the end, as in the book and the play, there's a silly, unfunny, low-comedy business of wrapping chains and locks around one palm tree as though any three-year-old child couldn't wrench it away. It's ridiculous, that's all."

Leland said, "You're right, Josh," but I didn't stop.

"And that great scene where Doc tells Roberts about the captain's name-signing contest, what happened to that? And that horrible, horrible, *horrible* nurse scene. Oh, God, Leland, it's not a picture, it's a rape. And you let it happen, my friend. *You know you let it happen.* If I killed you, I'd be exonerated. Tom would make room for me in hell." Oh, boy, was I enjoying my revenge.

He said, "You don't know what I went through, Josh. You can't imagine what I went through."

"What in Christ's name did *you* go through?"

"Listen, pal," he said, "on the first day of shooting on Midway Island I noticed that Ford was cutting out all the jokes between those enlisted men, so I said, 'What about those jokes?' He said, 'Don't bother me, asshole—get out of my way.' Then the fight was put in an ineffective long shot, and Fonda, who was accustomed to the laughter and action and excitement of the play, suddenly realized that none of it was taking place. It was all deadweight. And then what do you think happened?"

"Fonda spit in your face," I said.

"Worse than that. That night at the officers' quarters, Fonda was sitting in his cabin with a couple of the cast, having a drink, and Ford comes to the door and says, 'Well, Hank, what do you think of the day's shooting?' And Fonda said, 'I think it was shit,' at which point Ford stepped forward and punched Fonda in the jaw, knocking him to the other side of the cabin."

I said, "But Fonda is much stronger than—"

Leland said, "Sure, sure. But several guys grabbed Fonda and told him not to hit an old man, and others held Ford back." Leland watched my amazement. "That was openers. Josh, whatever I did wrong, I got paid for it that day. The rest of the picture was shot with Ford and Fonda in an armed truce. But from then on neither of them showed any enthusiasm for the project. Ford went a bit crazy. He began filming scenes that had nothing to do with the plot such as—like you say—men diving in comic, striped bathing suits, natives hugging the side of the boat in war canoes and shinnying up ropes, native girls wiggling through all the crew's quarters. But I didn't dare question him. He's a genius, Josh, and he seemed to know where he was going, although I'll admit he also seemed goddamned nervous."

"When did he go off the wagon?" I asked.

"In Hawaii—eight days later. Hank must have been too much

for him, too rigid, too unforgiving. And from then on Ford let everything go. And from then on we were all in a kind of churning, washing-machine limbo. Nobody knew who was in charge of what. Ford was pissed all day. Ward Bond, for Christ's sake, was directing the picture. At least he kept the cameras turning when Ford came to and until he passed out again. Eventually, someone got news that Jack Warner had said we've got to replace Ford. 'Replace John Ford!' I said. 'You can't replace John Ford—he's a giant!' But Jack did replace him, and the obvious choice was Jack Warner's close friend and troubleshooter, Mervyn LeRoy, who had wanted to direct the picture in the first place."

I said, "Leland, if you've got any picture today, that troubleshooter got it for you."

"Mervyn couldn't understand why Ford had begun to shoot Frank Nugent's fancied-up script—it made no sense to him. So he decided to throw it away and film the play straight from the published playscript. But poor Mervyn was stymied when he got to the scene where Doc reveals the details of the captain's name-signing contest. William Powell—he's an old man, Josh—had learned the crapped-up Frank Nugent version of the scene and was unable to unlearn it in a short time. And so, to keep the picture from running even further over budget, LeRoy filmed Nugent's version."

Leland kept flinching as he talked, like a cowering, whipped dog. He knew that whenever he put on that wounded-animal look—"Help me, will you, I'm in trouble"—you somehow believed him and went to help him, which is what I did, God forgive me.

I was given a cutting room and a cutter, and I took the film from the word go and started.

Mervyn insisted I help him shoot some retakes the week following: I worked each day cutting and most of the nights rewriting bits of scenes to match the mood and intent of the original play with this disparate footage.

I gave changes in close-ups to an actor or had lines spoken off-camera to the actor who would react to them. Some of the lines I put over the deck loudspeaker or squawk box. And to try to keep one of the swimming sequences, which was beautifully shot although totally against the spirit of the floating prison, I had the squawk box announce beforehand, "Now hear this! All men who have not been put on report for a week will now be allowed to swim for ten minutes. Hurry it up!" Then we could cut to Ford's swimming sequence for a few frantic dives without losing the prison mood.

I worked with Mervyn and the actors for several days on bits and pieces of dialogue and reshot the last scene of the picture, when Pulver knocks on the captain's door and demands that he give the crew movies tonight. It was the one scene in which Jack Lemmon had seemed weak originally.

We also reshot the soapsud scene, which became even more hilarious than onstage because we could go down below and see the companionways filling with suds.

The greatest tragedy of the picture, to my mind, was that Ford and Nugent and my pal Leland had decided to rewrite the nurse scene and bring in six nurses instead of one. In our play, one pitiful little nurse had been lured onto the boat by Ensign Pulver with the express intent of getting her down into his bunk. But she sees Mister Roberts and the result is a semiflirtation in which Pulver almost loses her. The crewmen hear there is a woman on board, and suddenly the entire ship's complement is crowded on the deck or hanging from ladders. Then comes the famous line, "I got a hundred bucks says she's the one with the birthmark on her ass." This causes the girl to leave, and all the crew's hopes of seeing naked women are finished—and Pulver is doomed to live another year of celibacy.

At the end of this scene, she signals her boat to go back to the island to tell the girls to pull down the shades in the shower room. The crew will be denied its greatest visual joy. The men disperse. Roberts, left alone, sees a pair of binoculars, shrugs, picks them up, and puts them to his eyes.

The entire scene was ruined for me by having six girls come on and destroy the sexual intimacy of the scene. Jack Warner promised to let me shoot the scene over again.

But halfway through the second day of the reshooting, I got a message from Jack Warner that he wanted to see me. It was to urge me to keep the existing nurses' scene. The background was so beautiful, he said; it was one of the only full scenes shot out-of-doors, in the Pacific, with an island showing. And even though he agreed that it wasn't as good as the original scene, if we reshot it on the little stage we had for the retakes, it would look like a smaller picture.

Leland urged me to give in, and I did, but it was painful.

Frame by frame, going from Ford footage to a LeRoy close-up to retake footage and back to LeRoy, then back to Ford, with added or subtracted sound tracks, the cutter and I finally put together a spit-and-toothpick version of *Mister Roberts*.

The picture, of course, was LeRoy's, since his were the only scenes that sounded like *Mister Roberts*. There are two obvious Ford touches, one magnificent, the other horrible. The magnificent one was a great leap on a motorcycle that a sailor made on the night of liberty, overshooting the pier and landing bike and all in the water. It was a hilarious bit of moviemaking and stunt work. The awful one was the ghastly nurses' scene.

To me, the picture belonged to Jack Lemmon, as Fonda had been more or less destroyed by Ford's treatment of the character of Roberts. Bill Powell had been directed to play his part as a drunk, which helped not at all, and one of the world's great actors, Cagney, had been persuaded to become a kind of Walt Disney character. The only thing to do about him was to pare him down as much as possible, play part of his scenes over reactions of others, and to play heavy "scare" music under all his entrances and exits.

Because two-thirds of *Mister Roberts* had been shot from our original play, Leland decided that as a reward for my efforts in reshaping the picture, I must have screen credit. Of course I couldn't be one of three directors, so he got me half credit for the screenplay. Screenplay by Frank Nugent and Joshua Logan, it said. What a joke! In this film, I longed to be forgotten. I didn't want my name or Tom Heggen's connected with this second-rate work.

But, as is the case with many stories that are fundamentally good, it is difficult to make them completely bad. I'll admit that if I hadn't known in maddening detail how good the play was, I would have liked the movie better, and the ironic part of it was that I had helped to make that movie.

But nothing about the venture depressed me as much as walking on the stage of the Writers Guild to receive an award for "the best comedy writing of the year," an award I "shared" with Frank Nugent, who, thank God, was not there. I couldn't have looked him in the face. I only accepted the award because Jack Warner asked me to, but I was blushing the entire time—all the way up and all the way down the platform—and then as I sat down beside him I gave Leland a crucified look. And he and Nancy looked as though they understood.

I sat there in a daze. All the work I had done was in desperation to avoid catastrophe. It wasn't a true *sound-as-a-nut Mister Roberts*. It was as stringy as old chewing gum. On the whole, I disliked it even though I'd worked for weeks to save its neck and, incidentally, mine.

But I had had my revenge. They had to send for me.

Revenge!

Who got revenge on whom?

This mock-up movie version of *Mister Roberts* was a hit. Not the great historic smash it should have been—but strong enough to make Leland a "successful" producer, to give Jack Warner a right to cut another notch in his gun, to win Jack Lemmon an Oscar.

The only true revenge was, unfortunately, on my close friend, Henry Fonda: a walking monster of revenge in the form of John Ford. Certainly their disagreements lessened Fonda's performance, and he must have felt it.

Although until recently he never said a word to me of his physical fight with Ford and the damage Ford did to the play he loved, I knew all along, and I'm sure he knew that I knew, what we both felt.

LAUGHING
WITH
FRIENDS

FORTUNATELY FOR ME, most of my friends are funny. And I've dined out on them for years. So let me share some of them with you.

While I was growing up in the South, there used to be an unspoken rule about telling Negro stories. You weren't allowed to tell any old secondhand Negro story, something from a joke book or a minstrel show. It had to be something that actually happened to you, something that you experienced.

I think I should apply that rule now to Dorothy Parker stories. I guess I've heard hundreds, and so have you. We all know what she said about Katharine Hepburn's performance in *The Lake*, and her poem about a madonna in a niche which she wrote after visiting San Simeon, but I accumulated a few of my own when I knew her during World War II and a bit afterward.

I'd imagined her to be sharp and somewhat tough, with a kind of acid edge to her voice. Instead, she was a beady-eyed dumpling, the sweetest-voiced of the mama dolls; also there was always a gush of emotion as she delivered barbs as though it killed her to say them.

"Oh, the *darl*ing," she would say, not quite meaning it, but somehow giving the impression that she *meant* to mean it.

I first got to know her when she and her husband and collaborator, Alan Campbell, invited me to have a drink with them
at "21" just at the beginning of the war. They had written a play
they wanted me to direct. Unfortunately, I was already booked
for a long bout with Uncle Sam and so I never got to read their
play. But the three of us began seeing each other for drinks. She
was full of concern for the boys who were going off to war; no
wisecracks about that, just true despair. Then I was inducted,
and so was Alan; I ran into him in a chow line in Miami, and
he and I began to pal around frequently because we were theatrical birds of a feather.

Just before Alan and I were admitted into Officers Candidate
School, Alan and Dorothy gave an enormous bash at their
rented apartment for all of their Army friends and their girls.
I would estimate that more liquor was drunk that night than
generally is consumed in all Miami even at the height of the
tourist season. The next day, most of us were varying shades of
green. Dorothy was a pale gray-green. Her cheeks throbbed
slightly and her eyes were more rheumily tearful than usual.

Alan and I were scheduled to be on a GI radio show on one
of the piers in Miami, so Dorothy, Alan, and I staggered down
and settled on a bench, waiting for the show to begin.

Dorothy looked so drawn and miserable that I decided to be
a Good Samaritan. I said, "Dorothy, there are several bars along
the beach. I'll go out and get you anything you like—a double
Scotch, a double rye, whatever. I might even find a little bottle
of gin."

"Oh, Josh," she said, "no wonder you have a Biblical name."

So I ran, having only about fifteen minutes, peering toward
the shore for an open liquor store, but I couldn't get off the pier.
Once GIs were signed in, for some stupid Army reason we
weren't allowed off, and there was no liquor bar on the pier. So
I combed all the various soft-drink stands, wondering if there
was anything that might bring her a little surcease or at least
calm down the nervous twitchings of her cheek. The only thing
I could find was Coca-Cola. I bought a bottle and put a straw in
it, then came back to Dorothy—rather sheepishly, I'm afraid.

"Dorothy, I couldn't get off the pier. I know Coca-Cola's not
strong enough to cure anything, but it's all I could get."

She said, "How sweet. Coca-Cola. I'll try it. I've never had a
Coca-Cola."

She took the bottle and sucked the straw, getting quite a large swallow, and then pulled the straw sadly from her mouth. There was a special concentration in her eyes.

"Did you swallow some?" I asked.

"Oh, yes, I took quite a large slurp."

"And did it help?"

"No, but as it was going down I learned a deep, abiding truth about drinking Coca-Cola."

"What's that?"

"Never send a boy on a man's errand."

Two weeks later we had another rollicking Good-bye-to-Alan-and-Josh party, and Nedda, who was to do a play, got off rehearsal for a day and came down for it. Dorothy and Alan soon had an open and terrible fight which ebbed and flowed all evening.

When Dorothy met Nedda the next day for lunch, she had a black eye. She started chirping. "They don't need us, Nedda, dear. They have their dear little Army, they have all their little squadrons and their silly guns to take apart, and their marching. They don't need us anymore at all."

"Nonsense, darling," said Nedda, trying to cover up the fact that she had noticed the bruise just below Dorothy's eye.

"And look—look what's happened—a beloved little mouse on my eye. That's not very pretty, is it? Not very pretty at all."

"Oh, don't let little things like that bother you, Dotty. It's a stressful time for all of us and besides, dear, we're all in the same boat."

"I know, Nedda, but my boat's leaking."

A year or so later I was with Alan in Paris where we had been assigned by some strange military miracle to offices in the same building. I was by then in charge of soldier shows and Alan had something to do with military information.

He had just returned from two weeks in London, and was reading a V-mail letter from Dorothy as I walked into his office.

"Look at this," he said. "It should go into the Smithsonian. Have you ever seen such a document in your life?"

He handed me the letter. The V-mail system had been invented so a large letter could be reduced onto a film strip by the postal service and then blown up to readable size again. The message of a V-mail letter had to be typed or written to fit exactly within the blank printed square on the V-mail form.

Typed by Dorothy, the message in the six-by-five-inch square read, "Dear Alan. For several weeks now I've been hearing about . . ." and then it went on sentence after sentence of tidbits like one I remember: "Kermit [Bloomgarden] whom I met on Fifth Avenue tells me that Lillian [Hellman] has been to Moscow." The "Yrs. Dorothy" came nearly at the end of the space allowed.

But there was a bit more space, and on it she had written: "P.S. If you will read the first letter of each sentence in this epistle you will find my real message."

And reading the first letters of these sentences spelled out these letters: F U C K Y O U.

But, since there was still one line of space left, she put an extra postscript. "PPS. Lucky I ran into Kermit. I was in trouble for a K."

End of letter. It fit the V-mail form perfectly.

* * *

I find it difficult to believe that such a thing as genius exists, but Fulco, the Duke of Verdura, shakes my disbelief.

He can create an effect with gold and precious stones unlike any other. In his workroom, he not only designs his rings and bracelets but paints miniature pictures of medieval ladies in costume that are jewels in themselves.

I discovered his great gifts once when I saw an antique ivory chessman that he had encrusted with jewels. The original chess set had been carved in ancient Persia, and the pawns were small warrior figures dyed red. Fulco took tiny diamonds, rubies, pearls, and bits of gold, and redressed his warriors in splendid fashion. I bought one for Nedda—a great success.

In the course of time, Fulco and I got to know each other not only at the shop but at parties or dinners. I found him to be as much fun and as outrageous a man as I'd ever met. He told me what has become a classic story in our family, about another friend of ours, the sensitive Cecil Beaton, designer and photographer.

Once, Fulco, perish the thought, went sailing in a small skiff with Cecil Beaton. Thinking of the two of them adrift on an ocean was to my mind as though Wynken and Blynken had left Nod and were on a wild spree. Fulco told me that as they sailed along, a squall came up and the boat began to rock in a violent fashion. So active was the movement that Cecil soon became physically ill and began vomiting rhythmically. Fulco scurried for a little bucket to catch the unpleasant stuff, but when he got it under Cecil's chin, Cecil screamed with pain. "Take it away," he wailed, "it's blue plastic."

* * *

Moss Hart and I grew to be very good friends early in my career, and then his wife, Kitty Carlisle, and Nedda and our children began to know each other. But one of our hurdles was that the Harts used to spend their summers down on the Jersey shore and we were far north in Connecticut. Once, Moss said, "Why don't you come down for the weekend?"

I said, "But, Moss, it would take a full day to drive there."

He said, "You can fly. The Westchester Airport's not too far from you. A plane should get you to us in an hour and a quarter at the most, and we'd meet you at our airport."

Since our children were small and had a fine nurse, we decided to go. Nedda and I climbed aboard a tiny plane which was to be piloted by a young man. It was scarcely larger than a toy model and seemed to be made of the thinnest silk. The near-adolescent pilot assured us it was in flyable condition and would get us there easily. We took off, feeling most squeamish as it rocked about in the air, especially as we each had the feeling that we could punch a hole through the walls of the plane with our elbows or fingers. We had been flying for about an hour, not too smoothly I might add, when the pilot, too, became rather nervous. He looked out of his window and down—too frequently for our complete peace of mind.

Finally, he turned his ashen face to us and said, "Do you recognize that racetrack down there?"

We both looked, and of course we didn't. Nedda said, "Maybe it's Monmouth. That's in New Jersey. But I have no idea."

He said, "Well, it's not here on the map," and he handed us the map. "I think I better glide over to the ocean and follow it down from there."

Nedda said, "Yes, and while you're doing that, could you instruct us what to do in case anything happens to you?"

He said, "Just push this lever and land, that's all," pointing to something in the front of his cockpit which neither of us saw. By this time Nedda and I would have gladly made a parachute escape if there had been a parachute.

When we got over the shore he looked down again and said, "I'm awfully sorry to ask you again, but is that Asbury Park or Atlantic City?"

We looked down and although I was beginning to have double vision, I figured it must be Atlantic City, although it seemed to me it could easily be Asbury Park. We wandered about along the coast, searching for the little airport where Moss and Kitty were to have met us half an hour before. All of us were too petrified to talk. Eventually, we saw the airport and eventually we landed and stepped upon the welcome earth.

As Nedda got out she said, "I will never go in a plane with only one pilot as long as I live."

"At least your kids know you're all right," said Moss. "I called your house when I finally saw you in the sky."

We drove to their comfortable house on the beach and had a lovely weekend with the two of them, going into the big waves or just talking—talking theatre, swimming, and then talking theatre some more until it was time for our trip home—on land this time, by bus.

* * *

One of my neighbors on Long Ridge Road was Joe Mankiewicz, the famous movie director and screenwriter. In the old days he used to come back from Hollywood to visit his pals on Broadway: Moss Hart, George Kaufman, and Marc Connelly. But none of them wanted to know what he was writing or directing in far-off California because they were too busy discussing the problems of their latest play.

Once, Mankiewicz broke in heatedly, "What's all this crap about how hard it is to have a hit on Broadway? I never heard so much talk. Someday I'm going to take six months off from Hollywood and write a hit just to show you how easy it is."

But somehow he never found those six months.

Years later, George Kaufman got very ill and was sent to the hospital where he was kept for quite a few weeks. One night there was a rumor that he was going to die before morning, but he passed through the crisis and in a few days he was allowed to have his first visitor, Moss Hart.

Moss told us the story. "I opened the door and looked into that room and had a terrible feeling I was seeing a ghost. It was all white—a white sheet and coverlet, George's white face against that sheet, with a pale white sun coming across the bed and spilling onto the white, white walls, and all rather dim. George looked like a corpse.

" 'Is that you, Moss?'

"I said, 'Yes, yes, George, it's me—Moss.'

"George said then, 'You thought I was going to die, didn't you?'

" 'Yes, I did. George, we all had the most terrible feeling you were going to die. The doctors couldn't tell what was wrong with you and we were worried, but thank goodness, you're all right now.'

"And then George said, 'There were other people who thought I was going to die, weren't there?'

" 'Yes, yes, all your friends—all of us—we all thought you were going to die. All of us thought it.'

" 'You should have reassured them, Moss.'

" 'What do you mean?'

" 'You should have told them I wasn't going to die until Mankiewicz had a hit on Broadway.' "

* * *

Leland Hayward was my producer on *Mister Roberts* and on several shows after that, but he had been my friend, my agent, and my general sounding board for so many years that I never knew where being a producer stopped and being just a friend began.

One of the things that always used to amuse me about Leland was his rather tough professional attitude when asked about certain subjects—namely, flying. The moment he had to talk seriously about flying, he became so professional, so offhand, so sure of himself that he was infuriating.

At one point, many years ago, Leland and I had to fly to the Coast. I had never really talked to him about the aviation side of his life, but I vaguely knew that he owned part of a West Coast airline, that he was a professional pilot, and that he sometimes flew his own plane either for pleasure or for business. Since the whole idea of flying was both repellent and terrifying to me, I never brought up the subject. But now we were passengers together in a plane headed first for Chicago—this tidbit of Hayward history took place quite a few years ago when planes stopped at least twice on the way to the Coast—and there was nothing to do but face the fact we were flying together.

As we took off, Leland and I occupied the two seats next to a window. I was really nervous, but Leland was only interested in the fact that we would soon be flying over Indiana where I had gone to military school at Culver Military Academy. He had just started to ask me about it when the pilot came by and spoke to him in a quiet, guarded voice.

Immediately, Leland put on his invisible flight commander's cap. The pilot leaned down and mumbled a few words in his ear. I was positive the engine had failed or something. Leland looked as though the pilot was giving him the most worthless information in the world, and after a shrug toward me he answered back in a mumble. Then the pilot mumbled a bit more, they shook hands, and the pilot went on down the aisle.

I looked at Leland immediately, expecting he would pass on the information, but no. Finally, I said, "Why don't you tell me what the pilot said, Leland?"

He said, "Because it's unimportant."

"Nothing is unimportant to me. Not in a plane."

"What he said is unimportant. He only told me as a matter of course because I happen to be another airman and would understand."

"What did he tell you?" I said nervously, almost shouting.

"He said that there was going to be a little 'weather' between here and Chicago, and that's all there was to it. He told me not to be surprised. Absolutely nothing to worry about."

"What do you mean, 'weather'? Does that mean bad weather? I'm worried enough right this minute to get off the plane. What do you mean, there's nothing to worry about?"

"There's *nothing to worry about!*" said Leland emphatically. "It's hard enough piloting professionals, those who know what it is to go through a little weather once in a while."

I said, "Why do you insist on calling it 'a little weather'? Why don't you just call it what it is: 'bad weather'?"

"Well, bad weather then."

"Do you mean to tell me that hearing that doesn't scare you just a little bit?"

"Of course not," said Leland. "I've been through it all my life. Oh, for God's sake, let's talk about Culver."

"No, wait a minute," I said. "How soon is this weather going to happen?"

"It's got to be at least an hour or more. Look how calm it is out there."

At this very moment, there was a stupendous crack in the sky. A long bolt of lightning shot down from above and wrapped itself like molten steel around the wing. I could feel that the plane had been jolted at least five hundred yards off its course.

Leland still tried to pretend calm but I was in panicked misery. "There you are!" I said. "That's what it is, and you said it was nothing."

"Well, that's nothing. That happens all the time, lightning going around a wing. It doesn't mean it's going to crash or anything like that." And as he was looking out, he said, *"Jesus Christ!!!"*

"What's the matter?"

"Another plane flew right under us—only a few feet away! Holy Christ! What's the son of a bitch doing up there in the cockpit?"

Leland turned around and saw all the passengers looking at him. He said, "Wait a minute. Look, they're all looking at us. Let's go on talking. I mean calmly."

I looked around, and everybody in the plane was quiet, slightly green colored, and it seemed they were struck dumb.

"WHAT TIME DID YOU USED TO GET UP WHEN YOU WERE AT CULVER?" Leland said, not realizing he was screaming.

I answered him in the same loud tone of voice. "Oh, five-thirty in the morning. That was early, you know."

"What did you have to do, did you have to FORM REVEILLE THEN?" he yelled.

"Oh, yes, we had to form REVEILLE. THEN THERE WAS sick call."

"That's a very interesting schedule," said he. By this time his voice had lost some of its force because he was talking without using up any air.

He said, "I'm going to call up that goddamned Jack Frye when I get off this plane and tell him what a lousy airline he runs. I'm gonna tell him. I WAS IN IT, I know what happened. I know how to land this plane—they shouldn't be going through all this weather. They should fly around it. That's terrible. GOD, LOOK!"

We both looked out and the clouds in front of us parted and we could see several stories of a skyscraper in Chicago with lighted windows—and I was looking at one girl who lifted her eyes and looked out of the window and then went back to her typewriting.

"My God, if we can see typewriters, we're flying through the Loop. Oh, my God, let's pray he can land the thing! Let's pray he can find another hole in the cloud!"

We landed, and Leland and I got out of the plane. I said, "Are you gonna call Jack Frye?"

He said, "You call him. I'm going across the highway there. They can't sell liquor on the airfield. So I'm going where they can."

The two of us sat guzzling Scotch until we could not walk, and when we were sure we could not walk, we held onto each other and staggered back into the plane where we found two seats and slipped into welcome oblivion and stayed there for the rest of the trip to California.

* * *

Marcel Pagnol was much more familiar with English than I had ever imagined him to be. He had even taught Chaucer in the original Middle English. But sometimes this member of the French Academy had his own version of the language.

While we were casting *Fanny* for the screen, I wrote to Marcel and suggested a French girl I had seen who, although she was not a star, seemed very charming and right for the lead part. Her name was Edith Fargay. After a while I got his handwritten reply with its surprising reversion to Middle English:

"Edith Fargay is a charming, lovely girl with great wit and ability, but she has breasts no bigger than mine, and I'm sure you agree with me that the girl who plays Fanny must be eminently and conspicuously fauckable."

* * *

When David Merrick entered the Broadway scene, it was a fairly dull street. But not for long. He brought back some of the excitement of Barnum and Ziegfeld. He not only produced plays but he sold them to the public.

David Merrick loved to get free publicity. For instance, on *Fanny* he noticed that some of the pedestals in Central Park which carried our statesmen had statues missing. David had a plaster statue made of Nejla Ates, the show's belly dancer, and put it up in the park in the middle of the night. This, of course, got the police out the next day, and it was photographed for the newspapers, and even got a three-page spread in *Life* magazine —and all with David's wicked mind, not his money.

When he produced *The Matchmaker,* shortly after *Fanny,* he had another brain wave. He bought an old English taxicab, with its high gates on either side, and had it transformed by a fine garage so that it could be driven from the rear seat without anyone noticing that the supposed passenger was actually driving. And in the front seat, attached to a rudderless steering wheel, he had a chimpanzee in a chauffeur's hat, with his hands strapped to the wheel as though he were steering. On the side of the cab was a sign which read, "I'm driving my master to see *The Matchmaker.* " The cab was driven all around Times Square four or five times a day, and had a hell of an effect. And pretty soon the entire theatrical district was talking about the latest Merrick stunt.

There was one outrageous hoax he pulled that he warned me about ahead of time, before it got on the front pages of most of the New York papers. David protected himself from being accused of perpetrating the stunt by leaving for London the night before. So he was safely abroad when at his Broadway production of *Look Back in Anger* a lady sitting in the first row suddenly became so infuriated that she got up and shouted at the leading man to stop treating women that way. She climbed up over the footlights and began to beat him on the head with her pocketbook. The stage manager pulled her away, the police were sent for, and she was booked on charges of disturbing the peace—charges David's office took care of. But of course she never would admit that she was in the employ of David Merrick.

David figured out very early in his career that anything said against the critics publicly and honestly in the way of attack was going to be greeted with delight by the ticket buyers as well as the actors and artists who worked in the theatre. So, he made it a permanent war: David Merrick versus the world of critics.

When one of David's musical shows opened and was pretty weak, the critics all said so, and vehemently, in their opening-night reviews. But the next day there appeared an enormous ad in *The New York Times* quoting what looked like the New York first-string critics, raving about what a great show it was, how much they loved it, how they felt the public was going to beat down doors to see it.

The only difference between this ad and a legitimate ad is that though John Chapman, Richard Watts, all said it was great, it was a different John Chapman, a different Richard Watts, etc., all down the line. David had gone through the phone book and found people with the exact names as the New York daily critics. He had brought them in to a preview, had treated them to a big dinner at Sardi's, and had urged them to say how much they liked the show, and if they liked it enough, they were going to get their names and pictures in the paper. And they did. Next to each name was a personal picture. It was surely one of the funniest tricks ever played on people by a theatrical producer.

When I congratulated David on doing this, he said, "But you know, I had to wait two years from the time I first got the idea."

I said, "For what?"

"For Brooks Atkinson to retire. To save my neck, I couldn't

find two Brooks Atkinsons in the world, much less in America."

But my favorite critic-baiting story of David is when he carefully seated the critics on opening night and just as carefully placed in front of them the center and forward players of the New York City college basketball teams. I never tried sitting behind a Wilt Chamberlain, but I can imagine it doesn't make for comfortable theatregoing.

* * *

Arthur Kober, with whom I collaborated on *Wish You Were Here*, was a droll man and we enjoyed each other enormously. Once he told me about the time he spent a night within the paper-thin walls of the Garden of Allah, the old hotel in Hollywood where the great stars of the twenties—Valentino, Theda Bara, et cetera—had wild parties.

Arthur had been married to Lillian Hellman, and the divorce had just been announced. It was practically his first night in a bed without a wife next to him. In the middle of the night, he woke up and he heard a sleepy, female voice close by saying, "Darling, would you get me a glass of water?"

He pushed his feet over the side of the bed, stood up, and padded dutifully to the bathroom where he filled a glass and came back to the bed and handed it toward the pillow. Much to his surprise, there was no one there.

But Mrs. Maxwell Anderson's voice through the walls said, "Thank you, darling."

* * *

The lush Hollywood, the ripe Hollywood, the Hollywood of the big studios with the biggest and most beautiful stars under contract to them, the Hollywood of Louella Parsons and Hedda Hopper, the classic Hollywood, is gone.

It has been watered down or it has just disappeared like invisible ink in front of our eyes, and now it's a different-colored place altogether, even though movies are still being made by the hundreds and grossing more than ever.

But fortunately for me and Nedda, we got a taste of that Hollywood before it had stopped glistening, and that was mostly due to Bill and Edie Goetz and their fantastic house on Delfern Drive in Holmby Hills, the heart of deluxe Hollywood.

Bill and I were making preparations to do *Sayonara*, so we had to spend a great deal of time together, and a good deal of that time was spent in their beautiful home. Edie—Edith Mayer

Goetz—was the daughter of Louis B. Mayer and was a kind of heiress or princess. Bill Goetz was a bit more sturdily self-made, but still from a strong movie family, and he had made millions of dollars in motion pictures. Their home had been decorated by the ubiquitous Bill Haines, and it had the traditional Haines signature—cabinets of Ming pottery and statuettes of Tang Buddhas. But the Goetzes had something even more spectacular, a collection of Impressionist and post-Impressionist paintings that was hard to rival in any private home in the world.

Their front hall, which extended from the entrance door toward the left about fifty or sixty feet, was hung heavy with Fauves, great Derain scenes on the Seine in the wildest of colors, equally spectacular Vlamincks, and two extraordinary Fauvist Matisses.

I used to make a pilgrimage to that Fauvist gallery every time I could and just stand while the colors washed about me.

The famous part of the collection was a little farther on in the great living room. The room itself was perhaps not of the most exciting shape. It was too long, too high, and tinted a faded turquoise; without the Impressionists it would have been quite ordinary. Arthur Hornblow called it an "elegant shoe salon." But on the walls was such a glory as is seldom seen. Entering the hall, I would pass a tall glass case with a little bronze by Degas of a fourteen-year-old ballet dancer. This imposing statue had a real cloth tutu. Of course, as in all of the dozen or so copies of the statue, the tutu had faded to a rust-brown; it still is one of the most touching and amusing objects in the world and certainly one of the most valuable. The room itself had two Cézanne landscapes, one enormous—a beach scene with the flags of the 14th of July by Monet—a large flower piece by Renoir, and in the corner the great Harlequin painting of a young boy, Picasso's son, by Pablo himself.

There was a large grand piano, and in front of it a white teddy bear cloth couch. There were low couches and divans all over the room, which when dinner was over was transformed into a cinema palace. The guests would arrange themselves in a comfortable seat close to one of Edie Goetz's great porcelain boxes of spectacular candy. Edie herself always stretched out on the couch to the right of the room facing the screen. But where was the screen?

When we were all settled, Bill pressed an invisible button, and music—rich, full melody—came up to us from all parts of the room, louder and louder as the lights grew dimmer. The 14th of

July Monet, plus the flower piece of Renoir, along with a marvelous painting by Toulouse-Lautrec of a French actress, all three paintings began to tilt in a frightening manner as they were sucked up through the wall to make room for the projectors behind them. It was all gruesomely mechanized. By the time everything was slitted and slotted into its proper place, the lights were totally out. Then a screen glided down almost invisibly from the ceiling from the far end of the room and the projection of the picture began.

This type of showing was known disdainfully in the profession as the Bel Air Circuit. I'm afraid it was not very popular, as the reports always came back that nobody liked the picture. The watchers were too busy making wisecracks for the delight of the group or for those who stayed awake.

Every time we dined with Edie and Bill it was an exciting occasion, not only because of the superb food but mostly because of the company. Beautiful ladies were in abundance—Claudette Colbert, Rosalind Russell, Natalie Wood, Ginger Rogers—and equally glamorous and famous couples—Gary and Rocky Cooper, who lived down the road, Clark Gable and Kay, Laurence Olivier and Vivien Leigh, Danny and Sylvia Kaye—but I think the most exciting and certainly the most lively night we spent at the Goetzes was when Edie asked us to pick up Sam Behrman at our hotel and bring him with us to dinner.

The great and fabulous Sam was in town conferring about writing another picture. He had scripted most of Garbo's. He was very suspicious of us all the way to the house, and kept saying, "Who on earth is going to be at this feast? I hate those pretentious affairs."

I said, "You know that it's got to be big, Sam—we're dressed."

He said, "Alas, but I don't like to be caught in a corner with people I hate."

As the butler opened the door, Nedda and I stood waiting for Sam to enter first. Sam simply peered through the door and looked beyond, trying to see into the room where they were serving cocktails.

"I won't go through that door," he said.

"Why not?"

"Look who's in there!"

We looked through the door at an angle and could see quite a few people. Among them was Mike Todd.

"It's Avram Hirsch Goldbogen."

"Who?" said I.

"Well, now he calls himself Mike Todd and even that doesn't keep him from being a Niagara of boredom, and I'm not going within five feet of him."

I said, "Oh, come on, Sam, we'll protect you," and Nedda urged him to come in, too. "You can lose Mike Todd in the crowd," I said. "Look how big it is."

But for some reason, Mike Todd was determined not to get lost. He was then in the midst of filming *Around the World in 80 Days* and he wanted publicity. His hands were constantly shuffling 8 x 10 glossies of shots of the various scenes and of people he had persuaded to play cameo parts in the film, and he never stopped rattling away about what a brilliant job his son was doing as a coproducer on the film. If there was the slightest pause in the conversation, Mike would say, "My son told me the other day . . ." or "My son said something brilliant the other day that I . . ." and unfortunately he would get most of the story told before someone could change the subject.

Dinner was even more turbulent. We sat at a table that was stretched as long as The Last Supper, with the most exquisite silver cups and bowls holding arrangements of fruit and flowers, marvelous candlesticks lighting up all our faces, and beautiful eighteenth-century china bowls of salted nuts and candies. Again, there was no conversation because that was still dominated by Mike Todd, who told us over and over again how he got the idea for the picture—never giving any credit, of course, to Orson Welles, who had done the musical with him on Broadway—and then how he got Marlene Dietrich to play in it, and Frank Sinatra, et cetera, et cetera.

Sam Behrman was not a reticent man. He loved to be in a conversation and he loved more to lead the conversation himself, but he always led it with an originality that was beyond compare. Listening to Mike, he was like a geyser that had a cap screwed on it.

Mike turned to Sam and said, "What's the matter, Sam? You don't look very happy. I know I've told most of my stories over again, but still, now really, be honest, what would you prefer to sitting there listening to me tell you stories of *Around the World in Eighty Days?*"

Sam looked at him with blazing eyes and said, "Solitude."

There was such a laugh around the table that Mike Todd turned green, brown, and then purple with anger. After that he shut up for a while at least.

Soon afterward we were asked to go back into the living room for coffee, and then the men separated from the women according to the best tradition of England and the Bel Air Circuit. Sam and I stood waiting for our cups, and to my surprise looked down to where Mike Todd sat staring furiously at Sam. Mike Todd lashed out in a way I had never heard him. It was a vicious street fighter talking, but he couldn't seem to think of anything more to say to Sam than, *"You're a Jew."*

I was sick with embarrassment and hated to think of what Sam was feeling. I expected him to turn to me and say, "Please take me home," but instead he said, in a very calm voice, to Mike, "That's right, and my name is Samuel Behrman," and then after a slight pause he said, "And it always has been."

* * *

One of the loveliest ladies I know is Dorothy Rodgers. She has a classic quality about the way she looks and dresses. Her voice is quiet, cultivated, and perfectly modulated. Because of her madonnalike looks, few realize that she really has the same kind of mind as most of us and that she enjoys a good joke as much as the next. During World War II, for instance, while everyone else was sending me V-mail letters with bits and pieces of theatrical news on them, Dorothy's weekly V-mail letters contained the latest bawdy joke. She knew it would be fun to swap it around with the other members of my Air Force outfit. I will always be grateful to her for those funny stories.

But I think the most original thing she ever said was years ago when she was on her honeymoon with Dick and visiting the huge dairy farm of Pat and Donald Klopfer, the famous publisher, in upper New Jersey. Eventually she was led to a shed where a team was milking cows. This was before the days of milking machines.

The city-bred Dorothy was fascinated. She had never actually seen milk coming out of a cow before.

Someone said, "Would you like to try it, Mrs. Rodgers?"

"Yes, of course." She sat on the little stool and was told exactly how to squeeze the cow's teat in the proper rhythm.

She tried it with enthusiasm, but after a while she looked up, quizzically, "I must be doing it wrong. It doesn't seem to be getting any bigger."

* * *

Many exciting people came to our lovely house in Long Ridge, and some of the best work I ever did was done in the living room or in the study with a book collaborator, composer, or lyricist.

But perhaps the most history-making event that occurred there was the day when Laurence Olivier called me up at the New York apartment and said, "Would you mind if Joan and I spent tonight at Long Ridge? We have to be in Connecticut tomorrow."

I said, "Of course. I'll call Carl and Selma, our couple, and they'll have it all ready for you."

Carl and Selma were the most perfect of perfectionists, and put everything in top shape. They went to the greenhouse and picked some beautiful orange-pink carnations to put in vases in all the rooms.

The next morning, Larry and Joan were called for very early, and before they left they posed for a photograph outside our house, wearing some of the carnations. The photograph was sent to us in a few days with a note, "Because of you, we were able to get married this morning. We could never have made it if we had had to come from New York. Thanks for the corsage. Love. Larry and Joan."

Much later, we were asked, "Is it true that Joan Plowright and Laurence Olivier spent their wedding night at your place in the country?"

"No," I said. "Not their wedding night—their dress rehearsal night."

* * *

Tom Prideaux is one of the best and brightest friends we have. He seems to be bursting with laughter always, or making us burst. He has a constant zestful gleam in his eye as he gathers the reactions to everything he experiences and files them away in the back of his mind for future use. He is one person who truly raises my adrenalin level whenever I even think of him. He speaks as he writes, with the exact word that he means, an accomplishment that was only equaled in my experience by Sam Behrman. We first knew Tom when my sister, Mary Lee, joined *Life* magazine and she and Tom became friends and coeditors in the theatre department of the magazine.

When Nedda and I flew to glorious pre-Castro Cuba in 1946 and rented a spectacular Spanish house near Havana, we soon made friends with some of the fine, patrician-looking Cuban families who were still allowed to live in Havana at that time. Our special favorites were the Arrellanos. One day the grandmother, a dark-haired, beautiful woman with an off-white porcelain face, flaming lips, and simple black dress, invited us to their customary Sunday luncheon for all her children and grandchildren.

I can see that gathering now—sixty or seventy of them, all darkly attractive—babies, toddlers, sons- and daughters-in-law —all unselfconsciously sitting in striking groups that might have been painted by Boldini. They were our dear adopted family. Yet we once came within an inch of embarrassing them beyond compare.

It started when Tom and Mary Lee flew down to spend a week with us. As we watched them descend the stairs from the plane, Tom's bow tie suddenly burst into brilliant light. Little flashlight bulbs in his tie were connected to a small wire behind his collar which led into the pocket of his trousers where it met a battery wire. When the two wires were pressed together, the tie could be seen for quite a distance.

We ached with laughter, as we always do when Tom reverts to the teenager.

Tom said, "Don't be jealous, I brought you one, too." I immediately took off my tie and was wired into my new light-up variety. I practiced turning it on by pushing my hand against my right pocket.

That night we were to have dinner with the Arrellanos and we were told to bring Tom and Mary Lee. Tom and I decided they would enjoy seeing the ties light up and so we wore them.

But the Arrellanos were really in no mood to laugh. Their very good friend, the mayor of Havana, had been shot that day and was lying in state at the city hall. They asked us to join them in going to pay honor to the corpse.

So Nedda, Tom, Mary Lee, and I packed into their cars, and pretty soon we were in the gracious, old, water-stained coral building that held the mayor's open casket. There was a vast central room two stories high, surrounded by the tallest, most overweight flower arrangements I had ever seen. I don't know how they were put together—or even squeezed into the room— but there were eight or ten of them, all at least two stories high. I thought, Those Cubans knew how to mourn. In the center of this vast room was the coffin, revealing half the mayor's body.

The mayor's lean widow stood by the coffin in a simple, short-sleeved black dress, her hair pinned back, wringing her hands, weeping, knocking her head against the coffin, and kissing the hands of friends who came by. A nurse stood by her.

On both ends of the casket were ten soldiers in full regalia, holding upright rifles with bayonets attached. There were armed military guards on the arched, second-floor balconies looking over the room. I don't know whether they expected some kind of riot or demonstration, but it seemed as though they felt the ceremony needed top protection.

We stood in the long line of mourners for quite a while as the people ahead of us paused by the casket, spoke to the widow. It was a most impressive and moving sight. But as we got closer, I could feel Nedda growing more and more nervous. Nedda has never looked upon a dead man or woman in her life. She just doesn't believe in the principle of looking at the dead.

Then Tom, behind Nedda, tapped me gently on the shoulder and said, "Don't touch your right pocket or we'll all be shot."

Good God! I remembered the bow tie. "Oh, no, I won't." I held my arm crooked and away from my right pocket to form a barrier against an accident. Nedda was behind me, whimpering. "I've never seen a dead person, I *can't* look at a dead person! What am I going to do?"

We were only two places away from the keening widow and her extremely dead husband, so I said, "Hide your eyes, pretend you're crying."

I was at the casket, the corpse slightly below my eye level, when I felt a terrific jerk at my right pocket. It was Nedda pulling my handkerchief out.

I noticed a strange expression on the widow's face as she stared right below my chin.

My God, the electric bow tie must be alight and gleaming! I smiled weakly and nodded to the widow. After a second she nodded back—tearfully, warmly.

After we passed, and none of the soldiers had pointed any guns at us, I whispered to one of the Arrellanos, "What on earth did the widow think? Oh, God, how awful!"

He said, "Well, the way I figure it was, she knew you were an American from the way you're dressed, and she must have thought this is an American custom at funerals—something like placing a candle or a flower around the casket."

But I was a wreck, and I took off Tom Prideaux's tie right there and then in the city hall, and I never put it on again.

DISASTERVILLE

WHAT HAVE the following got in common? *Tall Story, There Was a Little Girl, Ensign Pulver, Ready When You Are, C. B.!, Tiger Tiger Burning Bright,* and *Rip Van Winkle?* They are all part of Disasterville—my movies and plays that failed to pay back their production costs.

I make no excuses for them. I have a few reasons that I think make sense, but on the whole, when failure enters, it walks by itself. It doesn't need much aid.

Yes, I gave young, wildly talented Jane Fonda a very poor start to her movie career in *Tall Story,* and right on top of that a shaky debut on Broadway in *There Was a Little Girl.* I tried to tell myself that just bringing her to the attention of the theatre and movie public was enough compensation for me, but deep in my heart I knew it wasn't. I wanted to bring her to success. I thought she was bursting with talent, youth, and beauty. I cast her because I wanted those qualities and certainly not through any generosity to a young friend.

Jane Fonda is not really my godchild. We just kid about it sometimes because I was the godfather of Brooke Hayward, Margaret Sullavan's firstborn and a very close friend of Jane's. The two girls have known each other since they were babies, and I was very close to both their sets of parents long before the girls were born. I had watched Jane at various times since she was a little girl, and I must say that at all ages I found her to be irresistible.

When she grew up, she worked for a while for Warner LeRoy, New York's most spectacular boniface and Mervyn's son. Nedda invited the two of them out to our country house for Sunday dinner, and Jane sat there tossing her lovely head about and making long pronouncements about how she would never go on the stage or have anything to do with the theatre. Aside, Nedda said to me, "But she's got to be in the theatre. She's too heavenly to waste on anything else. She'll change—she's got to."

And sure enough, when I read in the fine print of a column one day that Jane Fonda was studying acting with Lee Strasberg, I knew Jane's life had taken a serious turn, because certainly no young people would remain in that atmosphere unless they were serious about going into the theatre.

I had agreed to do a film for Warner Brothers called *Parrish*, and for the young male lead I was hoping to make a discovery. A young man who had just played in a stock company production of *Compulsion* had made an impression, and I sent for him. He was all a director could hope for: tall, humorous, extremely male. He even sat down at the piano and played and sang. His name was Warren Beatty, and I decided to use him, though he had never been on the screen before.

Seeing him, I thought that now that Jane Fonda was interested in acting, she might be perfect for the girl. I made tests of both and signed them to personal contracts for *Parrish* and several pictures more. However, when I got the first draft of the screenplay I was so disappointed with it that I asked Warners if they would give *Parrish* to some other director and switch me to some other story they owned.

I learned that they had bought a flawed hit by Lindsay and Crouse based on a basketball scandal in which a young man is persuaded by gangsters to throw a game, and is adored by a little girl cheerleader who helps him clear his name. Julie Epstein had written an amusing René Clair type of script.

The part of the love-crazy pom-pom girl I offered to Jane Fonda, and she agreed to shift to *Tall Story*. Naturally, I wanted to use Warren Beatty for *Tall Story* as well, but I was persuaded by my agents to take an established name instead. I wasn't at all happy about losing my contract with Warren Beatty by not switching him as I had Jane, but I finally agreed to settle on one of my agent's clients, Tony Perkins, whom I had admired since his teenage days as an actor.

Although Tony was delightful as the basketball player, I was sorry again later not to have used Warren, as I would have avoided one mistake. During the filming of the picture Tony came to me and asked if he could go off privately with Jane to work out the love scenes with her alone. He would take the responsibility for the direction, but, of course, I could change anything later that I didn't like. He was so eager and enthusiastic that I said yes.

They worked very hard, devotedly in fact, on their intimate scenes. When they showed them to me they were strangely slow and full of pregnant pauses, but apart from that quite attractive, so I filmed them as rehearsed. Unfortunately, when cut into the picture they were endless and, I think, hurt the picture almost more than the charm of the two people in those scenes helped it.

Another young man played a small part, but made it stand out, as the football-playing married student. His name was Tom Laughlin, later of *Billy Jack* fame.

The picture *Tall Story* was certainly not a hit, although it will get its money back soon via television reruns. But it did get me one asset: a contract for several more pictures with Jane Fonda.

And, in addition to Laughlin, I made another great find in that picture. It was Hank Moonjean, the producer, who was then my first assistant director. I would say that if ever a gold statue is made to an assistant director, Hank Moonjean has got to pose for it.

While shooting *Tall Story*, I had visits with Dan Taradash, who had written the original screenplay for *Picnic* and who had just adapted another book into a play. When I read *There Was a Little Girl*, it was so fascinating and true that even though I knew it would shock most people, I wanted to do it.

It was about a young girl of a nice family who agreed to sleep with a boy in a motel room. The boy at the last minute is frightened, so he stops the car at a roadhouse for some Dutch courage. The girl is sexually aroused and insists that he stop stalling, but he has worked himself up with drink into an angry scene, and eventually gives her the keys to the car and shouts, "Go home by yourself." She takes the keys, and is followed out to the parking lot by a couple of young hoodlums who accost her, rape her, and leave her standing in pitiable confusion trying to flag a ride by the side of the road.

From then on, we are horrified to see the rest of the town, including her family, beginning to believe that she herself has invited the rape. In other words, the victim now becomes the culprit.

As it turned out, the subject shocked not only most critics but many in the audience, and though it had some avid defenders, *There Was a Little Girl* closed after three weeks.

But the important thing about the evening was Jane's performance. She was playing a lead, of course, for the first time on Broadway, but she was an instant professional. She wanted to be so perfect for the part that she warmed up by listening to meaningful music while putting on her stage makeup.

The Jane Fonda who later became so controversial was nowhere to be seen in those days. She must have been there somewhere, but the Jane I knew never gave a glimpse of her opinions on public affairs one way or another; she simply dedicated herself to being a good actress, a goal I think she has achieved to a degree that none of us ever dreamed of.

* * *

And Jane wasn't the only talent who helped lift me through some of my low spots.

I directed smiling Jack Nicholson in one of his early movie stints, a sequel to *Mister Roberts* which Peter Feibleman and I wrote called *Ensign Pulver*. He played Dolan, a crewman, with that same infectious verve that he uses so effectively in *One Flew Over the Cuckoo's Nest*. But Jack also appointed himself my "assistant producer": he helped me cast some of the other actors as well as Millie Perkins, the leading lady. He's more than an actor; he's an entrepreneur, tummeler, and an inspiration.

We thought we had everyone in the picture that anyone could ask for—Walter Matthau as the funniest Doc possible, Burl Ives as the Captain, Robert Walker, Jr., as Ensign Pulver, Millie Perkins and Kay Medford as nurses, Diana Sands and Al Freeman, Jr., as natives, Larry Hagman and Peter Marshall as officers, and James Coco, James Farentino, and Tommy Sands as crew. But we had left out the most important thing: the catalytic agent, Mister Roberts. And without him, the story falls into shreds. No one really cares about the others enough to create suspense as to the outcome.

The picture is still out and is often shown on television reruns, and, like *Tall Story*, it will earn all of its money back, but although it was really very funny, it will never be a completely satisfactory entertainment, no matter how much we enjoyed making it.

* * *

To my mind Susan Slade's little fabrication, *Ready When You Are, C. B.!,* as produced by David Black, was a cleverly made play of the spit-and-toothpick school.

Julie Harris, that most extraordinary of actresses, gave prestige to the project by agreeing to play the fussbudget loner lead, and Lou Antonio played the flamboyant movie star (modeled on Brando) who came to New York to escape from his studio's command to work in a cheap Roman epic. He wanted to hide in her nondescript apartment so as to avoid the picture sleuths and autograph phalanxes.

It was quite funny and a bit slapstick, with two dominant characters, and I would say if it had one fault it was because Susan Slade insisted we keep the unhappy ending. Some plots are strong enough, important enough, such as *Two for the Seesaw,* to make a sad ending believable, but this was fluff, and I think it should have ended in happy fluff. As it was, it led the audience along, promising a lollipop, and at the last moment jerked the lollipop away.

The joy of working with Julie Harris was great and as rewarding as the one-dimensional role allowed. And there was another remarkable actress, Estelle Parsons, who gave character and substance to another rather shallow piece of character writing. Lou Antonio was a fiery, funny Brando type.

I am sure this play would have gotten a good run if I had been strong or clever enough to get the author to give some kind of growth or self-revelation to the Harris part. Even as it was, however, it bumped along for a month or so before closing, and I'm told it lost very little money.

* * *

The only all-black play I have done so far, *Tiger Tiger Burning Bright,* certainly had the most distinguished cast of black actors ever assembled: Alvin Ailey, Robert Hooks, Diana Sands, Cicely Tyson, Roscoe Lee Brown, Ellen Holly, and Al Freeman, Jr., supported the central character, Claudia McNeil, who played the old rhinoceros of a mother.

From the start of rehearsal, Claudia was so full of all kinds of defensive feelings that I found it more difficult to direct her than an arena full of people. She twisted everything I said to her into some kind of prejudice or cant. We did a bit of shouting, I'm afraid. It's the only thing that worked.

Aside from that obstacle race, I thoroughly enjoyed working with the rest of the cast, and especially with young Peter Feibleman, the author, who wrote hard and well. Eventually, it was a fascinating evening. Feibleman had written a beautiful family story with no reference to time.

But good as it was, it had a terminal flaw: it opened during the newspaper strike of 1962, and none of the fine notices the critics wrote for it could be read by the public. Consequently, it closed in three weeks. What a loss.

* * *

Two of my biggest musicals closed quickly, one on its out-of-town tryout. They lost more than their initial investment, and yet I think everyone connected with them would count them to be near-misses.

Hot September seemed to be a smash when it opened in Boston. It was a musicalization of the play *Picnic* combined with the movie I had made of it. Paul Osborn did the script, and the score was by two young people with enormous talent. Kenneth Jacobson, a lean, aquiline young man, was the composer; Rhoda Roberts did the lyrics. She was stalwart, poker-faced, with very sharp, raisin eyes. Bill Inge had described her to me: "Valiant is the word for Rhoda."

Leland Hayward had brought the project to me, but we both agreed that we could use the help of David Merrick, who stepped in to make joint decisions and carry joint responsibilities. The entire backing was supplied by a record company.

At first, we were unlucky with the casting as M-G-M would not free Chad Everett from his obligation to do a picture for them. He was a big loss, I'm positive, but Katherine Hayes made a lovely Madge, and we had extraordinary people in the surrounding parts. Lovelady Powell as Rosemary was made by God for the part. Eddie Bracken as Howard and Lee Lawson as Millie, the younger sister, were perfect. The whole production was a joy to me, with two exceptions.

Number one was the dances. The composer and lyricist had brought the story up to date, which really meant that the dialogue had the nostalgic sound of the fifties but the dancing was up-to-date mid-sixties, with all the twisting and separation of bodies to a loud rock beat. That type of sound made Hal's and

Madge's romantic dance anachronistic, like an exhibition ballroom couple on a nightclub floor.

And the other, and subtler, mistake I feel we made was when we had Hal and Madge sing several songs to each other early in the play, establishing a contact which should have been saved until their coming together for the first time late in the story.

With these faults—and a few more—we opened in Boston to a cheering audience and good reviews.

But the real killer for the show was the fact that my producer pal, Leland Hayward, began to get nervous over our beautiful Madge, Katherine Hayes. He felt she wasn't strong enough, and she in turn felt his disapproval. Leland worried over her so much that after we opened in Boston he and David Merrick got together and insisted that we try another girl in the part.

I loved Katherine Hayes, but I finally succumbed and a new girl went on. The very pulp of life went out of the show that night.

After much talk, the producers agreed that the only way to turn the show into a solid hit would be to take it on to Wilmington or Philadelphia, which would have meant spending another $250,000 on fixing it. But since there was very little interest at the box office either in Boston or New York, Merrick and Hayward decided quickly to close it and cut their losses. I was sick, as I could clearly see how with time I could make the show work.

The moment everyone gathered onstage to hear the announcement of the closing, my collaborators turned to me and let me know in no uncertain terms that they felt the whole thing was my fault. Perhaps it was. Perhaps I should have fought Leland harder on the girl, fought to have them spend the money to continue the road tour. I still feel it was a near thing, that show. I can still hear the applause for Rosemary and for little Millie, and the lovely melodies that filled the score. But money allows no argument.

The other big loser was *Look to the Lilies,* Jule Styne's and Sammy Cahn's musicalization of *Lilies of the Field,* which had been a very successful movie ten years before starring Sidney Poitier among some German nuns.

I was not in on the beginning of the writing of this musical, so I never really caught up with it. I felt as though I were running ten yards behind them all on a treadmill. Somehow, the book by Leonard Spigelgass didn't work as easily as it had in the motion picture, and the songs, good as they were, didn't quite lift it into topflight entertainment. I worked hard, but it seemed as though I were going against the current.

Shirley Booth was a bit remote, and Al Freeman, Jr., who played the young black vagabond looking for work, and who had been so brilliant as the subnormal brother to Alvin Ailey in *Tiger Tiger Burning Bright,* was my Waterloo.

He had been so much fun to work with earlier that I was enthusiastic about being with him again. I used all the force I had to get him the part. But I regretted the decision almost immediately, as something seemed to have happened to him since those days. There was a superiority and an antagonism about him from the moment he walked onto the rehearsal stage. The warm, cozy friend had vanished. I felt that I was directing a personal enemy, a porcupine. He kept saying, "You're a bad director. You never tell me what to do."

Meantime, the book was not improving either, although the songs soared. I kept feeling I ought to be able to help it, but each day it grew more confused. To me, it was my personal failure.

But then, all directors can take the blame for failure, as it's generally their fault. The moment a director agrees to direct a story he has played the first card in his hand. His taste is up for judgment. The casting is quite obviously his fault, as it is impossible for the world to know how many people were tried before there was acceptance. And if the scenery is bad, that's the director's fault, too. He has had a chance to discuss it with the designer and he has seen the model. When an author has written a boring scene, it's still the director's fault; he should have cut it or speeded it up some way.

What a director does is so personal, so spiritual or ephemeral, that no one should see it, and therefore it is seldom seen. A good director makes everything he does look like nothing. A director edits fellow artists' work, shortens scenes, simplifies scenery and performances, controls the attention of the audience, tells that audience what to feel, whom to like, whom to hate, whom to forgive, whom and what to care about; also, what to be afraid of, what to dread.

If a play is wrong, sometimes he can convince an author to rewrite, or a producer to buy a new set of costumes. But mostly, his work is emotional. He must encourage gently or praise extravagantly—yes, sometimes fight with an actor to get the proper attitude for a scene. He must teach, coach, counsel, be a confessor, an analyst, a father.

* * *

Moss Hart was once asked, "When exactly is a play a hit or a flop? At what exact moment? When it opens in New Haven? In New York? The first time it's read aloud? The first dress rehearsal?"

And Moss said, "A play is either a hit or a flop when the author wakes up one morning and says to himself, I'm going to write a play about . . ."

Oh, but it's so hard to judge at that moment, as I discovered. A man I hardly knew named Ray Stark called me and said he was going to become a more active producer and wanted to see me. When we met, he asked me to consider an idea that he had of doing the story of his wife's mother and father—Fanny Brice and the gambler Nicky Arnstein. The thought of trying to capture Fanny Brice with someone less talented seemed unimaginable. I actually felt sorry for him for having such an impossible idea.

Funny Girl became one of the great successes of all time and established the hottest box-office star of her day, Barbra Streisand. I'm still embarrassed at my lack of foresight, but Ray, with whom I later did *The World of Suzie Wong*, never kidded me about it.

When I turned him down about Fanny Brice, he asked, "Is there anything you'd like to do?"

I said, "There's a movie I've had a lifelong passion to do."

"What's that?" he said.

I said, "Now hold your breath. It's *Tom Jones* by Henry Fielding, one of the earliest novels ever written."

He said, "Oh, *Tom Jones*. I think I remember that novel from school."

I said, "I read it as a freshman in Princeton and fell on the floor laughing. It's got the most outrageous situations possible, and they're quite up-to-date. There's even a period in it when poor Tom thinks that he's been to bed with his mother."

Ray said, "Great. I'll try to get it, at least. I'll register the title."

I said, "Register every possible kind of title there is. *Tom Jones Bastard,* anything that might keep other people away from it."

When I next saw Ray Stark, I said, "There's only one thing I want to hear. Are we in business with *Tom Jones?*"

He said, "I hate to be the one to tell you this. Tony Richardson and John Osborne have not only registered *Tom Jones*, but, more than that, Osborne is halfway through the screenplay and Albert Finney is going to play the lead."

My heart sank. I had been trying to get producers to do that book for years. I had even acted bits of it out in Jack Warner's office, in Buddy Adler's office, in Harry Cohn's office, while they watched me with blank or crossed eyes. The only answer they could think of was: public domain. "We can't do anything that's in public domain. The moment we start it, someone else can start it."

Well, the only people who didn't let that stop them were Tony Richardson and John Osborne. I knew *Tom Jones* was going to be a success. The pain of it was knowing it wasn't going to be mine. There's not a day that I don't still think about it.

* * *

In my time I did not have a rosary of failures; they were separated by a middling-type hit or even big hits, but there were a goodly number of duds, as you can see. However, each one of them started out as promising as the biggest success I ever had. It was impossible to predict which way they would go. The fact that so many of my shows went to the top was one of the miracles of my life, and I have lived through miracles.

Some of my failures—or disasters, as we call them—were deserved. They were bad ideas when we first got them and we should have recognized them as such before we went into rehearsal or, better still, before we raised the money. And some were near-greats, so close to being successes that we didn't know they were collapsing until the moment before they did.

Blue Denim definitely was not among the disasters. (I do not refer to that botch of a movie based partly on it.) I loved every moment of my work on the play.

James Leo Herlihy and William Noble wrote it, and it was offered to me by James Hammerstein, Oscar's and Dorothy's son, and by Jimmy's partner, Barbara Wolferman, a bright girl who had helped us before on casting and in various other ways.

It was a very personal play about a young boy, Arthur, played by Burt Brinckerhoff, who lived with his family without any real communication.

Arthur has a tender affair in the cellar with a fifteen-year-old girl played by Carol Lynley (who was herself fifteen) and when his love becomes pregnant, Arthur goes to his man-of-the-world friend, Ernie, for advice.

Ernie, played by Warren Berlinger, is a teenage sophisticated know-it-all. He gives authoritative answers to all professional questions asked him. He loves being Mr. Big.

But when Ernie is actually confronted with the word "abortion" he collapses and admits that he knows absolutely nothing. Eventually Arthur has to steal money from his father for this forbidden operation.

We found marvelous actors for the father and mother and sister: Chester Morris, June Walker, and Pat Stanley.

Rehearsals went well and by the time we got to Philadelphia the play showed great promise.

But as I studied it, I realized that the whole abortion thing was not as climactic as it could be, and I went to work with Herlihy to see if we could fix it. Jim Herlihy rewrote the third act one afternoon and Bill Noble, his coauthor, approved it, and we put it in.

The New York notices were all we could wish. But for some reason the play never did quite have a real impact on the public. It sold out only on weekends.

Twentieth Century-Fox bought the movie rights very cheap. They argued that because of censorship they could not use the central idea of the girl actually having an abortion. They had to save her from it at the last minute.

By shirking that ugly situation they took out the truth, the guts, the intestines, the liver, all the vital organs of the story.

Another moderate hit, but one which I feel could be a perennial, was *Rip Van Winkle*, which I did with Ralph Allen for the Kennedy Center Bicentennial season.

Ralph and I studied all the versions of the play, plus Washington Irving's story and all his writing around the area and period. We went back to the original story, and tried to keep to its humor while we extended it to a full evening. I decided it would enhance the evening to add five or six songs, which we also resurrected from period tunes.

Anthony Quayle, the distinguished British actor, played Rip, and I learned what it means to have a proven artist to call on. It seems he can do anything—any accent, any dance steps. Having played everything from vaudeville to classic theatre, he was a treasure chest of quips, jokes, snatches of song, and comic pantomime.

It was a lovely production, except that the deck stage meant the play needed two days to set up, and we were forced to close just as we were ready to tour the country and play Broadway for a limited run.

But that is just another iron in the hot coals of my fire. I have lots of plans. Any of them could land in Disasterville, but today they look in the distance like beautiful, snow-capped mountains.

Emlyn Williams, Richard Halliday, Mary Martin, Albert Hague, and Josh discussing *Miss Moffat* in Rio de Janeiro.

Miss Moffat. Bette Davis teaching class. Dorian Harewood in dark suit. (Françoise-Marie Benard)

Miss Moffat. Bette Davis and her prize pupil, Dorian Harewood.
(Jos. Abeles Studio)

Henry Fonda visiting his daughter, Jane, on the set of *Tall Story*. (Warner Brothers Pictures Distributing Corporation)

Tall Story. Jane Fonda as cheerleader. (Warner Brothers Pictures Distributing Corporation)

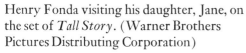

Tall Story. Jane Fonda and Anthony Perkins discovering the joys of a trailer. (Warner Brothers Pictures Distributing Corporation)

The set of *Blue Denim*. Burt Brinckerhoff, Carol Lynley, and Warren Berlinger. (Eileen Darby–Graphic House, Inc.)

Ensign Pulver. Front row, left to right: Walter Matthau, Robert Walker, Peter Marshall, and James Coco. Larry Hagman behind Peter Marshall. Missing: Jack Nicholson, Burl Ives, and Tommy Sands. (Warner Brothers Pictures Distributing Corporation)

Ready When You Are, C. B.! Josh, Estelle Parsons, Lou Antonio, Arlene Galonka, Betty Walker, and Julie Harris. (Jos. Abeles Studio)

Josh in action. (John Swope)

MISS DAVIS REGRETS

BETTE DAVIS has given close to fifty years of great performances on the screen, and yet to my mind none of these compares to the performance she gives off-screen.

The true story of Bette Davis's career is surely one of the most complicated, turgid, and confusing ever told. In fact, I'm sure it hasn't been told, and probably never will be. This is partly because she has been protected by her co-workers, producers, and agents, and partly, I deeply believe, because she has concealed great areas even from herself.

She's madly talented, with a God-given gift for sharp wit, humor, and vitriol. She can play any role to which she is physically suited better than anyone else in her profession. On the screen she can be convincingly warm, even joyfully so. But many who have worked with her have come to believe that all that joy and warmth are saved for the money public: they feel that there is little wasted on co-workers.

Perhaps she has an aversion to the soft, a loathing for the sentimental. It is as though, whenever she enters any room, she is compelled to use her favorite silver screen expression, "What a dump."

Because I was going to direct her, I went out of town early in 1974 to see her successful one-woman show. It was revealing. As she answered the questions shouted at her from the audience, it was as though she had become an amalgam of all her screen roles plus all her impersonators. Her trademark has become the big inhale and the slow exhale through the nostrils like an exquisite dragon. Her voice gets hoarser, the smoke bellows and billows about her, and sharp nasality whips out the bull's-eye answers when questions are fired.

"How old are you, Miss Davis?" was called from the crowd.

"I'm sixty-six years old. Next question, please." Puff-puff, snort-snort, and eyes rolled to heaven. Applause from the public amazed and delighted by her blatant truthfulness.

Soon the theatre is awash with honest candor and sharp judgment.

Her opinion of Errol Flynn?

"He was pretty but he was no actor."

Giggles of shock, disapproval, and wicked enjoyment.

Her opinion of a certain director?

"He can't direct himself out of a paper bag."

By now, the audience and the stage had become giddy with the ebb and flow of Davisiana. Even the drinking fountains seemed to have been spouting truth serum, and everyone had a sip. It was a bacchanal of raw personal exposure, a mass baptism of pumped-up candor. She finally exited and came on again for her bow. There was a standing ovation. She went offstage. They sat. She came on again. They stood again. They were cleansed, saved. Amen.

She was so bright, so sharp, witty, direct, so positive about her quick answers that to my eye the public was completely under her spell. They were convinced that she is that way always, and, of course, in one sense they are right.

She can be spontaneous, brittle, hilarious, and thrilling—*if* she doesn't have to learn lines or play parts as the author wrote them. That's hard concentrated work, the kind of work that turns her into an entirely different kind of person. The French have a perfect phrase for it: *un cheval d'autres dents* (a horse of different teeth).

I had nearly met Bette Davis back in 1952 when I got a call from Jerome Robbins, who was in Detroit directing *Two's Company,* a revue. It starred Bette Davis and had music by Vernon Duke and lyrics by Ogden Nash and Sammy Cahn. But Robbins, brilliant as he was, was having great difficulty solving the show, for Bette Davis had ideas of her own. He had asked her permission and that of her then husband, Gary Merrill, to have me fly out, and he said they both agreed and that I should bring along someone who could write. I brought Paul Osborn, a man I have always trusted as a playwright, especially brilliant as a troubleshooting playwright.

Paul and I arrived in Detroit, went to the theatre, and sat down to see the show. I must admit I was terribly excited at the prospect of seeing the stunning Bette Davis onstage, hearing her sing, perhaps even dance. I sat back, prepared for a great evening, no matter what Jerry Robbins's fears were.

The show started and continued, and I kept waiting for Bette Davis to appear. Finally, the first act was over and she had still not appeared onstage once, although in the program she had been listed at least six times. I couldn't decide whether I was more frustrated or infuriated. The trip from New York had been hard enough, but the trip through that first act was the Gobi Desert. I went to Jerry at intermission. He said, "She won't come on. She says her first-act scenes aren't good enough, so she just told the stage manager to cut them tonight."

I said, "But doesn't she have any sympathy for the audience? That they paid money to see her?"

Jerry simply shrugged his shoulders.

In the second act she appeared three times and was marvelous each time. She sang one song, making the points as expertly as a Bea Lillie might. She did a hillbilly character with blacked-out teeth who sawed at a bull fiddle with a crazy kind of bumpy rhythm. She was all that I dreamed Bette Davis might be in a musical.

Paul and I were taken back to her dressing room by Jerry. But the only one we got to see was Gary Merrill, who had been in *This Is the Army* with me. I was hurt that Bette would not see us, not even long enough to thank us for coming. Possibly that's the real reason she didn't appear. She didn't want us to come, so why thank us? Her honesty syndrome again.

I left town with Paul, and Bette's show went on selling out in Detroit, and eventually came to New York City and played ninety performances, some of them without Bette Davis. The producer told me that Bette was sick and missed a large number of performances. No one seemed to be able to find out exactly what her illness was, but in March 1953, she discovered that she possibly might have an infected wisdom tooth.

The producers were relieved, thinking that as soon as the wisdom tooth was removed Bette would come back to the show a new woman and miss no more performances.

But she never came back to the show. It closed, losing most of its initial cost. It was rumored that she had a very bad bone disease called osteomyelitis which might necessitate having part of her jaw removed.

Broadway almost went into mourning. For years, rumors reverberated that Bette Davis would never appear again, that she was the victim of an incurable disease, that her looks had been destroyed by an operation on her jaw, and that she could neither talk nor act anymore. Fortunately, none of this was the case.

In 1959, Bette Davis and her husband did a reading of Carl Sandburg's poems arranged by Norman Corwin. She toured for months and to everyone's surprise *she never missed a performance.* Although she and Gary Merrill decided to separate in the midst of the Sandburg readings, she continued to appear, and Leif Erickson replaced Merrill onstage.

The producer expressed regret to me that the critically successful tour lost money, which must have upset her enormously because she had been one of the greatest box-office draws in the country. But at least she performed constantly and with no signs of the reported illness of a few years before—happily not even an uneven jawline.

Perhaps her most spectacular stage performance was as the fleshly Maxine, proprietor of the Mexican fleabag hotel in Tennessee Williams's *The Night of the Iguana.* The night I saw *Iguana,* Bette made the evening for me. She was svelte, handsome, voluptuous, wicked, wise, raffish, slightly vulgar—in fact, she was ideal for the part and gave the play an added dimension. I immediately made plans to bring all my friends to see the show.

But before I could arrange it, Bette Davis left the cast. There were rumors that she was sick again; there were other rumors that she wasn't sick at all. Whatever, Bette Davis was no longer in the cast. Cause unknown.

Then came another rather extended period when Bette played a few oddball and aging women in increasingly poor film melodramas. A couple of them were financial successes, but Bette, uncomfortable in "trash," seemed to have reached a stalemate.

Kismet took over my life at that point, for through a series of mishaps, I landed on the boulevard of broken dreams, or Bette Davis Alley. But it was a long voyage.

It started happily enough with a telephone call from Brazil from Richard Halliday, Mary Martin's husband.

"Josh," he said, "find something for Mary. She's dying to work, and I'm dying for her to work. She's only happy when she's busy, and I'm sure you can find a story that she'll like. Please do it, and call me if you get any ideas at all."

I was thrilled that they wanted me. I told Dick I'd get after it at once. I made several calls to friends of mine whose theatre knowledge I trusted. One of them 'was Margalo Gillmore.

"Margalo, can you think of some story that might interest Mary Martin—as a musical, of course?"

"What about *The Corn Is Green?*" said Margalo. "It seems to me I've heard something about her interest in that story, and I think she'd be marvelous."

I pondered the idea for a while. Certainly, Miss Moffat, the Welsh schoolteacher, was the right age for Mary, and the story was full of emotion, which would lead naturally to songs.

I called Richard. If I could clear it, would Mary be interested in *The Corn Is Green?*

"Oh," he said, "she loves *The Corn Is Green.* We both read it recently."

I wrote a long letter to Emlyn Williams, its author, explaining the interest that the Hallidays had in the property, and asked him if he would consider turning the play into a musical. He replied that the only way he would consider it is if I would read the unproduced version he had written in 1964. He had changed his locale from a mining town in Wales to the cane fields of the American South, and had transformed Miss Moffat's most talented pupil, Morgan Evans, into a black field hand. He mailed a copy of *Miss Moffat*, as it was now called, to me immediately.

I let it lie on my bedside table for several days, in craven fear of reading Emlyn's idea of Southern dialogue. Finally, Nedda read it out of growing embarrassment that I was taking so long, and she told me emphatically, "If you don't read this wonderful play, you'll regret it the rest of your life."

And she was right. My doubts were groundless. I was enormously impressed with Emlyn's ability to assume the American idiom, even my own Southern idiom, and I was reconvinced of the basic power of his story.

He had even written trial lyrics in order to demonstrate songs he envisioned. I found these trial lyrics so strong that it seemed to me he didn't need any other lyricist.

There was a startling lyric toward the end when the young black student, Morgan Evans, now on his way to Harvard, thanks Miss Moffat for giving him all the books she wanted him to absorb. He said, "Those books are always in my mind. I can see and feel them, and sometimes, funny as it sounds, I even smell them. Yes, that's the strongest feeling of all," and then he started to sing Emlyn's words.

> In *Wuthering Heights,* the smell of the mist;
> The smell of poverty, in *Oliver Twist. . . .*

and it continued to the final line, when he sang,

> I will never forget
> The debt I owe . . . to you.

There was an equally moving song for Miss Moffat after that, when he goes away to college and leaves her. As a teacher, her happiness is not finished. "I shall experience it again," she sings:

> No, I shall not resort to grieving
> That a very special boy is leaving.
> I shall experience it again.

The thought that Emlyn might be the lyricist appealed to me enormously. But I knew a composer might be unwilling to take on a new lyricist.

At that time I was having daily conferences with the composer Albert Hague. He had written the music for two very big hits, *Plain and Fancy* and *Redhead.* He was an important composer but I decided to take a flier.

"Albert," I said, "would you be willing to write on spec four or five songs based on some lyrics by a new lyric writer, the great and distinguished Emlyn Williams?"

He said, "Just give me the lyrics and get out of the way."

I was leaving in a week or so for Europe and I wanted, if the songs were finished, to take Albert along with me to play them for Emlyn and receive his blessing. And that's what happened. Albert finished five songs, including the marvelous "The Debt I Owe" and "I Shall Experience It Again." Soon, Nedda and I found ourselves in our new apartment in London with Albert, playing the score for Emlyn. Emlyn was captivated by Albert's music and his personality.

In a moment of enthusiasm, I financed a trip to Brazil for

Albert and myself. Emlyn had already been booked on a South American tour of his one-man show as Dickens, and so I thought that if we could work out a proper time schedule the three of us could go to Mary Martin's home and play some of the songs for her.

Albert and I flew to Rio de Janeiro, met Emlyn, and the next morning flew to Brasília, where we were to be met by a chauffeur who would drive us north to Mary's home.

I had always imagined Brazil as lush and tropical, something from a Douanier Rousseau painting, but as our plane started lowering for its landing at Brasília, I saw in front of me what looked like a leafless desert, in the center of which was a cluster of tall, ultramodern buildings. It was as though a gargantuan child had played in a vast sandbox with a new Erector set. Brasília from the air was all clean, mathematically perfect metal and glass; but it seemed as though all vegetation had been destroyed for miles and miles around by some defoliating enemy chemical.

When we were all packed in the car, we took off on one of the most arid rides in the Western World. We passed vast stretches of sandy soil on which, spasmodically, a few thirsty tufts of crabgrass grew. There was not a tree in sight the whole way, and nothing that resembled one—not even a bush. Along the road, no happy peasants walked carrying baskets on their heads; the roads were deserted. As we rode on and on, we saw no villages, no homes, no houses, no cars, no animals—there was nothing but the long stretch of macadam cutting those arid, sandy wastes in half.

Eventually, three hours later, we came to a pitiful, bleached-wood town with a few dusty, ramshackle buildings looking out on backyards filled with broken bottles and rusty tin cans. This was the resting place.

After a warm Coca-Cola, we took off again for another half hour's ride to the Halliday house. Suddenly, there was a patch of green in the distance, and as we approached it, we saw bamboo trees growing out of the yellow-gray sand. Over a gate were the words Nossa Fazenda, Portuguese for Our Farm, and I knew by the painting on the sign of their signature, two clasped hands, that it belonged to Mary and Richard. Clasped hands were their symbol. They had many: marble, ivory, wood, and bronze.

We drove into the bamboo and were in another world immediately. Mary's and Richard's home was an anachronism. It shouldn't have been there, but it was. Everything was green: there were flowers, bushes, trees, and two small lagoons. Chickens and ducks were plentiful, and we could see quite a few cows. It wasn't a house, exactly; it was a doll's compound. Each room seemed to have a separate roof. One house was a living room. It was all charming, open, and terribly original, an atmosphere only Richard and Mary would create.

Mary ran out to meet us and she hugged and kissed Emlyn and me and was gracious to Albert. Richard was charming as always, but it was apparent that they in their way were just as nervous as we were about the approaching audition.

Dinner was delicious, and served by three of their twenty-nine servants. After dinner, we repaired to the wicker music room. Albert's head was turning like an owl's.

"Where's the piano?" he finally said.

"There," Mary said, pointing to an enormous bulge of white wicker.

"No, no, I mean the *piano,*" said Albert.

"That's the piano. We had it covered with wicker because we don't think upright pianos are pretty."

"Oh." And sure enough in a sort of pregnant cocoon which could be broken open near the keyboard was a rather apologetic little piano. Unfortunately for Albert, the wicker cover which opened up from the keyboard would not stay up, but a wire coat hanger remedied that. Then there was no place to hold his music; a music rack was improvised.

Finally, Albert sat down to play, and suddenly I saw pink blotches appear through the pallor of his cheeks. He whispered to me that there was no action whatsoever as he pressed the pedals.

When the sound came out strange and discordant, Mary said, "I've tried to have it tuned, but of course it's awfully difficult because the mice have eaten all the felt off the hammers."

I thought Albert was going to turn to liquid and form a puddle at our feet.

Dick announced that he was going to have a beer, and filled the glasses of the rest of us with gin or whiskey or whatever was ordered.

Mary and Dick listened to the first song as though they were in a catatonic trance. I hoped that was because they were trying to concentrate properly. I knew one thing: Mary was not going to leave her desert paradise for something she did not want to do with all her heart.

I later learned to my shocked surprise that she had no idea that Dick had called me to find a show for her. She must have thought we were just being pushy. It was a mixed-up time.

After the score had been played and after Mary had politely asked to hear one or two songs over again, and after Richard had replenished our drinks, we all went to our respective beds, hoping that the next morning we would get a clear-cut reaction to the evening.

Around the breakfast table we all talked nervously about nothing except how nice the farm was, and soon Richard was driving us around it, showing what could be done with it if they bought just a little more land, and then the two of them drove us across the arid crabgrass and sand to a nearer airport, where we had about an hour's wait.

As the time for our takeoff grew closer, I began to panic. Suppose we'd made this entire trip without finding out how they felt? I called Mary and Dick aside and said, "If you never want us to bring up the subject of *Miss Moffat* again, say so now and we won't—or, if you want us to go back and work on it and play it for you later, say so now, so that we can go back to work."

And wonderful Mary was equally clear-cut. "We would like you to go on working on it, but we can't say yes or no in the present condition of the score. There's just not enough of it yet to hold onto."

So we left with semihopeful hearts, and when Emlyn finished his tour of South America, the three of us met in New York and added more songs to the score, until we felt it was complete enough that we could play it again for Mary.

The next time, however, Mary and Richard met us in Rio and we stayed at a hotel with a very good piano and a room to work in. We played the score again. Mary sang several of the songs. We could tell how exciting she would be in the part.

While we were driving back to the airport the next night, Richard sometimes stopped talking in the middle of a sentence. The first time this happened I looked at Mary questioningly and she said, "He just has to hold his breath a moment because of the pain."

I said, "What pain?"

And she said, "Oh, he has a terrible pain in his stomach."

Later, I got Mary alone and urged her to make Richard go to a doctor, but she said, "Oh, God, if he only would. I'm sick with worry. But you know how strong-willed he is, and he can be very stubborn about anything concerning his health."

Emlyn invited us all to his home in Corfu in June. We could go over all the fine points. We all agreed. It was a hopeful good-bye.

Two weeks later Richard was dead.

Oh, my God, poor Mary. I could see a fading picture. Nossa Fazenda was tangled in bamboo, the clasped marble hands lying on the grass, broken apart.

Mary tried, according to Richard's wishes, to have him cremated, but in a Catholic country that was not easy to do, and so she flew his body to Florida. While there, she called me in the midst of her grief to say she knew we were holding up our plans for her but that she wouldn't be able to do *Miss Moffat*—that she couldn't do anything serious or sad without breaking into tears—and that would certainly be the case with Emlyn's moving and beautiful lyrics. I could easily understand why our story had become impossible for her to do.

But what could we do now? We had to find not only a star but one who would be willing to tour the United States before coming to New York. It's the only way we could work on it properly. Who would have enough drawing power to make that kind of tour feasible? There were only two who were famous enough to fill the bill: Katharine Hepburn and Bette Davis.

Hepburn read the script and liked it, but after thinking it over, felt it wasn't for her.

A number of people in the theatre begged us to forget Bette Davis because of her unfortunate attendance record on the stage. But she had played the part in the movie of *The Corn Is Green* when she was thirty-six years old, and now that she was in her sixties would really be nearer the age of the original actress, Ethel Barrymore, who had played Miss Moffat on Broadway.

Furthermore, Bette Davis remembered the script with warmth, and much to our surprise the thing she liked most about our project was that the locale had been changed. Bette, having a smidgeon of a Southern background, realized how effective a story could be made of the relationship between a black student and an older white teacher.

So, we drove out to Connecticut along with her agent, affable, pink-cheeked Robert Lantz, and Albert played them the score, and Bette said she was even more tempted by the songs. At that moment she just plain said, "Yes."

Bette and I got to know each other very well in the next few weeks. We had numbers of conferences, talks on the phone, and I began to realize her true brilliance, her originality of thought. The reasons for her enormous success in our profession became more and more obvious.

Despite the reservations of those others who had worked with her, we signed with Bette Davis. We told ourselves that she really loved our project and that things would be different.

From the beginning of rehearsal, she seemed aggressively frank, almost bluntly so. How refreshing to meet someone who says what she thinks, and more than that, *knows* what she thinks. And if she is wrong, seems to know that, too. I learned not to be surprised when she said one thing, took a breath, and said the opposite at once. "What on earth made me say that, I don't know —but I was wrong." It was a most endearing quality. It just had to be sincere.

One day, when she was scrutinizing a group of actors who were trying out for the part of Morgan Evans, I heard her approve vociferously of a young black youth who had just sung one of the key songs from the show. I liked the fellow very much myself, but there were two others who were going to try out and I didn't want any decision made until we had given them a hearing.

The second young man, Dorian Harewood, who wore a red shirt, had had less experience but had a beautiful voice and had learned three of Morgan Evans's songs. He hit the high notes thrillingly and with sure pitch. But he read the scene oddly, like a juvenile in a 1920 drawing-room comedy. Still, when he was singing, he had primitive passion and excitement.

When he had finished the third song, I went up onstage to tell him privately that I felt he was playing the part all wrong, and asked if he could come to my house the next day at eleven o'clock and work with me.

As we were talking, Gene Wolsk, my associate producer, came up to me, pulled me aside, and said, "Get rid of him."

"What?"

"I said, 'Get rid of him.' "

"Why?"

And then, with a little shrug of his head in the direction of the seat where Bette Davis was sitting, he said, "She doesn't like him."

"But he might be great," I said.

Gene insisted. "She can't stand to see him another minute."

At times like that I'm apt to like an actor more than I really do. I turned to young Harewood and said, "That still goes. Come to my house tomorrow at eleven o'clock." And he left.

Bette said good-bye at the end of the day, having approved of everyone but the actor who was to play Morgan Evans. The next morning, five minutes before Dorian Harewood was to arrive at my house, the telephone rang. It was Bette from Connecticut.

"I've been thinking," she said, "about that boy in the red shirt, the one who sang all the songs from the show so well. I thought if he can be made to put as much power into the scenes as he does into the songs, he might be wonderful. Why don't you call him and work with him privately a little bit and see whether you can get something more out of him?"

I said, "Thank you, Bette, that's a good idea. I'll do that."

These strong noes and these strange, contradictory yesses were beginning to reveal something odd, even a tiny bit anxious about her. But I told myself that at least she had eventually remembered something in this boy's work that was worth saving. Again, she was being instinctively professional, I felt.

The feeling began to grow in me that Bette was deeply frightened of something that even she couldn't find words for. Was it just plain old stage fright? Was it a lack of confidence, even a dislike of her own personality, her own self? She certainly never was willing to walk on the rehearsal stage without a script in her hand. Perhaps it was a paper security blanket. It became a game with all of us to try to get it away from her.

At first, I suggested that she might be nervous about the music, but she almost bit my head off. "Nervous about music? I'm a musician! I understand everything there is to know about music! And I'm very *very* good at it, so don't say such things."

When she talked like that, my heart sank. Because the one thing I did not want was to have her singing all evening long. To the public, she was an actress primarily, and I was hoping that she would use her great, unique talent to act the songs, even speak most of the lyrics—half singing the lines the way many people in the theatre do, Rex Harrison, for instance, or Walter Huston.

But Bette was hell-bent on singing, and to prove she could, on the first reading of the play, although Albert spoke most of the songs for the rest of the cast, Bette Davis insisted on intoning every one of hers. Because she was making such an effort, she did not do the songs perfectly; although on key, her tones were shaky and not very musical. But at least she proved that she knew her lyrics and that gave a lift to the morale of the cast.

She worked hard daily in rehearsal, but although I repeatedly urged her to act rather than sing her songs, she never seemed willing even to try. *"How will they know I can sing?"* she kept asking, and I kept saying, "They should never be sure whether you are singing or speaking. Just act each song as you would act a scene."

Two weeks into rehearsal, just before lunch, Bette asked to rehearse the song at the end of the first act, "The Words Unspoken Are the Ones That Matter." Without any warning, she began to act the song—gave it the full Bette Davis hot talent—and the cast and I were moved to tears and applause. This was why we had done the play, why we got Bette Davis. This was our dream. None of us could have believed then that she would never perform it that way again. The memory of it gnaws at me yet. For in those five magic minutes, I saw in my mind the potential and irresistible power of this story and her superb talent.

Yes, things were thoroughly promising—until the day we left our rehearsal room and held our first run-through in a theatre. Bette walked onstage and saw twelve to sixteen people scattered out in the auditorium.

"Good heavens," she said, "you didn't tell me we were going to have an audience."

I said, "This isn't an audience, these are your co-workers—costumes, props, scenery, wigs. They have to see what we're doing in order to get all their work done properly."

She said, "There are more than *that*—I'm not a fool."

"Well, there may be one or two more than that. There's my lawyer, and, if you must know, two or three people out there who've been brought in to see whether they'd be willing to put money in the show."

She said, "Do you mean to say you haven't got it fully backed?"

I said, "No, Bette, not yet. We've explained that to your lawyer. We're counting on some of these run-throughs to help sell it to other prospective backers." I didn't tell her how many people had turned us down because of what had happened with her previous stage shows.

She walked away, apparently forcing herself not to look at that audience. But she made her entrance, even though her drained face showed how upset she was. Once on, however, she rattled through the part, occasionally looking at the script she insisted on carrying, her performance growing vaguer and more and more unsteady as the play went on. To my horror, she also began to limp slightly. Then she began to call out to the other actors to enter or to exit more quickly. She seemed to me to be using others to camouflage her own problems.

Only the week before she had given the greatest performance I had ever seen of a song from *Miss Moffat,* and this afternoon she had given, to my growing unhappiness, a most embarrassing performance of the whole play. There were, as Emlyn Williams said, "breakers ahead."

Bette told me that she thought she had pinched a nerve in her spine several months before and that it had troubled her during that run-through. She also explained that it sometimes affected the left leg, which caused her to limp. I urged her to go to a doctor. She said if she wasn't any better, she would.

The next morning Bette went for an examination. Later, the doctor told me, "She might have a slipped disc. I've put her into Columbia Presbyterian. I don't know how long this will take, but she'll be under the care of the very best people in the country."

He explained that a spinal condition wouldn't show in X rays because cartilage doesn't photograph. Dye could be directed into the spinal column for what is called a milogram, but that would be very painful. Perhaps the condition could be relieved by traction.

Looking back, I feel we should have insisted on the milogram, for as it turned out we never really found what was causing her pain.

All of us—Emlyn, Albert Hague, Gene Wolsk, and the cast—walked about in hopeless, slow, and pointless repetitive patterns. The disaster incapacitated us all. At last, word came from the specialists that her hospitalization was going to last anywhere from three weeks to eight. No doctor would guess that there was a possibility of its being any less. This would be enough to destroy us financially.

We decided to rehearse and rewrite without Miss Davis for at least two or three days; it would be therapy for us, and we could put in the changes which did not affect Bette, and thereafter she could be easily rehearsed.

We moved about through our days like robots until Bette, in traction, called on all of us to come up and see her. Three or four of us went.

Gene Wolsk said, "Bette, please be frank. Do you want to continue with this or not?"

Bette said, "Of course! I love it. I'm passionately in love with it. I must do it. If you can wait for me, fine. If you can't, then I'll understand."

And Gene said, "If you want to do it, we'll wait as long as is humanly possible, so don't worry about that. Just try to get well."

She was sitting up in bed, in her nightgown and shawl. One of her legs was in traction. On her head was Miss Moffat's straw boater—a man's flat straw hat which had been sent to her as a basket for flowers by Robert Mackintosh, our costume designer. It gave her a cocky and humorous look, and pumped up more hope than almost anything else she said or did.

By this time she was crazy about Dorian Harewood and couldn't wait to get back to work with him. We promised to send the accompanist up any afternoon that Bette was free to work, and we got permission from the hospital to wheel a piano into her room.

I was meeting with Albert and Emlyn every other day, and we could scarcely look at each other. This play had meant many months of dedication and work on our part, not to mention personal expenditures.

"The mice got into Mary Martin's piano," said Emlyn, "and now they've got into our leading lady."

I couldn't join the gallows laughter.

We went on and rehearsed without her for a week, then laid off the cast for two weeks, and rehearsed a few days before going to Philadelphia. She was to come there on Sunday and we would open a week from Monday. She arrived on Sunday, all right, but we did not hear from her until the day was over. Her lawyer appeared and said that she had injured herself slightly over the weekend. We asked when and where.

"It was when she went up to Connecticut to see her grandson," he said, "but it was very minor and she'll be all right tomorrow morning."

We were astounded that, sick as the doctors had said she was, she would take the chance of that long automobile ride. Again we realized she was shooting with our dice.

She seemed all right the next morning, so we rehearsed in costumes and with scenery. Two or three days later, on a Friday night, we previewed the show in front of its first audience.

I believe that all of us had such buzzing in our ears from those deadly insects, fear and doubt, that we did not hear the show properly. The only thing I do remember was that Bette Davis entered without her script for the first time, and got an ovation at the end of the performance that I had never heard before for anyone. The entire audience rose as one, calling out, applauding, whistling, cheering, and they would have gone on for an hour had she allowed them to. But she bowed slightly and left the stage, only to be forced to return three or four times before they would quiet down. It was almost like a revivalist meeting on Grand Bayou in Louisiana.

What we really had in the making, to my eye at least, was a hit of enormous proportions. All the chemistry worked. Dorian Harewood as Morgan was a sure star with a great voice. The story was, I felt, even stronger to an American audience than it could possibly be in the Welsh idiom. Bette was perfect casting for the part, and as soon as her nerves were gone she'd be great. I loved the whole project.

She must have been as heartened as we were, for the next night Bette really gave them what they came to see. This was the night that *Miss Moffat* became in reality an enormous hit. She seemed more sure of herself, except for one or two small mistakes in lines; her performance was more clear-cut, and though not as good as I knew she could do, still, to the audience, terribly effective. And her music was handled in a much better way: she spoke a bit, sang a bit, spoke a bit, sang a bit, close to the way we had agreed. Maybe she was getting onto it. And that night she seemed to be a happy, stimulated woman. Oh, God, if we could only have frozen that evening.

She did not want to rehearse on Sunday, and I was grateful, for all of us needed a rest. On Monday we ran through the play lightly, trying not to talk about the fact that we were opening that night. But I could see that Bette's whole body had begun to sag; even her face seemed to hunch a bit. Did it forebode a bad evening? Yes, it did. The worst—the very worst.

That night, a wobbly *Miss Moffat* was seen by an opening night audience in Philadelphia, by critics, and quite a few visitors from New York—at a great disadvantage. Bette was right back to the insecurity she had shown in the first run-through. She was quite often difficult to hear. She repeated lines in lyrics or left them out entirely. She forgot dialogue she had never forgotten before, then giddily repeated what she had just said.

At one point she turned to the audience and said, to our

horror, "How can I play this scene? Morgan Evans is supposed to be onstage. Morgan Evans, get out here."

Poor Dorian Harewood, who still had minutes to wait before entering, nevertheless ran on and looked at her for a cue. Bette seemed startled to see him but started to talk. Almost at once she realized she had made a mistake. She turned to the audience at once and said, "I was wrong. I want you to know that. It wasn't his fault."

The audience, under her spell, cheered and applauded and laughed all through it, forgiving, even enjoying, any slip, any mistake.

Bette went on. "It was my own stupid fault, and Dorian had nothing to do with it. Go back, Morgan, and we'll start over."

He did, to more laughter and prolonged applause. The scene finally got going, but by that time the audience had lost its way. And the evening was growing long and longer. And the mistakes less amusing.

In another scene, she stumbled over the dialogue leading to a song and turned sharply to one of the children onstage, who thought she was looking for help. He whispered her line to her and she flew into a rage. "Don't you tell me my line! I know it! You're a naughty little boy!" The child was squelched and so was the song, which never went as badly.

Dorian Harewood, Dody Goodman, David Sabin, Marion Ramsey, Lee Goodman, and Nell Carter were rocks, solid palisades for her to hold onto, but she appeared not to see them. Her audience still adored her, but more quietly. She naturally had some brief moments of the great Bette Davis, but on the whole, that night she missed the boat. She just wasn't herself, nor was she Miss Moffat.

All in all, we found from the stage manager that the play had lasted seventeen minutes longer than it ever had before or ever did again.

I longed to run away and take a boat somewhere, but stayed because my military stepfather had taught me always to stay. To my surprise, friends from New York in the back of the auditorium told me it was going to be a hit. I couldn't believe them because I knew they had not really seen it—not anything like it could be—but to them it was enough.

That same night Bette sent a dark ultimatum to me via her agent and lawyer. I was to make *no changes for a week* so that she could get her mind and thoughts organized. Also, we were not allowed even to rehearse *the other actors,* which was unique in my experience of ultimatums. I was frustrated by that because I felt as I do with any play, no matter how good, that when a production is previewing out of town it should be treated as a patient with a temperature of 106 degrees. It needs constant attention, which means careful rehearsals, if for no other reason than for the morale of the cast. It's the best way of proving to them that the producer and director believe in the ultimate success.

I didn't feel there was a lot to do with *Miss Moffat,* but I was sure that now with costumes and scenery and props, we would discover dozens of little flaws to be repaired.

But anything to placate our star. No rehearsals for a week.

In the next morning's papers, the critics said what I would have said. I expected their irritation at how slow and repetitious the performance was. But they were all in awe of Bette Davis and blamed everything else but her.

One critic surprised me, however, by saying that the character of Miss Moffat seemed to him to be all sweetness and light: she won her early battles so easily that there was no question that she would win all the rest. Good God, why hadn't I seen that? He was right, but it could be easily fixed in a day or two with a small rewrite of the first scene.

By taking away or postponing her first song, "A Wonderful Game Called Reading," which could be called soft, and by going right to a characteristically Bette Davis belligerence in "How Lucky I Was to Get Out of the South," we felt we could strengthen the character and the play without adding any new lines. Emlyn and Albert and I decided to give a group of comedy characters the second song so that Bette wouldn't have to carry too much of the burden. Emlyn and Albert wrote a marvelous song called "There's a Stranger at the Doorstep." Then we held it in abeyance until rehearsals could start.

After eight days, Bette did come to rehearsal. At first, she didn't quite understand why we were taking out her soft first song, but once it was explained she became very reasonable, especially since the scene went well in rehearsal. Rehearsal also went well on Tuesday. We couldn't rehearse on Wednesday because of the matinee, but we did rehearse on Thursday, and by that time we were able to go through the whole scene with everybody speaking his lines and singing as before, except for Bette, who read hers as though they were new lines. She looked a little worried, I thought. Still, with weekend rehearsals, we should be able to get the new arrangement in the show by Monday night.

On Thursday night I went backstage to see her at the end of an especially successful performance—even with no changes she seemed to be getting better and better as the week went on, misplacing or forgetting only a few lyrics—and she seemed to be in a state of euphoria. The audience could always get her into this mood. In her dressing room she told me how much she loved the play, how she wanted to tour it all year and then play at least a year in New York and a year in London, and she said, "And then we'll make the picture. We'll make this whole picture all over again, with music."

I said, "That sounds marvelous." And I meant it. I felt closer and warmer to her than ever before.

"Thank God for this play," she said. "It's going to save me from those flea-bitten films. The last one I read, they had me hanging in a closet. *Miss Moffat* has saved me—saved me."

The next morning, I was summoned to her suite and escorted back to her bedroom, to find her lying on the bed with her face held rigid, her eyes unsteady. It was as though she had just lain down fully dressed.

She said, "Has the doctor phoned you?"

"Doctor? No, Bette. What doctor?"

"The doctor in New York. Hasn't he told you that I can't play it anymore?"

I stuttered a bit because I really didn't quite understand what she was saying. I said, "Play what? You mean, *Miss Moffat?* You mean, the doctor says you can't play *Miss Moffat* anymore?"

"That's right."

"But who told him to call me?"

Then she said, "I did."

"You did? But have you thought about the cast and the backers—and what about you yourself? Your reputation? You're famous! The whole country will be interested to learn—"

She lay back, stiff, with those wandering eyes. "I can't play it anymore. There's no use talking."

"You mean you've decided without actually going to see another doctor here that you're not going to play it anymore? That means tonight or the next night?"

"Or any night," she said.

I felt a burning flush go through me. I was walking naked through hell. But I managed to say, "Bette, I know this sounds silly to you, but for your own sake you can't commit this kind of professional suicide. You've become sick and made two important productions suffer before. There were hundreds and thousands of dollars of other people's money lost because of it and dozens of actors put out of work. You mustn't be blamed for that again, Bette. This might be the end of your stage career."

She said hoarsely, "I can't help it. I'm in pain. What can I do?"

"You can't do anything, I suppose, except perhaps wait a few days and maybe come back for—"

She said, "I'm not coming back—ever. I can't. The doctor will tell you I can't. So let everyone know, will you?"

I stood there with what must have been a pre-Columbian clay face. My feet and my brain refused to function. She still lay there like an alabaster queen on an alabaster coffin. There was nothing more to be said. I started out, and stopped. I thought, She's in pain. It's her spine again. If she's suffering, I must be civil at least.

I turned, leaned down, and kissed her on the forehead, and left.

Thinking back, I remember she flinched a little at that kiss— but then, perhaps I did, too. The whole scene was so hard to believe. I was lost and without a clue.

I went to a phone and called the doctor in New York. "Did Bette Davis call you?" I asked.

"Yes. She told me that she couldn't play the show anymore, and for me to tell you."

"Did you agree to tell me?"

"Yes."

"Why? Is she incapable of playing the show?"

"I wouldn't know without another exam," he said. "All I know is that when patients say they can't play a show, I'm powerless as a doctor to tell them to go up on the stage and play it. I'm sorry. I know how much this means to all of you."

I went upstairs to my hotel living room, which was filled with people sitting about in a blue trance. This scene I will always remember as I remember Sartre's bricked-up room in *No Exit*— the room of the condemned. All of us would be facing the electric chair at eight o'clock that night.

Nedda was with us in our living room, along with all of the production staff—Emlyn, Albert, the stage manager, and Gene

Wolsk. We sat all day long, "iffing," trying to think of what might possibly be done to make her comfortable and to save our play, to hold onto our livelihood.

There was no point in putting in a substitute. We knew that good as the play was, the public wanted to see Bette Davis. Had we put in our understudy, there would have been more bad talk phoned back to New York. "Don't go see it—it's no good without *her.*" If we brought in another star to consider while the understudy was playing the part, that star would have refused it hands down.

The blackest juices began to flow through my head and heart. On that gloomy afternoon I couldn't for one second weep for poor Bette Davis on her bed of pain. I didn't have time because I was feeling too sorry for myself and too embarrassed at having persuaded Emlyn to join me in this venture. He had written a great play and an enduring character. Another part of my agony was for Albert, the vulnerable, enthusiastic Albert Hague, who had written three or four of the most beautiful melodies I'd ever heard for *Miss Moffat*—"The Debt I Owe," "I Shall Experience It Again," "The Words Unspoken," and "I Can Talk Now." They were first-rate, melodic, dramatic, touching. Oh, my God, what a waste. And that great, blameless cast. What of them and their jobs gone askew?

As I recalled all the wildly successful moments in *Miss Moffat*, with audiences applauding and even cheering, I turned white-hot again with fury at the injustice of it. There had been lines at the box office ever since our ads appeared, and now the reports from the two next cities were the very best we could hear —sold-out houses, lines around the corner, enough money to pay back the production costs within a few weeks.

But finally I reminded myself that if she was sick we must care for her, and her pains, whatever they were due to, still required careful attention.

We all agreed a doctor must see her that day, and we finally found a highly recommended Philadelphia orthopedist who would come to her suite to examine her.

The doctor appeared. He described his examination step by step to us all, and said, "It is absolutely impossible for her to walk onto the stage tonight or to think of continuing playing or even getting to her feet for another six weeks to three months. During that time she mustn't move. She has to be carried to a physiotherapist and gradually be relieved of this painful condition she's in."

We asked him again. "You're sure she cannot do the play anymore—in a wheelchair, on crutches, seated in a fixed chair?"

"Not now. Not in the immediate future. She's in too much pain to walk. A year from now, perhaps. Two years from now, yes. But not now. Impossible."

He went over to Gene Wolsk to sign the insurance papers. Fortunately, we had taken insurance against the star's causing abandonment of the project. The investors would get part of their money back, at least. But we wanted our show and couldn't have it.

That night, we met the cast in the theatre just before they were to go put on their makeup. We told them the news, stood with them while they went through their first moments of distress, and then said we would have all plans worked out for them by the next morning at eleven o'clock, and could we have another meeting.

The next morning we were all there, except for Bette. The whole suffering cast was there, old and young, black and white. The company manager explained how everyone would get back to New York, and they just sat there. I wished Bette could see them there, trying to piece together their lives.

One of the cast, Nell Carter, a brilliant actress and powerful singer, who had been rehearsing the new song that was to go in the next Monday, asked, "Since we won't have a chance to perform this song ever again, maybe—maybe—we could do it once now?"

And four of them got up—Dody Goodman, Lee Goodman, Marion Ramsey, and Nell Carter—and while our musical director, Jay Blackton, played the piano, they sang "There's a Stranger on Your Doorstep."

Everyone watched and listened and tried to imagine it in front of an audience. They laughed and applauded and cheered when it was over. I couldn't look. I was trying to suppress the sorrow and anger I was feeling, and it was making my head ache.

That's theatre. That's the way theatre goes. That's the kind of ups and downs we have always faced and always will face. The only thing to do is get to work again—recast, rewrite, or do something new. I find I must always do it. It's my life or—yes, why can't I say it?—my destiny. My obligation. My joy. And thank God that whatever it is in me that keeps me going can't be killed—not by a star's illness, not by bad performances, not by bad notices.

I have always said, "If anything can stop you, let it," and now I was faced with that same admonishment to myself. And the answer is simple: Nothing can stop me.

I started to go to my hotel room to help Nedda pack, when I stopped and looked down the hall.

The long corridors of the Bellevue-Stratford were shadowed and almost empty. I looked down to Bette's suite, and wondered whether she was still lying as though on a sarcophagus.

Only a few days ago she had arrived with her secretary and companion, the bellboys carrying bouquets of flowers. "The Assyrian came down like a wolf on the fold, his cohorts were gleaming with purple and gold"—and now, defeat, pain, failure for her and for all of us: Emlyn, Albert, young Dorian Harewood who would never sing those songs in this show.

Why did I stand there waiting? I should leave. What more could I do? I had sent Bette many flowers. I had written her long letters, with never—from that day to this—an acknowledgment of any sort, neither to me nor to Emlyn, who had also written her of his feelings of sympathy and recalling their long friendship. All of the miseries of *Miss Moffat* would have been helped by one gracious word. Maybe it's an unfashionable thought today, the idea of being nice, gentle, gallant, or just plain polite, but it's a great medicine for failure and it helps unravel agony and fill the empty goblet with hope.

I thought of Mary Martin, for whom we had written *Miss Moffat*, and how different things would have been with her. Perhaps the play would have had somewhat different dialogue scenes, but the music would have soared and so would the spirits backstage.

In 1977, Mary opened in Tennessee in a new Russian comedy with Anthony Quayle. At the dress rehearsal, Mary fell backstage and tore a ligament in her leg. She never missed a performance, even though she had five different plaster casts in five days before a steel brace was set into her leg.

Mary is a great lady of the theatre. To me, artists are the aristocrats of today, and Mary is an aristocrat of aristocrats. A production is already blessed to have her as the star.

And what of Bette Davis?

This great, brilliant lady is a loner. At times she seems to have blocked out the rest of the world. Is she just incapable of acknowledging the inconvenience or loss she had caused, or is she perhaps not as tough as she pretends to be? Perhaps that forthright, seemingly opinionated veneer is just put on like lipstick and mascara.

We closed a show after fifteen performances that was on its way to success, with tremendous advances, and for Bette Davis one of the great roles of her lifetime.

A year later came a startling interview in the New York *Daily News*. It was by Rex Reed. In it, Bette Davis seems to have forgotten to mention that she left the show because of a bad back.

Rex asked her why she left *Miss Moffat,* and her reply is his article. He writes, "She became enraged when she talked about it," and then he quotes Bette:

> It [*Miss Moffat*] was a mistake. The audience stood up cheering and screaming every night, but I knew it wasn't what they wanted. They wanted me to be a bitch, not a middle-aged schoolteacher. The songs were wonderful. I sang them all and I was good at it, but it was nothing but hell. I had to carry the burden of the rewrites, and I spent three weeks in a hospital traction from the nerves and tension. The monkey on your back when you're carrying a show is wicked.
>
> Joshua Logan finished me off in two weeks. He was terrified of the critics and started changing things on opening night in Philly. I had one year on the road to do those changes, but I couldn't work ten hours a day and play a different show at night. They wanted me to learn forty pages in four days. I had to get my health back before I could concentrate on that kind of work. So we closed it down. I will never go near the stage again as long as I live.

Rex, who is an old friend, called me and gave me a chance to answer all this. And I couldn't wait. I quoted from his column and then gave him the facts.

Quote: *I had to carry the burden of the rewrites.*

Fact: There was no "burden of rewrites." We stuck to the lines she had already learned. We simply rearranged them.

Quote: [Joshua Logan] *started changing things on opening night in Philly.*

Fact: Her lawyer and agent can bear witness to the fact that she absolutely refused to change anything for the entire first week.

Quote: *They wanted me to learn forty pages in four days.*

Fact: What forty pages and what four days? She only rehearsed three afternoons in Philadelphia and we never finished staging the rearranged and far shorter first scene. I repeat, there was *no change of dialogue,* only a slightly different *order.* The rest of the cast, including the children, learned the new order in five or ten minutes, and four of them learned a complicated new song complete with dance routine in a day and a half.

Quote: *I had to get my health back before I could concentrate on that kind of work. So we closed it down.*

Fact: Who is "we"? No one else wanted to close it. And why didn't she mention her painful spine? Wouldn't a more accurate statement be, "My back was so painful that I closed the show"?

Quote: *Joshua Logan finished me off in two weeks.*

Question: Does that imply that I gave her the bad back?

What an odd woman she is—so loaded with emotional talent. What a sharp comment on life she had! Why should she be forced after the closing of *Miss Moffat* to abandon the theatre, to go on with television jokes from *Laugh-In* or question-and-answer shows in front of an audience of worshippers?

"How old are you, Miss Davis?"

"Did you like playing with Errol Flynn?"

I've written enough about Bette Davis. She's a book I'm trying hard to close. But that's not true of *Miss Moffat.* Even after these years, it's still alive to me, pulsating, musically superb. It contains poetic lyrics and roles that jump to life when inhabited by the right actors. Somewhere there is another star for it, too. And we'll find her. No, I haven't given up *Miss Moffat.* In Emlyn's words from her last song in the play:

> So this is no time for tears—
> And as for regret—never.
> The happiness I knew
> Will repeat itself—as new
> As ever!
> I shall experience it again.
> I shall experience it again.

THE REST
OF ME

I COULD HAVE led a black and white life without
Nedda, but not a life of full, unabashed color such as it's
been. We live in a blissful armed truce, making daily com-
promises and never fully agreeing on anything. The only thing
about us that is nearly equal is each one's opinion of the other.
But I'm her champion and she's my trainer. She would fight for
any principle I believe in like the ferocious *La Défense* on the Arc
de Triomphe.

I think she's as capable as she is beautiful. She knows everything there is to know about the theatre, acting, writing,
composing, casting. Her father was a famous actor, playwright, and lyricist, and her mother's father wrote music to
those lyrics and conducted the orchestra. She plays the
piano. She reads my plays and has her say, and often it is
helpful. She understands money, stocks, and can even use a
computer. She loves parties and knows how to give them.
She loves clothes and knows the right ones for her at first
glance. She's slightly insane on the subject of unhappy children. If a child is crying in a passing car, if she sees a hungry youngster on the sidewalk, she is overcome with dismay
and generosity. She loves dogs, horses, and gambling, goes

311

quite crazy around any one of them. But her love doesn't extend to rodents. I must go through any magazine first and vet it for pictures of mice or rats before she'll read page one. She doesn't even like Mickey Mouse.

She's seldom just sweet. Let's say she's tempestuous, raining epithets and deprecations and flashing her own brand of lightning. It takes a sturdy trudge in high galoshes and a strong umbrella to get through one of those storms, but it can be done, I assure you. And it's worth it.

* * *

Our children, Tom and Susan, were born one year apart. We took so many pictures of poor little Tom in that first year that I became fed up with all my cameras and took only half as many pictures of Susan, who was an equally beautiful baby.

As soon as Tom arrived, we knew we had to have a house in the country that would not be too far from New York, so that he could be brought up in the country and I could still work in the city. We gave ourselves three stipulations: the house must be less than an hour away, on the water, and must have an expansive view. What we settled on was a house an hour and ten minutes from town, nine miles from the water, and with a view only of the house across the street. But it was a street lined with huge maples and every house on the street was over two hundred years old.

The house that we fell in love with on Old Long Ridge Road near Stamford, Connecticut, was the epitome of a New England clapboard house. It was a reworking of an even older house. Everything about it was special to us. The floors were walnut and shined, taken from the cellar of an antique store in Pennsylvania. The two fireplaces were of the original rough stone and each had a workable Dutch oven. The window glass had been brought from Maine from barns and houses since torn down and were the original wiggly variety. The fixtures were adaptations of the antique ones.

There was a play yard near an old well which we covered over with concrete, and there was a jungle gym which I had seen at some friend's home, and in the back of the house was our chief madness, a vast swimming pool made from a large natural pond, surrounded by mammoth two-hundred-year-old willow trees whose branches hung down to touch the water. It was a large, irregular-shaped oval, fifty-five feet by seventy-five, and when filled and cleaned properly, it was a magic sight. There was one entire side that was very shallow, with a rope across to keep the kids from swimming into the deep end.

In spite of the generous proportions of the large garden, there was one problem when we bought the house. A small piece of land jutted straight into our vision from the terrace of the rest of the property. It was a chicken yard, alive with chickens, and an old barn right behind it. All this belonged to the people next door.

When we first asked about it, the real-estate man said that the man who owned it, a Mr. Weld, had refused to sell the property before because he didn't like the previous owner of our house.

He said, "Maybe someday you'll be able to make friends with him and get it yourselves. I can at least put in your request."

It struck me that one way to win Mr. Weld's favor would be to make Tom go to work for us the moment he could talk. We would teach him to say as his very first piping words, "Mr. Weld, I wuv you." This struck us as terribly funny and we said it to Tom who didn't have the slightest idea what we meant, but laughed anyway.

Of course, we had never met Mr. Weld, and didn't until Tom was old enough not only to talk but to carry on a conversation.

When the three of us went to call on him, it was a shock to find him in a wheelchair, most of his body paralyzed. He could barely talk, and when he laughed it was a crow—a quiet crow. But we stayed and told him all kinds of stories about our friends in the theatre and movies, and when we left he made us promise we would come back.

A year later we got a message from our lawyer that Mr. Weld was moving to Florida, and before he sold his house he wanted to sell us the chicken yard and barn, as he had heard that we wanted them.

We bought the land then, and I'm afraid it was not a very happy day for Nedda when I said, "I know! We'll make the barn into my studio and we'll turn the chicken yard into a Japanese garden."

But no one seemed to know how to build a Japanese garden until I ran into Mr. Frank Okamura of the Japanese garden of the Brooklyn Botanic Garden, who came out to see our patch of land. He was a slender Japanese whose daughter worked for a great Zen Buddhist. Frank studied the chicken yard carefully and I asked him whether he thought it would work, and he answered, "Rocks. Rocks must chase each other around garden."

I said, "Yes. Yes, of course."

"And pools. Have pools here with waterfall, and over there a house in the east. House in the east mean all poles face exact compass points but is earliest Japanese dwelling. Must be in all gardens. And another stair pool—oh, yes, here must be stair pool like mirror—and next to it we will plant willow tree so when it grow old enough, it twist, as though young girl looking at herself in mirror say, 'Oh, how beautiful am I. I did not know.' "

Naturally, I said yes to all Frank's suggestions for the house, but when the drawings came, the ground below the garden, with all of its pipes and electric cords, began to look like New York City when the subway is taken apart. Then I realized it was going to be more expensive than I had hoped. But we went through with it.

The Japanese garden was laboriously and elaborately finished by Frank's men. Its fountains were turned on and its circulating waterfall always visible, and the drip, drip, drip of the bamboo fountain perfectly regulated.

The old barn had been turned into a kind of large Japanese house which was now my studio and where we sometimes served drinks before a luncheon party. It was a wonderful playroom that even had a piano. Downstairs was a sauna and changing rooms.

Both children grew up swimming, and before Susan was six months old she had become the more powerful swimmer and insisted on going across the pool by herself. I had a terrible feeling that she would do anything to be noticed after the attention we had lavished on Tom.

Fortunately, there was a primary school across the street from us, and when Tom was nearly two years old he was allowed to go. He resisted it from the first time anyone mentioned it to him, and I can remember Tom reluctantly trotting after the nurse, calling out over and over again, "I don't want to go to kool—I don't want to go to kool." And Tom has never really wanted to go to kool, even though he finished Choate and the music college of Berklee.

Susan was far more gregarious and couldn't wait to see her friends.

When we first moved to the house on Old Long Ridge Road, the greenhouse was still filled with the previous owner's flowers and plants and our accountants said to us, "Either tear the greenhouse down or go into the flower business."

Well, it seemed very much simpler to go into the flower business than to destroy that beautiful greenhouse, and so we made a very giddy decision. We thought we could handle a retail florist shop and supply it with flowers, but learned, painfully and far too late, that we couldn't.

We rented a small shop in New York on the East Side and signed a short lease. Then we found a florist who was about to retire. She bought flowers at the market, and then in the spring we began to bring her armloads of daffodils and tulips. And she made arrangements. But our flowers always came in on the wrong day and there were far too many of them.

We would come in with laundry baskets bursting with spring flowers, fill the River House bathtubs half full of water for them. Every time we staggered into the elevator I had a terrible feeling we were going to be thrown out of the apartment building.

But somehow we lasted long enough to rent another shop and put a floral designer in it—and that's where the money went.

This great artist, Miss Pleasance Mundy, made French Impressionist floral arrangements for people and charged a goodly amount for them. But that did not pay the rent or for the wholesale flowers, nor any of the equipment, and as the years went by our status with the Internal Revenue Service changed. We now had two businesses, the theatre and flowers, and we had lost money on one for five years. We were taxed for all the years we had failed. When it came right down to it and we had finally closed our shop, we had lost almost half as much as I had made up to then in the theatre.

Another of my extravagances was a tree house for the children when they were two and three years old. I got a local carpenter to put a little house way up in a maple tree in a small wooded area and to build a long stairway-ladder sort of thing that would go up to it. The only trouble was that when I went to show it to the children, it wasn't there. Nedda had found it meanwhile and had it torn down before the children fell from it and broke their necks. But I was going to miss it.

* * *

We gave lots of parties because they were so much fun, for us as well as for our guests, and the lawn and the terrace were so easily suited for them. The children always joined us or were somewhere within earshot.

Perhaps the party to end all parties was given once when

Leland's friend Joseph Cotten told us that he had always given a Fourth of July party in California with a brass band. But he couldn't give one this year because he was in a play in New York. We decided we would take over the Fourth of July party and invite the Cotten friends as well as our own.

We hired a local band and put up a bandstand complete with red, white, and blue cheesecloth. The menu was dictated by the Cottens, and there were plenty of hot dogs about. The entire cast of *Wish You Were Here* had been invited along with their children—and bathing suits—as well as the entire town of Long Ridge. Two cops were on duty, showing people where to park. There was a baseball game going almost immediately on the lawn, and according to Cotten tradition mint juleps were served starting at eleven o'clock in the morning. I had been making them since ten-thirty, and when there was an extra one, I decided to try it myself. It was a disastrous decision, for quite soon afterward I staggered upstairs, flopped onto the bed, passed out —and missed most of the party. But, fortunately, no one missed me; they just went on having a good time.

But I think that's the party that knocked Nedda out completely. She had been so nervous for days ahead about giving a party out-of-doors that couldn't be moved indoors no matter what the weather that she was constantly waking up in the middle of the night and calling the weather bureau to find out the prediction for the Fourth of July. Just getting it all organized and done was almost enough to make anyone collapse. We never again had a party as big as that one. But we never forgot it either.

* * *

But it wasn't all parties. Trying to raise children while keeping up with a theatrical career required a bit of juggling. Shortly after Susan was born, Nedda and I flew to France on our way to England, where I was to direct the London company of *South Pacific*, and then on around the world to get back in time for the babies' first Christmas together.

We got off the plane in Paris, took a taxi, got to our room in the hotel, and Nedda said, "Now, I have to tell you something before we go any further. The nurse wants more money now that we have two babies; otherwise, she's going to quit. I think she's absolutely justified and I don't care what you say."

And pretty soon we were in an argument of such dimensions that I only knew how strong it was when Nedda suddenly left me, walked into the bathroom, and banged the door. It had been her habit for years to stop all arguments by just avoiding joining them, and the safest way, once they got started, was to go into the bathroom and lock the door.

I thought, Well, I'm not going to go and bang on the door and ask her to forgive me. I'll just wait until she cools off, and I'll enjoy myself in Paris while I'm waiting. I went out the door without saying anything and went downstairs and started wandering along the Champs-Elysées. I was practically alone at that time of the morning on that street, and I had a wonderful time looking in windows, buying a French newspaper, and getting a cup of coffee at a small stand, wandering farther and farther until I looked at a clock and realized it was now almost three hours since I had left.

I thought, Well, by this time Nedda should know how she feels. I went back in, went to the bathroom door, and rapped on it.

"Yes?" said Nedda. "Is that you, Josh?"

"Yes. I've come back. Are you all right?"

"I'm not all right!" she said. "I'm in a terrible state!"

"What's the matter?" I said, through the door.

"When I came in here I banged the door but I didn't lock it. It locked itself—and I haven't been able to get out of that damned door since you left. At first, I just lay down on the bath mat and went to sleep. But when I waked up and tried the door and it still wouldn't open, I was furious. I had no idea when you'd come back, so I thought there must be some form of communication between this room and the rest of the world. I looked around and suddenly I saw, right next to the bathtub, a wonderful white telephone. Old-fashioned, of course, and French, but a telephone nevertheless. And I went over, working myself up into a rage to speak to the manager, and when I put the receiver to my ear and pressed the button, water squirted all over me. It was a hand douche. But that was an hour ago. I'm almost dry now."

I was bumping all this time against the door. I bumped and bumped until finally it sprang open, and there was poor Nedda, bedraggled, miserable, but, I was positive, not defeated.

*   *   *

Although Nedda left school to go on the stage, she's brilliant, and can read faster and more clearly than any person I know. But she sometimes makes slips of speech which we call Neddaisms. They aren't malapropisms, they're not spoonerisms, and they certainly don't come from ignorance. They come from overenthusiasm, perhaps, or overemphasis, and they are peculiar to her. Like all slips of speech, there is always at their base a bit of truth.

For instance, on some of our trips abroad we had talked about going to Capri, but we never went, and when someone mentioned the Blue Grotto and we were naive enough to say, which Blue Grotto, they said, *the* Blue Grotto in Capri.

Eventually, we decided that as long as we were in Naples we would go to Capri come hell or high water, see the Blue Grotto, and become instant world travelers. We did so, and soon we were in a little boat which had squeezed through a hole in the rocky shore. We looked about and saw this beautiful bluish light reflected up from the ocean floor, emphasized by the darkness of the cave itself. When we had had a good look, we started back. We ducked our heads and bobbed out of the place, and Nedda said to me, quite seriously and enthusiastically, "Well, *now* we've seen the *Green Grotto* . . ." Of course, we both burst into laughter, but later on that night I began thinking, It was kind of green, wasn't it?

Once we were in Naples and I heard Nedda talking about a young lady traveler who had been lecturing us on art all afternoon, and very inaccurately. Nedda was more passionate than I'd ever heard her. She said, "But she's *wrong* so many times. She really doesn't know her hole from an ass in the ground!"

* * *

I had gotten in the habit of bragging that I could stand any kind of hot food there was. I said that my grandfather used to put Tabasco in everything, including my milk, which he did—and I did love hot food, except sometimes it got a bit too hot even for me, too.

But Nedda, poor darling, can't stand anything either too hot or too strange—strange vegetables, strange fish. She can only eat certain things. But when we found ourselves in New Delhi, India, and there was a very nice-looking young man from the tourist bureau who was talking to Nedda and putting his hand every once in a while in that prayerful attitude that means please or thank you or whatever, Nedda was absolutely captivated. She began assuming that attitude which I always call the French Ambassador's Wife—lots of gestures, lots of charm, total flattery—hoping, of course, to win friends for the United States, and this particular case was special because the man was so black, and the blacker he was the more Nedda felt guilty about the way blacks were treated in the United States and the more she gave to him of warm attention, admiration, almost adoration.

She said, "Now do tell me about your children. Do you have children or do you live with your family?"

He was just ready to answer her when I said to him, "Before you answer, maybe you could tell the driver to take us to a restaurant. I would like to go some place that is frequented only by Indians, not where foreigners go, or tourists. Is there some special place like that?"

He said, "Yes, yes, of course," and gave the driver a signal and the driver drove on. Then he turned to Nedda and said, in a very high voice, "Yes, I live with my family—my sister has forty-two family and in-laws and . . ."

"Forty-two!" said Nedda. "And they all live in the same house? What *fun*. I know you must enjoy that—all of you together. And you don't have to go see each other in a bus or a car. You're just *there.*"

She went on raving about it as I watched the countryside. When we arrived at the restaurant and walked past the white flaps which were on poles and divided it from the road, I looked inside and saw a vast mass of tables and benches, most of them filled with customers in Indian garb. As we got closer to the tables, I saw that nothing was made of wood. All was made of mud which had been pushed into a flat shape by hand in prehistoric days. The seats of the mud benches were shiny from bottoms of various sizes, shapes, and weights sliding across them through the ages. The tables were shiny because they had absorbed the grease of those same ages. I had wanted something Indian, not Biblical, I thought.

We were seated at a table by a waiter who, it was explained to me, was a Sikh—very tall—who never cut his hair; bits of it were sticking out of his turban at odd places.

Nedda, seeing all this, increased her comments and questions on the house and the cousins, obviously to cover her own nervousness.

The waiter was waiting for our orders, so I said to my guide, "You know, I really feel that I have never had proper Indian curry. Do you suppose I could order curry?"

He said, "Of course."

"And my wife wants something that isn't hot at all. She can't stand hot peppers."

"All right—good. I'll take care."

And he ordered a few things and left, while the French Ambassador's Wife continued her charm. I was hungry, so while I was waiting for my meal I noticed that they had brought in a small tray about the size of a pickle tray, and perhaps it *was* for pickles because what looked like two long green pickles were lying in the center. I figured that they were hors d'oeuvres or crudités, and I reached forward and picked up one green pickle and bit into it.

I have had few shocks like that. In spite of my grandfather's training, I had never tasted anything as hot in my life. I could feel the sweat coming out on my forehead and my eyes watering, but mainly I felt as though the piece of pickle I had put on my tongue was going to burn right through it and through my chin, and fall down onto the table somewhere. I pushed the tray away from me while I heard Nedda talking on, but I was gasping and I didn't know how to get rid of the gasp without embarrassing Nedda, so I just tried to cover it by looking away.

That's why I didn't see Nedda reach for the pickle tray. She was determined to show that she had no national prejudice, and as she was talking she reached down and picked up the other green pickle, which I knew would destroy her throat. I tried to reach out to stop her, but my hand wouldn't move. Then I tried to call, but my mouth wouldn't work, and before I could even close my eyes and hope not to see it, she bit into the pickle.

Her face was slightly gray, but she was so determined to make a good impression that she still had a pitiful smile preserved. I could see that she was going through some kind of extraordinary inner experience. She started to talk charmingly again.

"But your cousins—I'm just fascinated by your family. Hic."

Suddenly, she had the hiccups, and when Nedda gets the hiccups they never stop. She tried again. "You see, I was born into a large family, too. Ten. Hic."

Well, I thought, what can I do? I perhaps could ask for some water. Maybe we could get up and walk around the tentlike edifice. But finally I decided, I don't often get this chance to enjoy myself. I think I'm just going to sit back and listen.

"So, if your family and my family ever got together—hic—why then we could go on—hic—playing and having a good time for the rest of their—hic—lives. Hic—hic."

By this time we were all laughing.

* * *

South Pacific was playing in New York, London, and on the road, *Mister Roberts* was still playing to full houses on Broadway, and *Annie Get Your Gun* was hanging on, too. I felt extremely affluent for the first time in my life. Since our River House apartment was only half furnished, there were spaces yet to fill. Besides, I longed to buy some beautiful paintings.

But on our way to France from London I opened my mail and pulled out a letter from our accountant, who warned me not to take my hits too seriously, that I really had no money at all and whatever money I had must go to the government in taxes—ninety percent bracket, probably—and the main thing I must remember was Don't Buy Anything, Don't Spend a Cent.

I went on through the rest of my mail feeling a bit low, when suddenly I was brightened by a clipping that my secretary sent me from America. It was cut out of the front page of the latest *Variety* and the headline read, "Logan Making $40,000 a Week."

The only way to make that trip a success was to forget my accountant and believe *Variety*.

So, when Nedda and I had a chance, we went into the antiques section of Paris, at the corner of the rue Jacob and the rue Bonaparte. Along rue Bonaparte I saw a beautiful swan made of shells which would be lovely for a flower arrangement, sitting in the window. It was an antique, I was sure. I started toward the door of that shop, asking Nedda to join me, and not realizing that I was taking an important turn in my life.

As we walked in, the fat little man who was the proprietor was out of sight. He seemed to be busy bending down and doing things with his hands surreptitiously. I heard the tinkling sound of a music box and looked to my right. Three music boxes were hidden in three different antique bisque dolls about two feet tall, and each of the dolls was going through a little routine.

One lady, dressed to the nines, a marquise perhaps, with pearls hanging from the hem of her bouffant dress and a white wig, was sitting in front of a little dressing table, and as the music progressed she looked at herself carefully in a hand mirror held in her left hand, then more carefully still by leaning her head forward, closer to it. Then she turned, and I saw that in her right hand was a powder puff. She leaned way down so as to see herself in the mirror, and began pounding her cheek with her right hand. After a good emphatic last pat, she leaned up again and began the scrutiny of herself in the hand mirror.

It was so funny, so delicious, and so beautiful that I could hardly stand it, and I could see that Nedda was entranced.

The next doll, or *automate*, as the French call them, was an oh, so beautifully gowned shepherdess, looking very much as she might have had she been Marie Antoinette on one of her bucolic binges. This superbly costumed doll was very quiet and reserved, but the music was playing under her composure, and soon she turned her plumed head slightly, lifted her left hand which held a skinny little bouquet of flowers, and which pointed to a basket under her right arm. The right hand raised the front lid of the basket, and inside could be seen the head of a little woolly lamb. After a second, the lamb let out the tiniest squirt of a sound, a little "baa" that was so short you might not recognize it, but surely it was the funniest thing I have ever seen in my days of searching for props. I imagine the artisan woke up one morning and said, "I'm going to build the most beautiful doll in the world. She will open a little basket and a little lamb will go, 'Baa.'" Just the thought of it made me laugh.

But there was still another surprise to come that knocked the breath out of us both. It was a straight-spined, starry-eyed little girl with her feet spread apart and an old-fashioned pinafore type of dress in satin. Her eyes stared straight ahead, her cheeks were pink and sturdy, and her lips perfect curves. She was holding a shallow pewter cup, 2 inches in diameter, in her left hand, and in her right was a pipe stem. The music tinkled a tune and she dipped the pipe stem into the cup, lifted the other end of it to her lips, and blew a perfect soap bubble, then another, then another.

I went over to the man and in my very best French I said to him quietly, "Please do not tell me how much they are. I want all of them."

And that's how our collection of antique French dolls was started.

We gave one of the dolls to Marie-Louise Bousquet, our dear old friend who at that time worked on Paris *Vogue*, and we brought the others back to our New York apartment. Later, we had some gifts of other brilliant antique mechanical dolls. David Merrick gave me a blackamoor that could smoke tobacco from a hookah; Richard Rodgers sent me an intricate elephant doll that walked with a prancing gait; and Jimmy Stewart sent me a great boy doll who did violent somersaults. He said it was named George, in honor of the twenty-eight cats, each named George, we had while we were rooming together in our early Hollywood days.

Emlyn Williams and Laurence Olivier at a party at Long Ridge.

Nedda *inside* the Taj Mahal.

The house at Long Ridge with House, Jr. (for the children).

The back of the house at Long Ridge showing the swimming pool.

The sauna of the Long Ridge house. (Photograph for *Vogue* by Hans Namuth)

Josh's studio at Long Ridge. (Photograph for *Vogue* by Hans Namuth)

A corner of the red room at River House. Oliver Messel portrait of Nedda. Tobacco leaf pillow needlepoint given by Dorothy Hammerstein. Ventriloquist dummy from Japan on child's chair. (Horst)

Blackamoor magician automaton, gift of Coco Chanel. (Roy Pinney)

Antique French mechanical doll powders her nose. (Roy Pinney)

Four automatons, circa 1840: a shepherdess with her lamb in a basket, a fishmonger who reveals her dreams, a blackamoor who smokes a hookah (gift of David Merrick), and a little girl who blows bubbles. (Roy Pinney)

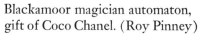

Henry Fonda, Jimmy Stewart, and Josh sing "Minnie-Ha-Ha" (from their 1931 Triangle Club production) at a gala tribute to Josh Logan.

Nedda Logan. (Raphael)

A year or two later Nedda and I spent days searching the antique stores for mechanical dolls and none were for sale. Our dear friends at Damiot, the shop where we had bought our first ones, decided they were such an attraction they would not sell any more: they made a museum of their collection and charged for looking at them.

We were still searching when we met Marie-Louise Bousquet at a spa just outside of Paris. She was sitting with another woman. She rose and said, "Did you find any more *automates?*"

I said, "No, they don't sell them anymore. They keep them."

She turned to her companion and said, "They have the most wonderful collection of mechanical dolls," and the lady rose quickly and said, "How chic. I have only one. It's theirs."

It was the famous Coco Chanel, and she sent us a most elaborate little magician the next afternoon. I finally understood what that French expression meant, *"Quel geste."* We had never met her before, and yet she gave us an outstanding part of our collection.

That little blackamoor doll plays a special variation of the shell game. He holds two little cups upside down on a green felt table and lifts them, sometimes one at a time, sometimes together, to reveal his treasures: under the left cup a little doll, under the right an ivory elephant, then under the left a die, under the right a button, under the left three gaily wrapped packages, under the right nothing, and at once a rooster and three coins. He even varies his routine as to which are exposed together and which separately. And all the while he turns his head from side to side, wiggles his eyebrows, winks an eye, and keeps up a constant—though silent—chatter.

So we had a doll collection, and we put it right in our living room, each one in its special place—on pedestals, tables, one on the piano, and two on bookcases.

But as a manic collector, I can't be satisfied with just one collection, even so special a one. We also have a collection of balloon plates that we started in Paris many years ago, each with a marvelous painting of historic balloons. Dorothy Hammerstein is responsible for our great collection of tobacco leaf pattern porcelain, because she knew we loved the wildness of it. She would buy single plates or pairs at all the auctions and send them to us at Christmas or for an opening night. It's probably now the most prized china in the world.

And that isn't all. I collect liqueur bottles, *Kitsch Tassen* (bad taste cups), shells, embroidery, needlepoint pillows, beaded flowers—and more. After all, as I remind Nedda, when she gambles, she throws money away, too.

My painting collection started with a smallish pointillist Pissarro of three children painting watercolors in a garden, which I found in Paris. As I said, I was feeling flush, but even at that I was cautious before I paid a few thousand dollars for it. The fact that some years later it would be worth an enormous amount never occurred to me. Back in New York I found one of the most beautiful pastel drawings of four dancers that Degas ever made. That was slightly more, but I bought that, too, and it increased in value almost as I hung it on our wall.

I never dreamed of buying these paintings for investment; that commercial side came when other people looked at our paintings and began to estimate their worth. Finally, our banker came to cocktails, saw them on our walls, and said, "How dare you have those pictures! That's only for millionaires. You can't afford to have that money hanging on that wall. It should and must be making money for you. Sell those paintings and buy stocks and bonds—and quickly."

I paid no attention to him.

I had decided from the beginning that I was only going to buy top paintings by artists. No matter how famous or obscure the artist is, I would get only one of his masterpieces. Then I would have something I would be proud to own. I could never be accused of buying just for the artist's name.

I had been offered a Signac at the Marlborough Gallery in London. From first glance it was a masterpiece. It was the *Portrait of Félix Fénéon*, a French critic, and probably the strangest painting I had ever seen. M. Fénéon, seen in profile, was carrying a top hat and a stick in one hand and holding a cyclamen in the other. Behind him was a mad swirl of color and design, almost formalized, as though painted on a backdrop of a theatrical production. The whole thing was portrayed in the traditional tiny dots of the pointillists.

I was very happy with it, despite its high price, until the day my business associate came in and stood in absolute shock as he saw it hanging on the wall. I thought something had gone wrong with him physically and I said, "What's the matter?"

He said, "What are you doing with this painting on this wall? What are you *doing* with it—it shouldn't be *there*. It should be in a *museum.*"

I said, "But why should it be in a museum when I own it?"

"You shouldn't have bought that painting. That's not the kind of painting you can get rid of easily. It will fit in no drawing room and it's got to be accepted by all kinds of boards in order for you to give it to a museum."

I said, "But I don't want to give it to a museum. I want to keep it."

"No, no, you *mustn't* keep it. It'll only lose its value over the years. I would bet you couldn't sell it today for what you paid for it."

He was a kind of art collector himself on the side and knew everything.

He never stopped badgering me about that painting. "Have you sold it yet?" "What are you going to do with that painting?"

Finally, two years went by and a definitive Signac exhibit was announced by the Louvre in Paris. They asked me for the loan of my *Portrait de Félix Fénéon*, whose full title I finally had memorized: *Portrait of Félix Fénéon on the Enamel of a Rhythmic Background of Musical Beats and Angles of Tones and Colors.*

The portrait went off to the Louvre for a full year, and toward the end of that time, again my friend was after me.

"There's going to be a sale at Sotheby's right after the Louvre. That's the ideal time to sell it, after it's been exhibited at the Louvre for a year."

I said, "But I don't want to sell it."

"Of course, you want to sell it. You've got to get rid of that painting. I'm telling you—you must do it. That painting does not belong with you."

And after a great deal of backing and filling, I said yes, and it was sold at auction and at a price much to my friend's surprise and pleasure. But I felt it should have got much more than it did. It went to an unknown buyer in Switzerland and I kept hearing about it, and before I knew it, it had been sold back to the United States, and it now hangs in its full splendor on the wall of the Museum of Modern Art, with the donor plaque carrying the name Rockefeller. I wonder how much money exchanged hands before that happened. All I know is, I should have obeyed my greedy instincts and kept it.

It was partly the fact that we had our Impressionist collection that made us decide to paint the living room red, or to put it more exactly, that *I* decided to paint the living room red, because Nedda was too frightened of the subject to commit herself one way or the other.

Our living room does not get much light. It's mostly a dark room, and although Dorothy Hammerstein tried to lighten it once years ago by painting it a color which she called "dirty banana," it still was dark.

Most of our furniture had come from the rue Jacob in Paris and could be called Napoleon III. With the paintings and the antique mechanical dolls and our various other bits of collections—Battersea boxes, china, etc.—the room really did look a bit full, a bit cluttered, and not pulled together. I remember how my sister had reacted to our vast numbers of chairs: "Oh, I see you're giving a party for chairs."

The really stunning thing about the room was a drape that had been put across one end by the decorator, Bruce Buttfield, who took some old material that Nedda and I had bought at the flea market in Paris and added some material to it as though it were lining. The drape made the window look as though it covered the entire side of the wall.

On one of my trips to France I went to see Mme. Castaing in her antique shop, and saw several squares of Brussels carpet on the floor—dark red and black with huge pink flowers, roses. I brought Nedda to the shop and said, "Wouldn't that be a wonderful rug for us to have? If we could have this design on our floor, all of our Victorian things would fit in better." She agreed, and we ordered it from Madame.

When it was down on the floor it was superb, there was no question in either of our minds, except that it made the dirty banana even dirtier, and so we decided we had to pick some color from the rug and paint the room that color.

Nedda consulted Albert Hadley, who is one of the great decorators of all time, and she told him in the presence of my mother and of her old friend, Beth Merrill, that I was coming in in a few minutes and that she was sure I would want to have the room painted red, at which point both women squealed, "Red! Oh, no, you can't! Oh, please! That's terrible!"

Albert Hadley was trying to please Nedda, and went through all the colors in the rug to see if he could find one that he might suggest. Finally, he found a kind of olive green and a grayish olive green and a beige in the rug and said, "Well, I'm sure Mr. Logan will agree to paint it one of these colors."

At this moment I came in. Mr. Hadley pointed out the colors he had suggested for the wall, and I looked up at him in horror. I said, "Mr. Hadley, you can't mean you think that would be beautiful. I think it's terrible."

He said, "Well, think it over, and you can make up your own mind," and as he was leaving he turned and said, "Of course, really I think it should be painted red," and disappeared.

There was a cacophony of squeals from Mother and Beth Merrill, and Nedda switched immediately. "It's only a can of paint, Mrs. Noble. Why not red? If we decide we don't like red, we'll buy another can."

I called Hadley up and gave him the order for the painters, as we were going to have to leave for California in the next few days.

When we got back from the picture I was making, the room was red. All the pictures were down and most of the furniture had been moved about to keep it from being splattered. It was the most marvelous dark cordovan-leather red I'd ever seen. Somehow, Hadley's painters had given it a texture. It looked as if it had been stippled over in a kind of brown. Of course, we were looking at it late at night and without anything hanging on the walls.

The next morning, I again woke to find Nedda sitting in the living room, looking very sad. The room, with its little bit of light coming in in the morning, was a kind of dark prune color, and there was no doubt about it, it wasn't as attractive as I had imagined it would be.

I said, "Well, Nedda, you win. Let's call Mr. Hadley and go find something else. Maybe some golds, some flocked wallpaper that would fit with those curtains. I think we've just made a mistake, that's all."

So I called Mr. Hadley and said what I felt, and he said, "But don't you like it? I think the red is marvelous. Oh, don't make up your mind too soon. Please consider it a little longer."

I said, "All right, I will."

Nedda was very impatient to get it changed. I said, "I tell you what, Nedda. The reason we chose the red was because of the paintings, and the paintings aren't hanging. Carl will help me get them up, and then you can look at it again."

She said, "I'm not going to change my mind," and went back to our bedroom to sulk. Carl and I hung the paintings, plugging in the electric fixtures so there were little lights over each picture, and then I called for Nedda.

No, she said, she didn't want to see them.

I said, "But, darling, this is like climbing a mountain and stopping four feet from the top. You've got to get up far enough to look over the other side. Come on in and look at the room."

Nedda walked into the room and turned around to get the full effect. With the paintings and the light, the wall was rich and had various textures of red, and was dark and beautiful. Nedda was under its spell almost immediately. She sat down. I watched her.

She said, "I'm never going to leave this room."

And she seldom has.

* * *

Though my mother talked about Charleston all through my childhood—she was fascinated by her family history, almost all of it dating back to that city, which she had learned from old letters she had read—she had never been there. Her family had migrated to Louisiana generations before.

So, one year when Mother's birthday approached, Nedda said, "Listen, I have a sister-in-law and two nephews and nieces living in Charleston. Plus lots of cousins. Why don't we go down and see them over Easter, and take your mother so she can really see Charleston? We'll take Tom and Susan, too. They might learn something of the family history."

I thought it was an inspired idea, at least from Mother's point of view, so that's what happened.

We arrived in Charleston, met part of Nedda's family and had some grits and gravy, and then were taken immediately to St. Phillip's Church where most of Charleston's important graves are located. But to Mother a graveyard was not a graveyard. It was far more like a social gathering, and this one was extra festive, as though her ancestors had come together to have a mint julep and welcome Sue Nabors Noble.

Mother switched gears and soon was in the high, giddy state she got into only at large parties. "Why, that's Dorothea! I do not believe my eyes! I didn't know you were here, Dorothea. Now don't tell me that's Jim—oh, your brother's right *next* to you, how *nice*. I always knew you were in Charleston, but I had no idea you were jogging elbows with your brother. And here's an old, old friend and cousin—Sarah Hapgood. Oh, Sarah—how nice to finally meet you! Now, could you tell me where the first Joshua Lockwood is buried? Oh, here's somebody—oh, look!" All at once she leaped across a grave and reached down and touched the gravestone. "It's little Mary Marston! She was the niece of one of Josh's great-grandmothers." Mother kept on for hours.

She saw every grave in the ancient place. Then she had to go to St. Michael's and do the same, but we never, at either of those churchyards, found the grave of my ancestor, Joshua Lockwood.

The next day as the kids and I drove up in front of a park in downtown Charleston, I heard Nedda calling, "Josh, Josh— stop!" We pulled up near the circular church, the third most important church in Charleston.

"Come over here, Josh, and bring your camera. Your mother's discovered the first Joshua Lockwood's grave." There had been three Joshua Lockwood Logans and before them three Joshua Lockwoods.

But I knew that Mother was not just looking for Joshua Lockwood's grave, but for a Lee who had married one of the Logan relatives generations before. When I got to the Joshua Lockwood grave and saw all the data on it, I was thrilled. I was in the process of getting the focus on my camera when I heard Mother's voice calling.

"Come here, Josh, and see what I have discovered!"

I said, "But, Mother, I'm photographing my great-great-great-great-grandfather's grave!"

"I know," she said, "but this is the one that's *important.* This is *my* ancestor John Lee's grave, and he's the one *that makes us cousins.*"

At that moment I realized something about Southerners that I hadn't before—that they don't care about larceny or even a bit of incest—it's just having good blood that matters.

*　*　*

My sister, Mary Lee, had been the thorn in my side when I was a child—I was jealous of her beauty, her power over my grandfather, her persuasiveness with my mother, and her natural ability as an athlete—but she grew up to make me very proud of her. She was with me in the University Players, and met her husband there—one of my closest friends, Charlie Leatherbee. He died a year after their marriage, and from then on, she made her way on her own. She worked up the ranks of *Life* magazine, became the editor in charge of two of the special annual issues —one on entertainment and one on the movies—and both of them spectacular successes. And she created a new department for *Life,* called Travel. That way she could turn her favorite hobby into her job. She traveled everywhere with photographers and then wrote her own breezy accounts of what she had seen. She gave those articles a humor and reality that few magazine pieces had.

She took wild chances in her travels because she had always loved adventure. She was a pilot, had flown with the WASPS in World War II, and now she flew over Holland in a balloon and wrote a dizzying piece about it. She went down the Colorado River over the rapids and again wrote her sensations. And then to the Amazon. She went up mountains and far below the water.

But one of her adventures was her last. She and two others met their death in an outrigger canoe in the tumultuous white waters caused by the tidal rapids around the island of Vancouver.

It wasn't too long after her death that the magazine collapsed. To me, it was as though it missed her zest and enthusiasm.

She was my mother's closest companion, and when she drowned and her body had been sent from Vancouver to Mansfield where we had flown to meet it, Eleanor, my cousin, called me up and said, "What kind of coffin should I get for Mary Lee? I don't want to do anything that would displease your mother."

I said, "Well, I think I should call her. Mother reads Ovid and generally goes by him. I know Ovid wouldn't want one of those big steel or bronze caskets. He believed in metamorphosis." So I got Mother on the phone and said, "Mother, you don't want one of those big bronze or metal caskets like Charlie Leatherbee's for Mary Lee, do you?"

"Oh, no," she said. "No, I want her to be buried in nice grained wood—but a wood that will eventually disintegrate and become soil. I want her in time to be at least part crape myrtle."

* * *

On Nedda's and my twenty-fifth anniversary we decided to give each other a party. It was to be at The River House and we invited about 150 people. We had a very fine Southern-born chef who had served several of our parties beautifully, and I consulted him about what we should have for this many people and suggested gumbo. Of course, I'm from Louisiana and gumbo means a lot to me. He felt the same way.

I asked Nedda and she said, "Well, I don't know anything about it, but if you like it, go ahead. It seems kind of odd to me."

Well, the gumbo became a kind of symbol of the party. It was going to be sort of Louisianan and people were going to be very informal. Edward arrived with his gumbo in the early afternoon and put it on the stove to keep it warm. He stirred it every once in a while and it certainly smelled delicious. I was looking forward to a great success with the Louisiana dish. Edward made his gumbo exactly the way I remembered it being made in New Orleans, with shrimp and crabmeat and bits of chicken and okra, but he included one more thing which I thought added greatly to the taste—tiny pork sausages.

Everything was going fine. We were all dressed and the party was ready to begin. The doorbell rang. It was the first two guests, who had come over early to see our apartment before it got filled up. We ushered them into the living room, and as we passed through the hallway there was a faint but rather unpleasant smell.

Carl signaled to Nedda and me to come into the kitchen. When we got there, poor Edward was stricken, standing next to the enormous tank of gumbo.

He said, "Come here."

He lifted the top, and the smell almost knocked us over.

"What happened?" I asked.

"I don't know. It spoiled. Perhaps it was sitting over the pilot light all afternoon and something went wrong. I don't know. It's spoiled. It can't be used."

I turned to Nedda. Her eyes were darting here and there as she thought. "What else have we got to serve?"

I said, "What we have to do first is get out the Rigaud candles and the Lysol spray and some of that Floris bath oil, and cover the apartment with it. We've got to do something to get rid of this smell."

She said to me, "Do you suppose the River Club could help us out?"

We had them on the phone in a minute. No, they had nothing. They had to prepare from scratch. Who would have something all ready?

"I know," said Nedda. " 'Twenty-One.' "

She called "21" and talked to one of the heads. "I'm Nedda Logan and I'm in terrible trouble. Have you got anything already prepared that you could send over?"

"Yes, we have some nice lobster Newburg."

"Fine."

"And chicken hash."

"That's good, too."

"And creamed chipped beef."

"That's fine."

"How many orders would you like? Six? Ten?"

"One hundred and fifty," she said. "Everything you've got. Just send it all over, and as fast as you can get it here."

I'll never forget the relief that came on everyone's face when the news got around that the truck from "21" had just arrived. In the meantime, the place smelled like a rose bower. There must have been a thousand little invisible Tinker Bells squirting lovely perfume in every corner of the apartment.

I said to Joe Curtis, "I liked it better when we could smell the gumbo."

* * *

Tom and Susan had grown up around theatre people, and mostly, of course, around the people who were working with me at the time. We had conferences in either our living room in the city or the one in the country, and the kids were free to walk in or out whenever they chose, or sit and listen. They didn't sit and listen very much because they always had something to do, but as they grew older they began to show an interest in the theatre and what we had liked and what we had not liked, and they began to see plays themselves.

I remember Tom standing on the seat beside me watching Mary Martin flying in *Peter Pan.* Tom was three, and Mary was singing and flying and obviously giving her all. I thought to myself, Tom must be getting an eyeful now. But he turned to me and whispered in my ear, "Daddy, when does the cwock-odile come?"

Susan proved herself equally undiplomatic years later. Both my children had gotten to know Harold and Florence Rome very well because, when we were working together on *Wish You Were Here,* the Romes rented a house across the street from us in Long Ridge and brought their children out as well. Generally, every afternoon there was a swimming party in which all of us joined.

Later when Jack Warner decided that musicals were not making money and so turned *Fanny* into a straight picture, it was a major disappointment to Harold. When I came back from Europe, after cutting the picture, I called him up and asked if I could come to see him. He invited me downtown to his studio.

I scarcely had a chance to open my mouth. He had obviously been spoiling for this conversation for quite a while, and he poured it all out in as vituperative and furious anger as I had ever heard. And he sustained it. He accused me of every form of dishonesty and lying, and eventually claimed that I had stolen his lawyer and his psychiatrist.

When he had finished, I knew how hard it was going to be for us to regain our close friendship.

About that time I was trying out *All American* in one Philadelphia theatre, and Harold had opened his show, *I Can Get It for You Wholesale,* nearby. I knew he was having problems with his leading man, Elliot Gould, who seemed to shock people every time he moved because beads of sweat sprayed out like little diamonds from his neck and arms. The person who made the biggest hit in *Wholesale* was a girl who played the small part of a secretary: she was Barbra Streisand, who would eventually marry Gould.

Anyway, Nedda and I were asked to come and see it. The children were visiting us, and so we took Tom and Susan and the nurse with us. I determined that no matter how bad it was I would find something good to say about it to Harold Rome or he'd decide I was still the same old villain.

Susan was standing with me at the end of the show when Harold came up to us. I said, "Hello, Harold—I think there's an awful lot of good in this show."

He said, "I hope you're right," then turned from me and squatted down to Susan's height. She was ten and was really thrilled to see him.

He said, "Sue, now be very honest, what did you think of the show?"

And then Susan came up with what she was sure was the going remark. At least she had heard it at conference after conference. She said, "It needs work."

Harold's face fell, and although I tried to cover for Susan, I got nowhere, for he just made some vague excuse and left us.

As the children grew and went away to school and college—Tom to Choate, Tufts, and the Berklee School of Music; Susan to North Country, Madeira, Sarah Lawrence, and Juilliard—we used the country house less and less.

We went so often to London, where we stayed in a suite at the great Connaught Hotel, that Nedda and I finally realized that over the years we had paid the hotel enough to buy a wing or an annex, and yet we had nothing but memories to show for it.

Molly Williams, Emlyn's wife, urged us to buy a flat. "You don't like resorts and you love it here. On your way to the airport, stop and look at the flat I have in mind. It's on the Embankment on the river—like your River House, only closer."

The flat was fifty yards from the river's edge, with bay windows and high ceilings, two large bedrooms, two baths, and living room, kitchen, and several small rooms. We liked it but were still hesitant about buying anything.

And then in a pell-mell rush, we made the big change. We sold the house at Long Ridge, bought the place in Chelsea, and shipped most of the Connecticut furniture to London. In six months we had a flat on the Thames—nine rooms—far easier to manage than an annex to the Connaught.

It's been one of our happiest decisions. Our friend Leueen MacGrath has the penthouse above us, and we have friends all over town.

London is filled with beautiful theatres. It was made for Nedda and me. Except, Nedda would have said once, for the way the people there talk.

She got over it years ago, of course, but Nedda used to have a terror of English people. I think it stemmed from the fact that she had stood at parties pretending to listen to various British actors or writers, and becoming increasingly embarrassed because she realized she wasn't understanding a word they said. It hadn't helped at all that her grandfather was born in England; she was far too young to remember his accent.

But I had pressed her to break her fear barrier, and told her, "You've just got to face the fact that there are certain English people who don't mind if you ask them to repeat what they've said. But they're wonderful friends and good fun, so let's not lose friends just because you don't understand what they're talking about."

She said, "Darling, you're right." Then she set her jaw. "I promise you, at the very next opportunity I'll get over it."

We had just flown back from London, where we'd seen quite a lot of plays, and one of them was a very entertaining mystery play called *Dial 'M' for Murder*. I had tried to go backstage and find out whether I could buy it or not, but on the way down the aisle, I learned it had already been bought and had been planned for production that season in New York by Maurice Evans.

Nedda confessed to me that Maurice Evans was one of the people she had great difficulty understanding, or even identifying. She said, "John Gielgud, Maurice Evans, and people like that . . ."

Arriving back in New York, we of course went to a theatre the first night. We found ourselves at the beautiful old Empire Theatre, which was soon to be torn down, where Shirley Booth was playing in *The Time of the Cuckoo*. At the first intermission we were standing back of the auditorium while everyone was sauntering out to the lobby.

To my surprise, I saw John Gielgud approaching us, and realized that he must have finished shooting his part of Cassius in Joe Mankiewicz's movie of *Julius Caesar*, and that he was stopping in New York on his way back to London.

He saw us, shouted, "Josh! Nedda!" and started toward us.

I didn't realize that Nedda, beside me, had immediately got into a panic. She had said to herself, I'm going to talk to him if it kills me, and then she looked up at Gielgud, who was almost at us by that time, and called out, "We're going to *see you next week* and you're going to be *absolutely marvelous!* That part was just made for you!"

It made no sense whatsoever. I couldn't imagine what she was thinking.

"We saw it in England and we loved it!" said she. "I don't know who you'll have playing with you, but I know you'll have good people. Oh, it's going to be such a big hit!"

By this time I was so embarrassed that I said in a very loud voice to Nedda, "What on earth are you talking about?"

She looked up at me, then back at Gielgud, and all of a sudden, with a gulp and a moan, she bolted into the ladies' room which was nearby. I still didn't realize she thought he was Maurice Evans. I tried to make some sense to Gielgud out of her strange remarks, but couldn't.

Later, when I was telling the story to my friend Paul Osborn, he said, "There was only one thing for you to say to Gielgud at that point, and that was, 'Who on earth was that lady?'"

THE BIG
OPTION

FREE! For the first time in my life.

Free from the fear I have waked up with since I was a youth: the fear of my illness, manic depression. It's not just an illness; it is like a ride on the giant swing at Coney Island. It swoops its victims from low to high without warning—from inky black depression where life is all hopelessness and despair to a wild state past happiness and joy of life to the upper regions of irresponsibility. All personal censorship shrivels like a burnt match. Free and unfettered willfulness takes over until the patient must be incarcerated to protect those around him.

I have been manic, or as it was once called, elated, twice, so seriously that I had to be hospitalized—once for four months and once for four weeks. But now, to put it simply, that will never happen again.

A chemical salt named lithium carbonate, derived from a white clay from the earth, came along to save me.

Lithium, as far as is known, can alleviate only one or possibly two types of mental illness. By a great stroke of luck, the first of these is my illness. I will always be a manic-depressive, but with lithium as a prophylactic or preventive I will never stray from normal again.

And, instead of having to sit for hours under the prying nose of a psychiatrist and trying to talk about myself, I simply see my doctor and have my blood tested every month to be sure my level of lithium is correct. I swallow my white clay in capsule form according to my needs.

Although I no longer ever reach an elated state where I make no sense, I am still as volatile as I have always been. I yell and jump around when enthusiastic. I can write or direct and cast plays or pictures with the same zest. Ideas pour out constantly. If I see an antique cup, I'm apt to buy it along with the whole collection. I buy enough diet drink to flood the apartment below. I talk passionately to actors. I am still recognizable as myself. I go far in my moods, but not beyond reality into fantasy.

From 1953, the time of my second manic breakdown, till 1969, I had no idea a preventive even existed, so I just kept on directing plays or films, praying that I would stay on an even keel, but I knew and Nedda knew that with too much pressure or not enough sleep, I might start fantasizing or exaggerating all existence again. If there was any sign of a high, I was advised by a doctor to take Thorazine, a new drug, or several other depressants, but they did the trick only temporarily.

In January 1969, we were in Hollywood finishing work on *Paint Your Wagon* when Nedda came into the room with a copy of the Sunday magazine section of *The New York Times*. She had it turned open to an article headed, "Help Found for Manic Depression." We both read the article eagerly, and immediately tried to find a doctor in Los Angeles who would prescribe the drug mentioned for me.

To our astonishment, no doctor or psychiatrist we tried knew anything about lithium except the name. Each of them advised us to inquire when we got back to New York. That was months away, but we had to wait. When we got back to New York, several prominent doctors who knew nothing of it themselves recommended hospitals or clinics which would know. After talking to doctors in several, we narrowed our choice to one named Ronald Fieve, up at Columbia Presbyterian Medical Center. He told me that lithium had been used experimentally in Australia and England since 1948 and in America since 1958, but it was still virtually unknown across the nation. Now a small number of doctors were presenting it and he himself had been treating an entire clinic population with lithium for several years and studying the results. He agreed that as a manic-depressive I should try it regularly, but I was to be very careful to have a normal salt intake daily to keep the lithium from becoming toxic. I should not, for example, take a steam bath, because I would lose too much salt. Lithium has its dangers and must be taken under medical supervision.

But as of now, I've been taking lithium nearly ten years as a preventive. The day I started, all my manic moods melted away. I'm a lucky man. I was given another life.

But what made me manic? Where did all this wildness in my blood come from? For many years, doctors thought it to be seasonal, brought on by fatigue, overwork, tension. Dr. Fieve and his associates say that the same doctors recently have come to believe that in most instances it is inherited.

That would certainly seem to be true in my case, since my father was surely at the height of a soaring manic state during the last months of his life. Unfortunately, no one then knew how to treat him; there were no psychiatrists readily available in the Bible Belt back in 1911. He was persuaded by faddist relatives to enter some kind of health sanitarium in Chicago, where he was given whole-grain wheat, honey, raisins, and dried figs—cure-all nature food. It didn't work.

My twenty-four-year-old mother came to see him, bringing my baby sister, Mary Lee, who was just six weeks old. My father was nervous and distracted by things far beyond his family. He kissed his wife and baby and went into his bathroom, pulled out a penknife concealed in his belt, and cut the arteries in his throat. He died two days later when the blood in his lungs brought on pneumonia.

Although I have never been tempted to take my life, mostly because I felt it would be too cruel to those I love, I certainly know how my father felt. He was a plunger, they say. He had many frustrations with oil and creosote companies, sawmills, and the vast purchase of timberland he made which he agreed to pay for with cut lumber: when he could not float a single log to the mill because no rain fell to fill the lake he had dug, he lost his entire investment.

Perhaps that can be compared to my frustrating and fiery activities with plays and films. Again, these things are not the cause of a manic state, I'm told—but they aggravate it.

Instead of locking my illness in Jane Eyre's tower, I decided to talk about it. I had been ignorant all my life about such things; at least I could tell others so they would never be as ignorant as

I was. And so I agreed to be interviewed about my illness, even by a group of doctors.

According to the doctors, even when manic people are healthy, they tend to be overachievers. Was that why I was able to do so much in such a short time?

Dr. Fieve in his book, *Moodswing,* points out those he feels are manic. He writes of the normal but almost superhuman achievement of, for example, Charles Bluhdorn of Gulf & Western. According to the doctor, he is not psychotic as I was, but is a manic type nevertheless. Other soaring dreamers and lightning-quick achievers in his book are Churchill, Lincoln, Teddy Roosevelt, and Howard Hughes.

Although I never have made the fortunes some of these men did, or won the glory, I am flattered to be in the club. It must have been stimulating just to attend their meetings or to read their notes.

So, being a manic-depressive, which had for so many years been a shaming stigma, has become, at last, possibly the mark of wild accomplishment.

* * *

In 1973 we were in our London flat, packing for a flight back to New York in order to be part of a panel on lithium for an American Medical Association convention, when a cable arrived asking me to appear with the same panel on *The Today Show* the Friday before the AMA meeting. I wired Dr. Fieve that I would be willing to do anything he approved of.

Sure enough, when we arrived at River House, Joe Curtis told us that I was to be on *The Today Show* the next morning.

Barbara Walters was still a mainstay of that program in those days, and as we are good friends, we chatted a bit before the show was filmed.

"This sounds interesting," said Barbara. "I wonder if you and the rest of them would do it for me on my other program, *Not for Women Only,* in the next month or so?"

"You'll have to ask Dr. Fieve," I said. "It's up to him."

"But remember this," she said, "if we do it, I want Nedda to be there. I want to be able to ask her what a wife's reaction is to this kind of mental illness."

I said I would ask her.

Our segment on *The Today Show* was fairly brief, but it did give a chance for Dr. Fieve to talk about lithium and to point me out as a functioning example of what lithium could mean to manic-depressives.

Then five weeks later, Nedda and I, along with several others, including Dr. Fieve and Dr. Nathan Kline, another specialist in lithium, gathered at the studio where Barbara Walters was filming the week's five segments of *Not for Women Only*. Each one of us was allowed half an hour. I was in the second spot and Nedda the third, and then the doctors divided the rest.

When I finished my conversation on tape with Barbara, I went down to sit in the auditorium to watch Nedda who, when she saw me, said, "Oh, no, I'm not going to do it if Josh is sitting there. He'd make me too nervous. I'm sorry, darling, but you've just got to go."

I said, "Of course, of course, I understand perfectly," and I went out the door and down the hall, looking for a place to sit and wait. I opened a door and found myself in the control room. There were all kinds of instruments, a number of people, and about ten or twelve different little television screens with individual shots of Barbara and Nedda as well as the two of them together.

I sat down and watched the entire show from this vantage point. Nedda was marvelous, beautiful, serene. She had on a red hat and a red scarf around her neck, pinned with her leaf pin, and she and Barbara made quite a sight on that screen. I was really amazed by Nedda, because somehow I'd always had a feeling that she was nervous about appearing on the stage or on the screen. She had shown nerves thirty years before when I directed her in *Charley's Aunt*. I had gone back to her between the acts of opening night and said, "Calm down," in a very loud voice, which made her even more nervous.

But now as I watched her here on the screen, she was the queen of this domain. She spoke with a rich voice but in no way a pretentious one. When a lady in the audience asked her, "How were you able to cope with a man with a disease like this? Why didn't you leave him? Why did you stay with him?" Nedda answered in a very quiet way, "Because I love him," at which point all the ladies applauded and ohed and ahed, and she was quite obviously a smashing success.

When it was over, I rushed backstage, trying to find her to tell her how much I liked her and to explain how really different I had found her. When I got to her, I said enthusiastically, "Darling, *why* couldn't you have been this good in *Charley's Aunt?*"

A reporter from a medical journal was interviewing me that afternoon.

"Suppose you were allowed to live your life over again—as a perfectly healthy, level-headed man who had never any vestige of manic depression. Would you choose that life to the one you had?" he asked.

I felt a cry rise quickly from my guts to my throat, almost choking me. "No! No—No—No! I would *not* want another life. Never. I don't want to be level-headed. I'd want this one, the way it was, every inch of it—the lows, the highs, the controlled and the uncontrollable—all of it, all of it."

To paraphrase the story of the bishop and the monkey, "It's a filthy little mania, but it's mine, all mine."

Without my illness, active or dormant, I'm sure I would have lived only half of the life I've lived, and that would be as unexciting as a safe and sane Fourth of July. I would have missed the sharpest, the rarest, and, yes, the sweetest moments of my existence.

Granted, there were at least five, maybe six, months when my illness was beyond control, when it stepped away from reality and I was, I suppose, psychotic. That was long before lithium was known or even available in America, and those who lived with me at that time—my family, the members of my casts, my co-workers—suffered agonies as they saw me fly off the handle, act willfully, stubbornly, even hysterically, to force a point or get something I wanted. I was Dr. Johnson, who, when his pistol misfired, would knock his opponent down with the butt end. It was embarrassingly painful to them, but it didn't seem even odd to me. I was soaring above life, whirling, swooping in a psychotic and wind-tossed free-fall.

But now my manic personality is under control and I am able to work like any normal man. The difference is that I will never be really normal. As I said, I will be a manic-depressive until I die. But ninety-nine percent of the time it didn't seem to show, and now, with lithium, it never will show.

My mind is constantly active, exhaustingly so to others, delightfully so to me. I'm a workaholic. Any kind of work is therapy for me—writing, directing, casting, painting, sculpting, repairing furniture, wiring lamps, gluing together bits of broken china, writing new English lyrics to *Carmen*—endless things. And the harder the work, the more concentration it requires, the better.

To some, I seem a bit larger than life, perhaps, surely now and then overemphatic, and always inclined to laugh too loud and too long. For inside my skin still flows manic blood which pumps a manic heart, making my dreams, my ideas, jokes, stories, tumble all over each other, allowing me to match the fantasies of the great men and women who were creating the shows with me.

For two collaborating writers, male or female or mixed, must have the same mental ability. They must be able to ride the wind together until they are high enough to look down and see the road (the line of the story) they are looking for, with all the cloverleafs looming ahead. It is a joyful and heady time, because thoughts are not allowed to settle, are kept suspended in solution; sentences do not solidify enough to be put down on paper. It is a time when "anything goes," when ideas fill the air like birds rising from a field, screeching and nearly blacking out the sky with their flapping wings. One co-worker's thought sets off a skyrocket in his partner's brain, and suddenly it is a mutually contagious creativeness, the true zest of writing together. It's thrilling. It's sex without sex. It's the closest two people can get to each other without thinking of some physical satisfaction. On second thought, it's better than sex because it can last for hours.

I literally lived for those hours, and I was at my best, I'm sure, during those mental ascensions and spiritual levitations. My manic personality seemed able either to follow or lead such discussions. I could not have kept up with these volatile minds I worked with if it hadn't been for my beloved illness. And so I must be grateful to that illness for many things.

Come along now and live through them with me:

Regular afternoon skyrides around the universe and back, writing *Fanny* with Sam Behrman—spirited discourse on how fathers felt about sons, or the ultimate melody of how boys felt about girls—those outrageous Marseillais expressions of Pagnol's and our equally outrageous translations of them . . .

Floating, long, comic lazy vacations down rivers with Paul Osborn while we worked on *On Borrowed Time*, searching along with Pud and Gramps for "where the woodbine twineth". . . .

A few short hundred years of ecstatic happiness with my second Sarah Bernhardt, Ethel Merman, while blocking out one song for *Annie Get Your Gun* . . .

Endless dizzying swoops up over mountaintops and dives into sweet-water valleys with Irving Berlin, hearing his classic Jewish jokes, his infectious enthusiasm, and his foggy, little-boy laughter . . .

That invigorating mental trampoline on which Oscar Hammerstein and I leaped and bounced and leaped again until we got high enough to see the solution to the "Bali Ha'i" sequence in *South Pacific* . . .

The melting and remelting sexual visions of their stolen love life while Lancelot sang "If Ever I Would Leave You" to Guenevere in *Camelot* . . .

Teetering on a Kansas grain elevator, then freewheeling through the Labor Day picnic, complete with games and amateur contests in the film *Picnic.* And doesn't it take a certain bit of centrifugal mania to fill a screen with a baby blowing spit bubbles? . . .

Whirling and twisting and spinning to hang onto the tail of that elusive shooting star, Larry Hart . . .

Getting lost in the warp and woof of Kurt Weill's music and then leading Walter Huston back through it, only to find that he was leading me . . .

Trying to lose myself in Maxwell Anderson's editorial maze of a mind . . .

Trying to catch Mary Martin's rarefied yet practical ideas of how a song should go. Pacing ahead of her, then running back, until we finally caught the idea we both wanted . . .

That tantalizing guess as to what the melody was when Dick Rodgers began composing the bass of a new song on the piano, while whistling soundlessly to himself what I was dying to hear . . .

I've worked with the greatest and had the temerity to suggest new endings to choruses of songs, or even different orchestrations. Dick Rodgers might set his jaw, but he listened, and soon was doing it not necessarily my way but a new way of his own.

What else gave me the courage to get up and stomp out the patterns of "There Is Nothin' Like a Dame" with the sagging knees of restless animals, with the men following suit, and all done and finished in five or ten minutes?

Wasn't it a manic mind in full flame that saw those fingers dancing in "Happy Talk?"

That made Cherie her own electrician, kicking switches in rhythm to control her lurid lighting effects while singing to the cowboys in *Bus Stop?*

That led to the wild arrogance of Brando waiting at the girls' bridge and making comic faces at the leading lady in *Sayonara?*

The theatre is a kaleidoscope, a hall of mirrors, a kangaroo, a Roman candle. It's like the weather in Kansas, reversing every five minutes.

A director must change hats and even costumes constantly: a preacher's collar, a trainer's turtleneck, a doctor's stethoscope, a cheerleader's megaphone. He must encourage, persuade, bully gently, argue, convince, inspire, flatter, fight—and above all he must win.

And so I am still putting as many irons in the fire as I can, hoping one will get hot. I'm going to revive *Miss Moffat*, and soon, just to see whether we were wrong about it or not. I'm writing, or rather putting together, a musical originally written by Edward Harrigan, Nedda's father, with music by David Braham, her mother's father and Harrigan's orchestra leader. My play will be based on the Mulligan series, which Ned Harrigan played with his young co-star, Tony Hart, on the lower East Side in the 1870s and '80s when immigration was in full flood. It's a tricky mosaic to put together, but so far it feels good. Jay Blackton, who has conducted many of my shows, is reworking the music, and my present therapy is revising the lyrics to the wild songs and the mad stories. And I've got a great movie already financed if I can find the right lady movie star to play it.

Choose another life? Never. I believe that high, wild side, that manic side, has given me a daring I could never have learned, and that daring has made for me a life I could never have dreamed of living otherwise. And so, for me, the future is still another story.

CHRONOLOGY

Josh Logan's role as
director, producer, and/or writer
is in italics above each title.

Director and coproducer
TO SEE OURSELVES, a play by E. M. Delafield
Produced by Jack Del Bondio and Joshua Logan
Ethel Barrymore Theatre, April 30, 1935
Cast: Patricia Collinge, Reginald Mason, Earle Larimore

Director
HELL FREEZES OVER, a play by John Patrick
Produced by George Kondolf
Ritz Theatre, December 28, 1935
Cast: Louis Calhern, John Litel, Myron McCormick

Dialogue director
THE GARDEN OF ALLAH, a David O. Selznick film
Directed by Richard Boleslawski
Released November 19, 1936
Cast: Marlene Dietrich, Charles Boyer, Basil Rathbone, C. Aubrey Smith,
   Tilly Losch, Joseph Schildkraut, John Carradine

Dialogue director and second unit director
HISTORY IS MADE AT NIGHT, a Walter Wanger film
Directed by Frank Borzage

Released March 28, 1937
Cast: Charles Boyer, Jean Arthur, Leo Carrillo, Colin Clive

Codirector with Arthur Ripley
I MET MY LOVE AGAIN, a Walter Wanger film
Released January 14, 1938
Cast: Joan Bennett, Henry Fonda, Louise Platte, Dame May Whitty, Alan
  Marshall, Tim Holt, Dorothy Stickney

Director
ON BORROWED TIME, a play by Paul Osborn
Produced by Dwight Deere Wiman
Longacre Theatre, February 3, 1938
Cast: Dudley Digges, Frank Conroy, Peter Holden, Dorothy Stickney

Director
I MARRIED AN ANGEL, a play by Richard Rodgers and Lorenz
  Hart. Music by Richard Rodgers; lyrics by Lorenz Hart
Produced by Dwight Deere Wiman
Shubert Theatre, May 11, 1938
Cast: Dennis King, Vera Zorina, Vivienne Segal, Walter Slezak, Audrey
  Christie, Charles Walters

Director
KNICKERBOCKER HOLIDAY, a play by Maxwell Anderson. Music
  by Kurt Weill
Produced by the Playwrights' Company
Ethel Barrymore Theatre, October 19, 1938
Cast: Walter Huston, Ray Middleton, Richard Kollmar, Jeanne Madden

Director
STARS IN YOUR EYES, a play by J. P. McEvoy. Music by Arthur
  Schwartz; lyrics by Dorothy Fields
Produced by Dwight Deere Wiman
Majestic Theatre, February 9, 1939
Cast: Ethel Merman, Jimmy Durante, Mildred Natwick, Richard
  Carlson, Tamara Toumanova, Dan Dailey, Jr., Alicia Alonso, Nora
  Kaye, Maria Karnilova, Jerome Robbins

Director
MORNING'S AT SEVEN, a play by Paul Osborn
Produced by Dwight Deere Wiman
Longacre Theatre, November 30, 1939
Cast: Jean Adair, Dorothy Gish, Russell Collins, John Alexander, Enid
  Markey, Effie Shannon

Director of sketches
TWO FOR THE SHOW, a revue by Nancy Hamilton. Music by
    Morgan Lewis
Produced by Gertrude Macy and Stanley Gilkey
Artistic director, John Murray Anderson
Booth Theatre, February 8, 1940
Cast: Eve Arden, Brenda Forbes, Betty Hutton, Keenan Wynn, Alfred
    Drake

Director and coauthor
HIGHER AND HIGHER, a play by Gladys Hurlbut and Joshua
    Logan. Music by Richard Rodgers; lyrics by Lorenz Hart
Produced by Dwight Deere Wiman
Shubert Theatre, April 4, 1940
Cast: Jack Haley, Shirley Ross, Marta Eggerth, Leif Erickson, June
    Allyson, Vera-Ellen

Director
CHARLEY'S AUNT, a play by Brandon Thomas
Produced by Day Tuttle and Richard Skinner
Cort Theatre, October 17, 1940
Cast: José Ferrer, Nedda Harrigan, Arthur Margetson, Mary Mason,
    Katherine Wiman, Phyllis Avery

Director
BY JUPITER, a play by Richard Rodgers and Lorenz Hart. Music by
    Richard Rodgers; lyrics by Lorenz Hart
Produced by Dwight Deere Wiman and Richard Rodgers
Shubert Theatre, June 3, 1942
Cast: Ray Bolger, Benay Venuta, Constance Moore, Bertha Belmore,
    Vera-Ellen, Nanette Fabray

Additional direction
THIS IS THE ARMY, a musical revue by Irving Berlin
Produced for benefit of Army Emergency Relief Fund
Broadway Theatre, July 4, 1942
Cast: Irving Berlin, Ezra Stone, Gary Merrill, Burl Ives, Julie Oshins,
    Hank Henry

Director
ANNIE GET YOUR GUN, a play by Herbert and Dorothy Fields Songs
    by Irving Berlin
Produced by Richard Rodgers and Oscar Hammerstein 2nd

Imperial Theatre, May 16, 1946
Cast: Ethel Merman, Ray Middleton, Harry Bellaver

Director
HAPPY BIRTHDAY, a play by Anita Loos
Produced by Richard Rodgers and Oscar Hammerstein 2nd
Broadhurst Theatre, October 31, 1946
Cast: Helen Hayes, Louis Jean Heydt, Enid Markey

Director and coproducer
JOHN LOVES MARY, a play by Norman Krasna
Produced by Richard Rodgers, Oscar Hammerstein 2nd, and Joshua
    Logan
Booth Theatre, February 4, 1947
Cast: Nina Foch, William Prince, Tom Ewell, Loring Smith, Pamela
    Gordon, Max Showalter, Ann Mason

Director and coauthor
MISTER ROBERTS, a play by Thomas Heggen and Joshua Logan
Produced by Leland Hayward [and Joshua Logan]
Alvin Theatre, February 18, 1948
Cast: Henry Fonda, David Wayne, Robert Keith, William Harrigan,
    Ralph Meeker, Steven Hill, Jocelyn Brando, Marshall Jamison, Harvey
    Lembeck, Murray Hamilton, Brian Keith

Director, coauthor, and coproducer
SOUTH PACIFIC, a play by Oscar Hammerstein 2nd and Joshua
    Logan. Music by Richard Rodgers; lyrics by Oscar Hammerstein 2nd
Produced by Richard Rodgers, Oscar Hammerstein 2nd, Leland
    Hayward, and Joshua Logan
Majestic Theatre, April 7, 1949
Cast: Mary Martin, Ezio Pinza, Myron McCormick, Juanita Hall,
    William Tabbert, Betta St. John

Director, author, and coproducer
THE WISTERIA TREES, a play by Joshua Logan
Produced by Leland Hayward and Joshua Logan
Martin Beck Theatre, March 29, 1950
Cast: Helen Hayes, Kent Smith, Walter Abel, Peggy Conklin, Douglas
    Watson, Ossie Davis, Bethel Leslie, Vinie Burrows, Alonzo Bosan,
    Reri Grist

Director, coauthor, and coproducer
WISH YOU WERE HERE, a play by Arthur Kober and Joshua Logan
    Songs by Harold Rome

Produced by Leland Hayward and Joshua Logan
Imperial Theatre, June 25, 1952
Cast: Patricia Marand, Jack Cassidy, Sheila Bond, Paul Valentine, Sidney
    Armus, John Perkins, Larry Blyden, Florence Henderson, Tom
    Tryon, Phyllis Newman, Frank Aletter

Director and coproducer
PICNIC, a play by William Inge
Produced by the Theatre Guild and Joshua Logan
Music Box Theatre, February 19, 1953
Cast: Ralph Meeker, Janice Rule, Kim Stanley, Paul Newman, Peggy
    Conklin, Eileen Heckart, Arthur O'Connell, Reta Shaw, Elizabeth
    Wilson, Ruth McDevitt, Joanne Woodward

Director and producer
KIND SIR, a play by Norman Krasna
Alvin Theatre, November 4, 1953
Cast: Mary Martin, Charles Boyer, Dorothy Stickney, Frank Conroy,
    Margalo Gillmore, Robert Ross

Director, coauthor, and coproducer
FANNY, a play by S. N. Behrman and Joshua Logan. Songs by Harold
    Rome
Produced by David Merrick and Joshua Logan
Majestic Theatre, November 4, 1954
Cast: Ezio Pinza, Walter Slezak, Florence Henderson, William Tabbert

Coauthor of screenplay
MISTER ROBERTS, a Warner Brothers film. Screenplay by Frank
    Nugent and Joshua Logan
Directed by John Ford and Mervyn LeRoy
Released July 14, 1955
Cast: Henry Fonda, James Cagney, William Powell, Jack Lemmon, Betsy
    Palmer

Director
PICNIC, a Columbia Pictures film. Screenplay by Daniel Taradash
Released February 16, 1956
Cast: William Holden, Kim Novak, Rosalind Russell, Arthur O'Connell,
    Cliff Robertson, Betty Field, Susan Strasberg

Director and producer
MIDDLE OF THE NIGHT, a play by Paddy Chayefsky
ANTA Theatre, February 8, 1956

Cast: Edward G. Robinson, Gena Rowlands, Anne Jackson, Martin Balsam, Lee Philips, June Walker

Director
BUS STOP, a 20th Century-Fox film. Screenplay by George Axelrod
Released August 31, 1956
Cast: Marilyn Monroe, Don Murray, Arthur O'Connell, Hope Lange, Betty Field, Eileen Heckart, Robert Bray

Director
SAYONARA, a Warner Brothers film. Screenplay by Paul Osborn
Produced by William Goetz
Released December 5, 1957
Cast: Marlon Brando, Miiko Taka, Red Buttons, Ricardo Montalban, Miyoshi Umeki, James Garner

Director
SOUTH PACIFIC, a Magna—20th Century-Fox film. Screenplay by Paul Osborn
Released March 19, 1958
Cast: Mitzi Gaynor, Rossano Brazzi, John Kerr, France Nuyen, Ray Walston, Juanita Hall

Director
BLUE DENIM, a play by James Leo Herlihy and William Noble
Produced by Barbara Wolferman and James Hammerstein
Playhouse Theatre, February 27, 1958
Cast: Chester Morris, June Walker, Carol Lynley, Burt Brinckerhoff, Warren Berlinger, Pat Stanley

Director and coproducer
THE WORLD OF SUZIE WONG, a play by Paul Osborn
Produced by David Merrick, Seven Arts Productions, and Joshua Logan
Broadhurst Theatre, October 14, 1958
Cast: France Nuyen, William Shatner, Sarah Marshall, Ron Randell

Director and producer
TALL STORY, a Warner Brothers film
Released April 6, 1960
Cast: Jane Fonda, Anthony Perkins, Anne Jackson, Marc Connelly, Ray Walston, Tom Laughlin

Director
THERE WAS A LITTLE GIRL, a play by Daniel Taradash
Produced by Robert Fryer and Lawrence Carr
Cort Theatre, February 29, 1960

Cast: Jane Fonda, Dean Jones, Joey Heatherton, Sean Garrison, Gary
Lockwood

Director and producer
FANNY, a Warner Brothers film. Screenplay by Julius J. Epstein
Released July 6, 1961
Cast: Leslie Caron, Charles Boyer, Maurice Chevalier, Horst Buchholz,
Lionel Jeffries

Director
ALL AMERICAN, a play. Book by Mel Brooks; music by Charles
Strouse; lyrics by Lee Adams
Produced by Edward Padula and L. Slade Brown
Winter Garden Theatre, March 19, 1962
Cast: Ray Bolger, Eileen Herlie, Anita Gillette, Ron Husmann, Fritz
Weaver

Director
MR. PRESIDENT, a play. Book by Howard Lindsay and Russel
Crouse. Songs by Irving Berlin
Produced by Leland Hayward
St. James Theatre, October 20, 1962
Cast: Robert Ryan, Nanette Fabray, Anita Gillette

Director
TIGER TIGER BURNING BRIGHT, a play by Peter S. Feibleman
Produced by Oliver Smith and Roger L. Stevens, in association with
Lyn Austin and Victor Samrock
Booth Theatre, December 22, 1962
Cast: Alvin Ailey, Claudia McNeil, Diana Sands, Cicely Tyson, Robert
Hooks

Director and producer
ENSIGN PULVER, a Warner Brothers film. Screenplay by Peter S.
Feibleman and Joshua Logan
Released July 31, 1964
Cast: Walter Matthau, Burl Ives, Robert Walker, Jr., Jack Nicholson,
Larry Hagman, Peter Marshall

Director
READY WHEN YOU ARE, C. B.!, a play by Susan Slade
Produced by David Black
Brooks Atkinson Theatre, December 7, 1964
Cast: Julie Harris, Estelle Parsons, Lou Antonio

Director
CAMELOT, a Warner Brothers film. Screenplay by Alan Jay Lerner
Released October 25, 1967
Cast: Richard Harris, Vanessa Redgrave, Franco Nero, David
  Hemmings, Lionel Jeffries, Pierre Olaf

Director
PAINT YOUR WAGON, a Paramount Picture film. Screenplay by
  Paddy Chayefsky. Music by Frederick Loewe and André Previn; lyrics
  by Alan Jay Lerner
Released October 15, 1969
Cast: Lee Marvin, Clint Eastwood, Jean Seberg, Ray Walston

Director
LOOK TO THE LILIES, a play by Leonard Spigelgass. Music by Jule
  Styne; lyrics by Sammy Cahn
Produced by Edgar Lansbury, Max J. Brown, Richard Lewine, and
  Ralph Nelson
Lunt-Fontanne Theatre, March 29, 1970
Cast: Shirley Booth, Al Freeman, Jr., Taina Elg

Director, coauthor, and coproducer
MISS MOFFAT, a play by Emlyn Williams and Joshua Logan. Music
  by Albert Hague; lyrics by Emlyn Williams
Produced by Eugene V. Wolsk, Joshua Logan, and Slade Brown
Shubert Theatre, Philadelphia, October 7, 1974
Cast: Bette Davis, Dorian Harewood, Dody Goodman, Avon Long, Nell
  Carter

Director, author, and lyricist
RIP VAN WINKLE, a play by Joshua Logan. Music by Trude Rittman
Produced by Ralph Allen
Kennedy Center, January 26, 1976
Cast: Anthony Quayle, Annie McGreevey, Michael Petro, Deborah
  Fezelle

INDEX

A page number in italics
indicates a photograph.